simon spector

YEARS AGO, I SAT DOWN AND THOUGHT ABOUT WHAT adventure comics might've looked like today if superhero comics hadn't have happened. If, in fact, the pulp tradition of Weird Thrillers had jumped straight into comics form without mutating into the superhero subgenre we know today. If you took away preconceptions about design and the dominant single form.

And then, a couple of years later, Alan Moore went ahead and did some of it with the America's Best Comics line. And Dan Jurgens did the rest with the Tangent line at DC.

The other day, I was thinking about response songs. Rappers taking shots at each other, covers that answer something in the original, art made in reaction to art. Which, you kind of hope, is not the same as being reactionary.

The small music labels 555 Recordings and Dark Beloved Cloud have singles clubs. People play down the importance of singles these days—they don't sell the way they used to, downloads bother the music business—but I love them. Sometimes one song contained on one object is all you need to move the axis of the world. Self-contained and saying all that needs to be said.

Singles and Tangent and ABC all kind of stuck together in my head, and I began conceiving of a response. The Apparat Singles Group. An imaginary line of comics singles. Four imaginary first issues of imaginary series from an imaginary line of comics, even.

This is what I think adventure comics would look like today if you blanked out the last sixty years of superhero comics. Yes, there would still be elements of great strangeness, because that's what the pulps traded on. There would be sf and high adventure and weird thrillers and occult journeys. But they would be of their time. The term "adventure" itself would have a dozen different definitions.

THE MAN

Doc Savage, man. The Shadow. The Spider. Ten or eleven years old, poking through the book rack at the Oxfam charity store in Rayleigh high street with some change in my pocket, and coming across a bunch of weathered old paperbacks from the Sixties. Fifty pee in my

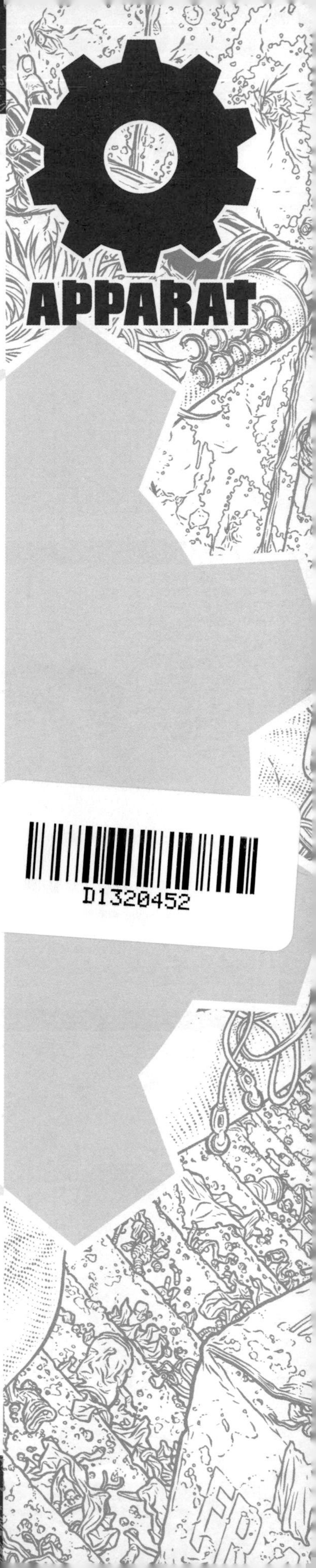
APPARAT

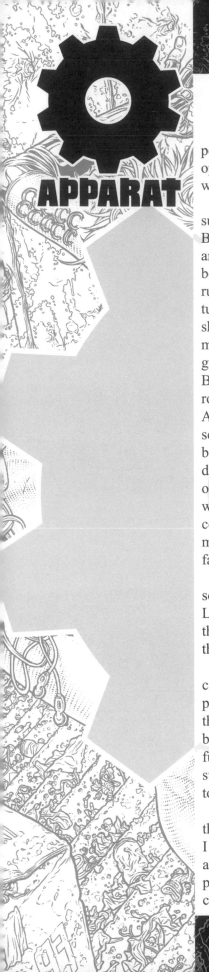

pocket. That's fifty pence or pennies, in British money, as opposed to having a pocket of collected urine. I walked out with ten of the things.

They were the guys. The antecedents of the American superheroes, and sharing something of a tone with the British stuff too. These were the guys who didn't screw around. They were stinking rich, mad as arseholes and so bored or otherwise up themselves that they couldn't help but run around and get entangled with bad guys. And did they turn the bad guys over to the cops? Did they hell. They shredded the bad guys with hails of bullets, often from machine-pistols they designed themselves to kill the bad guys more quickly and more messily. At best—at BEST—they *abducted* the bad guys and performed back-room *brain surgery* on them to Make Them Better Citizens. And then they'd go home to play the violin badly, shag their secret mistresses and, in Doc Savage's case, play with a little box of vials that even as a kid I was convinced contained drugs of some kind. I mean, would smelling little bottles of oils and powders make you a superman? Course it bloody wouldn't. Would snorting a bunch of weird and conveniently mysterious chemical substances possibly make you feel very strong and also make you think very fast? Oh, I think so.

They were all at it, you know. The Shadow? Out of south-east Asia. Where they have the good shit, oh yes. Look at the size of that man's nose. He could do a rail of coke the length of Broadway and still have room to park his car up there.

The great adventurers of pulp. The people that writers came up with when Allan Quatermain and his ilk looked too polite and staid and, well, English. The British characters, in the tradition of all British adventurer heroes, were dodgy bastards, on the sly. But the American pulp heroes were all full-bore freaks. These guys are the basis of the superhero subgenre—crime fiction nailed on to science fiction with a touch of horror squirted out over the top.

For those of us who loved the pulp heroes, but thought that back then things were a little too coy and way too white, I give you Simon Spector: superhuman detective-adventurer who is also, frankly, here to take drugs and kill people. He is as straight and altruistic as Doc Savage, his chemical turbocharge as devoted to the scientific method as

Doc's little box of things to sharpen his senses (and, frankly, it's not like Sherlock Holmes wasn't averse to a bit of the marching powder on his off days). And, like the Shadow, he doesn't mess around. Like all of them, there's something missing in his life. I'm hoping—despite the appearance of tropes you may recognise from comics characters, but which are sourced in the pulps—Simon Spector shows just a little more complexity, in conception and execution. While still providing one of the most important points of the Weird Pulp Thriller strain of fiction: a self-contained story. You have to bear in mind that the pulps are what people had before television, and people came to the newsstands looking for a stream of complete fictional experiences.

The execution was written, of course, for Jacen Burrows. I first saw his stuff ages ago, when he was working with the writer Miles Gunter *(NYC Mech)* for, I think, Hart Fisher. The other artist I discovered through Hart Fisher was John Cassaday. I probably owe Hart money. I've been writing for Jacen for years, and the weird thing is, I've never met him, never heard him speak, and barely email him. I write the scripts—*Dark Blue, Scars*—he draws them. That's it. I don't *need* to talk to him, and at this point I'm kind of afraid to disturb the odd equilibrium of it all. He's one of those very few, very rare artists who's somehow capable of telepathically photographing what's in my head. It's beyond drawing what's in the script. It's often as if he can see into my head and understand what I was thinking about when I wrote the lines. I think he's an astonishingly capable and flexible artist, and it baffles me that people aren't building shrines to him. I've thrown genuinely horrible things at this guy over the years, that lesser artists, and better-known artists, would have screwed up or walked away from. At this point, I'm convinced there's nothing that Jacen Burrows cannot draw. And that, in a business of clones and amateurs, is the rarest thing of all. *Simon Spector* was written for Jacen Burrows, the friend I never talk to and the collaborator I couldn't do without.

(And, after *Scars* and *Dark Blue,* I definitely owed him a book with a fight scene in it.)

—Warren Ellis

POST-APPARAT

warren ellis

What follows is a last-minute collection of notes and thoughts on the Apparat Singles Collection (or, as we now consider it from here in Teh F00tu7e of December 2005, *Apparat 1*):

Apparat probably started sometime in the late Seventies, when I was given The Encyclopedia Of Science Fiction for Christmas. A massive book with a lurid yellow cover by, I think, Chris Foss. Edited by Peter Nicholls. I remember the guy's name because his biography in the book claimed that he'd been wearing black since the death of F.R. Leavis, and I recall having to go to Rayleigh Library to look up the name. I think I may even still have the Encyclopedia, somewhere, even though the spine got broken around 1986 when my mother threw it at me in the middle of a tirade about drinking and having sex with girls. Which, you have to admit, is a different spin on the old "my mother threw them out" saw.

An updated version of the Encyclopedia was released in the early 90s, and that's probably the easier one to find, but you don't want it. You want the original with the yellow cover. Because, as I discovered, it was illustrated (and the subsequent version isn't, which I think is a crime). Among the myriad subjects it covered was the pulp magazines, and selected illustrators from the magazines, and it ran little black-and-white cover reproductions from each. I knew next to nothing about the pulps at the time. The cover shots and potted histories of these magazines provided just enough meat to set me to wondering what these things were really like. It was like discovering a secret history to the genres I loved. Which, of course, has become something of a recurring theme of mine, if you've read my serial *Planetary* from DC Wildstorm.

They still exist, of course, in a mostly ugly and attenuated form. There are a handful of crime fiction magazines in English, I believe. The sf pulps live on as *Analog, Asimov's, The Magazine of Fantasy and Science Fiction*, and a few others. They sell in the tens of thousands, and mostly by subscription. At age 37 as I write this, they are of course not going to hit me in the same way as those greyscaled little archaeological finds I pored over when on the edge of my teens. But in my limited personal experience, they've been dull, sparkless little things for the most part. Your experience may be different. But written sf has been generally acknowledged to be in something of a crisis for some years, no more so than in the field of short fiction, which pays peanuts, and, well, you know the rest of that line. I remember one disgruntled commentator putting forth his belief that the people sending in stories were the same people buying subscriptions.

EDITED BY PETER NICHOLLS
THE ENCYCLOPEDIA OF SCIENCE FICTION
ISAAC ASIMOV

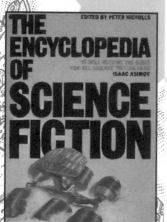

I neither knew nor cared about this, looking over that book that winter. I was interested in the *idea* of these things. That somewhere in the past there'd been an entire industry of people devoted to releasing a mass of submunitions of novelty every single month. Not just a veritable regiment of people hellbent on imagining the future, back when that was a new thing to do. But that each of these magazines was full of new stories, new ideas, fire-and-forget one-shots never to be returned to.

A lot of people still say that the real intent of comics is to produce habitual entertainment on a periodical basis. And, certainly, as much as many of us would like to be Joyce, the shape of the world means that we have to be Dickens, who of course wrote a great many of his books as magazine serials. Or, worse, that many of us have to be Conan Doyle, unable to give our heroes the mythical burial they deserve and then to move on to new things.

(God knows we'd be happy with Dickens' sales figures from those days. I dimly remember a story about crowds at the docks when magazines bearing new instalments of Dickens stories were shipped in to the States, mad to know what happened next.)

And if you'd like to know where bad comics come from, the answer is often simply this: that not every idea has enough give in it to go to a hundred episodes. Or even six. Some ideas only retain their power and charm in the short form.

I have a little stack of pulp magazines in the office. When I finally broke down and got a credit card in the late 90s, I went on eBay and hunted down the magazines with the covers that most haunted me from their little reproductions in the Encyclopedia. I found a bunch of them. One day I'll go back and get the rest. There's a stack right on the shelf to my left, from the Twenties to around 1970, when *New Worlds* was setting off its conceptual firecrackers. They all came wrapped in plastic bags, and it's hard not to think of them as little fossils of art, little prehistoric things sealed in amber. These days, I haunt eBay for actual tiny things sealed in amber, as my girlfriend has a fixation with the stuff. Some of it's fake amber, a handful of bugs and leaves embedded in a plastic amber-like resin, that comes out of China and sells for pennies. Which, I guess, is another way to look at the Apparat books.

Comics inherited a lot from the pulps. Some of the most influential editors in the medium, like Julius Schwartz, actually came from the pulp era, as editors or agents. Schwartz and Mort Weisinger ran a literary agency that represented the likes of Ray Bradbury and HP Lovecraft. (Alan Moore once told me that he discovered this over lunch with Schwartz in New York, in the mid-Eighties. Unable to help himself, Alan asked, "What was Lovecraft *like*?" Alan said that Schwartz' response was,

"Y'know, at the time, I really was thinking, I've gotta remember what this guy's like because in fifty years Alan Moore's gonna ask me.") This is how that great sf innovator Alfred Bester—and if you've never heard of him, understand that you don't get most of modern sf without Bester, and then go and look for *The Demolished Man* and *Tyger Tyger/The Stars My Destination*—writing the likes of Superman and Green Lantern for DC. (There's a depressing story to the effect that Bester was up for writing the first Superman movie, but was passed over for Mario Puzo because he was an "unknown." And if you want to know how groundbreaking sf writers end up, there's an even more depressing tale that he died alone and willed his estate to the bartender at his preferred drinking hole, who reportedly didn't even remember the man.)

And these guys knew that there was more than one genre in pulp, and a range of different audiences. Right through to the 70s, both DC and Marvel published war comics, sf comics, fantasy comics, comedy comics, tv- and film-based comics, horror comics and even romance comics in addition to their superhero lines. I remember my dad taking me into Terry's Paperbacks And Comics in Southend in the 70s and seeing a hundred-page-thick comic with a pink! cover, one of DC's "Super-Spectacular" romance compendiums. I didn't buy it, of course, because I was a kid and it was the 1970s and that would have made me a poof. Besides, I didn't have much money, and there was so much else to look at. (These were the years before 2000AD, at which point I stopped looking at American comics entirely for many years.)

Angel Stomp Future was kickstarted by a short story I wrote in early 2004 that just nagged and nagged at me. A two-minute glimpse of a comprehensively ruined future that hit me in the pub. This is that original short story, called "Biological":

Lavinia sits on the bench outside the local Starbs and swallows her antifutureshock meds with a soy chai latte. After a few minutes, she feels able to switch her shades from obstacle-imaging to full vision. The world slowly fades up from green and black wireframe to three-dimensional colour. She gazes blankly over the rail station, at the full-motion billboard ad for the new Speculum Bar down on Main Street, where warm drinks are mixed in and served from the muscular rectums of young Algerian girls.

A flock of Fuckit Kids clatter past Lavinia, videoloop John Lydon tattoos on their scrawny arms snapping out the words "fuck it" over and over. Some of them slow down in front of her. People under twenty-five or so aren't used to seeing pregnant women. One of them stops dead, scratches his scabby upper arm, making his fresh new talking John Lydon face bend and ripple.

Antishocked to the eyeballs, he still struggles to cope with Lavinia's alien curves.

Fuckit fuckit fuckit. The words lose their power, when they become a constant part of the urban soundtrack. The tat may be new, but the Fuckit Kid shows all the signs of having already tuned out the noise. Lavinia considers the boy. He's beautiful, in a crooked, dirty way. He's thin and wired and stupid and sniffs the air like an animal. It occurs to her that, on the days she'd forget to take her meds, he'd be attractive to her. The sort of boy she'd wipe her mouth on afterwards and toss back at the floor like a rag.

Sparrows skitter across the ground between them, playing ringtones.

She smiles, peels back her top to expose her belly. "Do you want to touch?" The words sound slow to her. She'd never realised, before she started experimenting with unmedicated urban experience, that everyone speaks slowly now. Sedated antishock drawl. He sniggers. Looks back at his crew, fuckiting off into the tangle of commuterhuman streams. Nervous now. Lavinia strokes her belly. "Come and feel it. It's weird."

He steps to her. Kneels. He's almost reverent. This is going to be special. This is going to be new. In his slow head, he can almost perceive a frame around the image, something timeless. This is how people used to be made, he thinks. This is biological history, this is.

Bark drops from the shade tree beside the bench, revealing slick pink vertebrae.

Lavinia takes his grimy hand and places it gently on her belly. "Just wait," she says. "You'll feel him move in a moment."

Her stomach distends softly. A bump, from a kick. His eyes widen in wonder. He feels it move. Again. Independent motion inside her body. He feels... he doesn't know what he feels. He feels.

And then he hears it move.

A whump. A beating sound. A deep, cupped clapping. Whump. Coming from her belly. Whump.

Lavinia smiles. It's not a nice smile anymore, she knows. She smiles and pulls the sonogram sheet from her bag. Rubs it together to release its conducting gel, and then stretches it tight over her belly. The sheet flickers to life, taking soundings of her womb. The image of her unborn child resolves.

Her winged foetus.

The Fuckit Kid retches and scrambles away. Lavinia throws the sonogram sheet on the floor. It freaks out for a moment, and then begins imaging the pipes, wires and dead animals under the paving slabs. She watches the Fuckit Kid almost fall over again in his eagerness to be back inside his flock of cultural clones. Winks to read the time off her eyelid. Time to go. Lavinia stands, leaving the sheet, leaving her bag and her drink, and walks steadily down the steps to the rail station, followed by a three-headed frog.

Just enough time to be on the tracks by the time the train arrives.

APPARAT

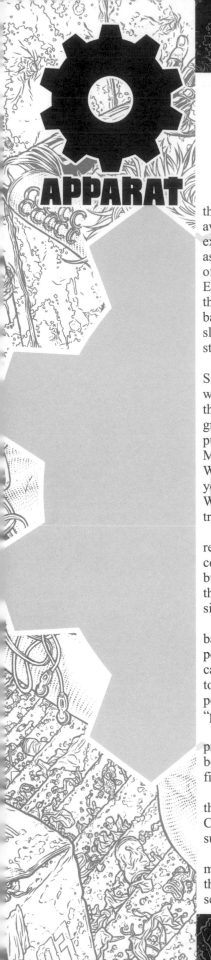

APPARAT

Singles:

Perfect 45 seconds: the last 45 seconds of "Peter Gunn" by the Art Of Noise and Duane Eddy. There's the final fusillade of awful fakey sampled trumpets, the bass walks down, the last explosive flourish of snare; and then the snare just keeps snapping as Duane Eddy starts to improvise. He stays way down the neck of the guitar—he always said the deeper strings record better. Each riff is just a bar or so; an improv off the theme riff, pause, then another, until fade-out. Just perfect. Like Dick Dale banging out "Fish Taco", playing around within the riff, finding a slightly new angle on it each time, then screaming back up the strings to start again.

You kind of beg for better engineering: I was listening to Sinead O'Connor's first single, "Mandinka", again the other week, and you can hear Marco Perroni's plectrum sliding back up the string at the end of each riff, this gorgeous SKREEK noise that grounds the bullshit lyrics Sinead is testing her range around and puts you right there in the studio. And the violinist/thereminist Meredith Yayanos pointed out to me the other day that Tom Waits' *Mule Variations* is so perfectly mic'd and engineered that you can practically hear Waits scratching his stubble on "Cold Water." No faking, no slickness. Perfect clarity of intent. Perfect transparency of creation.

I think that's why the Pixies hit me so hard in the 80s (I remember buying their first release on 4AD because I liked the cover). Three guitars and a drumkit is as simple as you can get, but they wrung the most astonishing, pure and direct sounds out of them. Clarity of intent and incredibly affecting work with the simplest, most transparent tools.

I had this weird kind of epiphany/seizure about five years back, that that's what single comics should be: the three-minute pop song. A replayable complete experience. I even started calling the standard 32-page comic unit a "single", which seems to have stuck with a lot of people, possibly because it's not perceived as being as deprecating a term as the more literal "pamphlet" or "floppy."

(I'm suddenly put in mind of the writer friend who proclaimed around 1994 that we were living in the cyberpunk age because he could buy floppy disks down the local street market five-for-a-quid.)

The four Apparat books were all, in their way, attempts at the three-minute pop song. I termed this book The Apparat Singles Collection, though at this point I don't know if that bit of play will survive the design process.

I'm only interested in two different kinds of single. In my more megalomaniacal/drunken moments, I sometimes proclaim that there should *only* be two kinds of single: self-contained and serialisation-to-book. The latter, of course, is Dickens: a finite

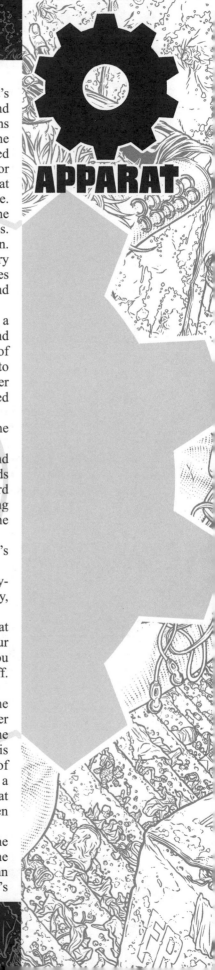

APPARAT

serialisation of a book in chapters. A close-ended run. What's always bugged me—and it's an aspect of franchises and company-owned works, where commercial considerations mean the work has to be permanently open-ended—is the "never-ending" book, where nothing can be completely resolved or concluded. What begins as a heroic struggle or a search for love or a quest for peace becomes a Sisyphean ordeal, a fight that cannot be won paced out in years or decades like infinite torture. Further, in order to provide little optimums, peak events in the lives of the characters become an accretion of barnacles. Because the characters cannot be allowed to age, grow or learn. Ultimately, you can't enter the work without knowing the history to which it is forced to refer. This is how long-running tv series die; the creators end up writing to the continuity and the fans, and potential new audiences are shut out.

Apparat was also something of a response to that. In a commercial medium becoming choked by crossovers and Events and writing directly to those invested in the history of those things, here were four brand new books that you had to bring nothing to but your mind. It's okay to like those other things, but try this: a three-minute single that you don't need Cliff's Notes for.

(Which would be fairly unusual in music today, too, with the rise of the record-collection band, but there you go.)

All of which is to say: these four books are just keyboard and ink. Lou Reed inscribed on his album *New York* the words "nothing beats two guitars bass and drums" and the old bastard was quite right. Sometimes you just need to strip everything back and hopefully remind people why they liked the noise in the first place.

Juan Jose Ryp might be the drums, but only if the drummer's Keith Moon.

And I'm in the back, still trying to find those perfect forty-five seconds. That's going to be my job until I die. And, frankly, there's nothing better.

It's the openings that haunt me. I've always been aware that I only have the first couple of pages, at best, to grab your attention. And, to my shame, I work like that with music. If you haven't got me in the first thirty seconds, I'm turning you off. Terrible, really.

(Here's another Old Fogey moment: I remember hearing the first play of the Cure's "Inbetween Days" on the radio. Ever heard it. The first forty-five seconds (again!) are among the most perfect openings ever. Big clatter of drums, and then this loping Peter Hook-style bass, and then another explosion of drums and this huge fucking rhythm guitar comes in, with a keyboard striking points of light between the snare and the hi-hat and... Anyway. You heard that and you weren't moving, even when Robert Smith starts whining.)

Carla told me that she had a perfect reference point for the *Frank Ironwine* opening; trying to get her kid out of the cot in the morning. Which just fits Frank so wonderfully. Laurenn photoreferenced *Quit City* in Oakland, of course, but it's

APPARAT

watching her power-chord her way through that opening that teaches you that photo-reference isn't what makes an artist great. What makes an artist great is having the eye and knowing what the hell to do with it. I kind of tripped Jacen up with the low-key opening to *Simon Spector*, but watch him go once Simon starts work. Ryp had the hardest opening—as you can see by comparing "Biological" to *Angel Stomp Future*, I transferred some of the hardest and most complicated images from story to script. You know Ryp produces one complete inked page a day? He frightens everybody.

As I write this, I'm working up to the first burst of real activity on what you might call Apparat 2. I've always had a fondness for the novella form, that no-man's-land between the long short story and the novel. Possibly because I just like short books. I've always thought JG Ballard had much more action on the path of the culture than Mike Moorcock because you can carry Ballard's major books in your pocket, whereas Mike's major books require some kind of cart or pack animal.

So the next wave of Apparat books will be forty-eight pages long, released with spines and card covers. So they'll go on a shelf next to this book. There may eventually be an Apparat Vol 2 collection for the bookstore market, but that's many years into the future.

Are they still singles? Hey, "Like A Rolling Stone" was six minutes long. So was "Heroes." I swear to god I'm not going prog rock on you. You can all come and beat me up if I ever announce an opera, The Apparat Concept Album or Apparat On Ice, okay?

You'll be able to buy the new Apparat books in comics specialty stores, which really aren't as frightening as they appear to be from the outside (or from "The Simpsons"). Okay, I'm lying. Some of them are. But they mean well, and you are my brave little soldier, aren't you? Course you are. In America, you can dial 1-888-266-4226 to find your local comics store, or (and for the rest of the world), you can steal someone's internet connection and go to http://www.the-master-list.com/.

Thanks for reading. My name's Warren Ellis.

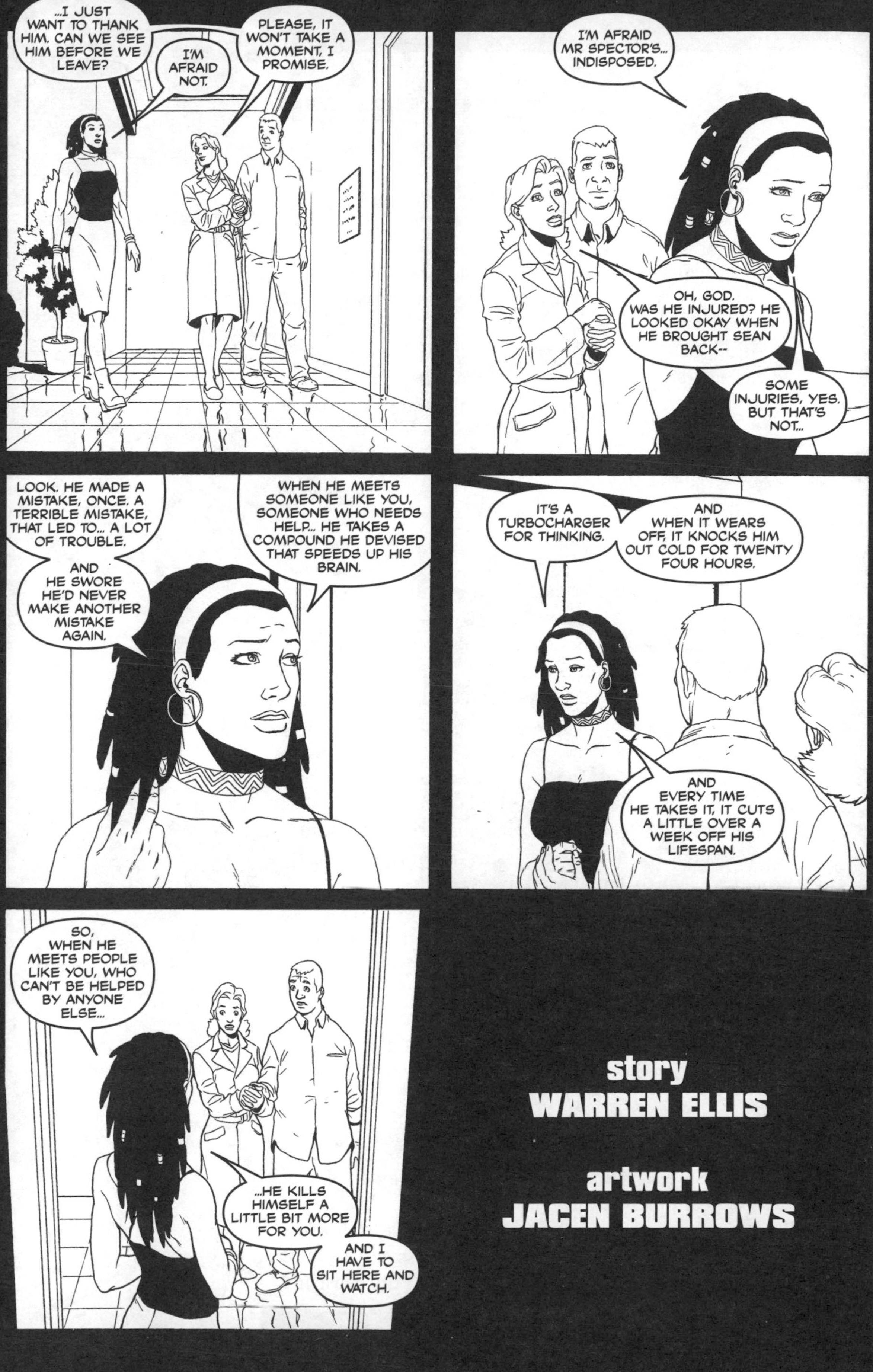

...I JUST WANT TO THANK HIM. CAN WE SEE HIM BEFORE WE LEAVE?
I'M AFRAID NOT.
PLEASE, IT WON'T TAKE A MOMENT, I PROMISE.
I'M AFRAID MR SPECTOR'S... INDISPOSED.
OH, GOD. WAS HE INJURED? HE LOOKED OKAY WHEN HE BROUGHT SEAN BACK--
SOME INJURIES, YES. BUT THAT'S NOT...
LOOK. HE MADE A MISTAKE, ONCE. A TERRIBLE MISTAKE, THAT LED TO... A LOT OF TROUBLE.
AND HE SWORE HE'D NEVER MAKE ANOTHER MISTAKE AGAIN.
WHEN HE MEETS SOMEONE LIKE YOU, SOMEONE WHO NEEDS HELP... HE TAKES A COMPOUND HE DEVISED THAT SPEEDS UP HIS BRAIN.
IT'S A TURBOCHARGER FOR THINKING.
AND WHEN IT WEARS OFF, IT KNOCKS HIM OUT COLD FOR TWENTY FOUR HOURS.
AND EVERY TIME HE TAKES IT, IT CUTS A LITTLE OVER A WEEK OFF HIS LIFESPAN.
SO, WHEN HE MEETS PEOPLE LIKE YOU, WHO CAN'T BE HELPED BY ANYONE ELSE...
...HE KILLS HIMSELF A LITTLE BIT MORE FOR YOU.
AND I HAVE TO SIT HERE AND WATCH.

story
WARREN ELLIS

artwork
JACEN BURROWS

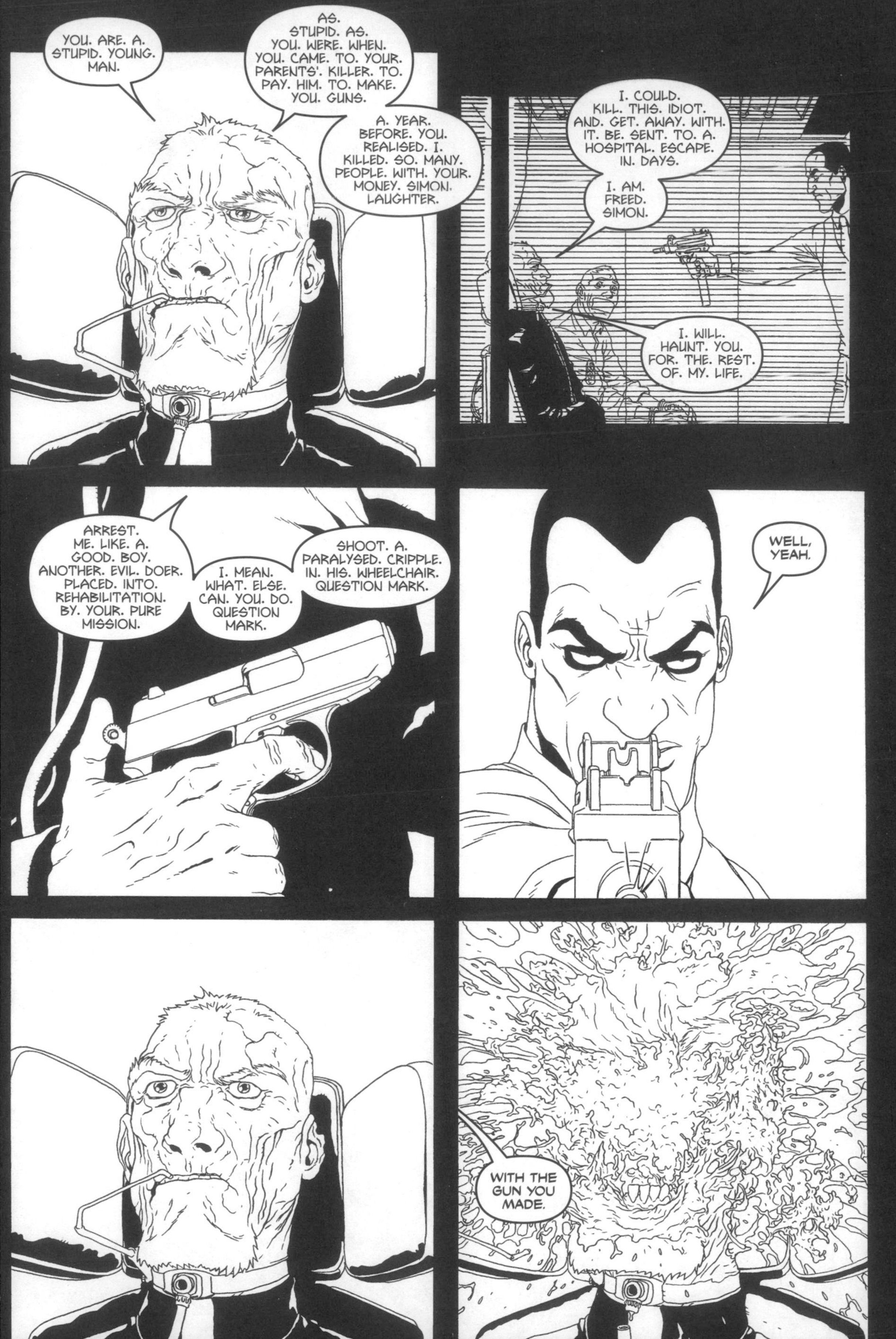
YOU. ARE. A. STUPID. YOUNG. MAN.
AS. STUPID. AS. YOU. WERE. WHEN. YOU. CAME. TO. YOUR. PARENTS'. KILLER. TO. PAY. HIM. TO. MAKE. YOU. GUNS.
A. YEAR. BEFORE. YOU. REALISED. I. KILLED. SO. MANY. PEOPLE. WITH. YOUR. MONEY. SIMON. LAUGHTER.
I. COULD. KILL. THIS. IDIOT. AND. GET. AWAY. WITH. IT. BE. SENT. TO. A. HOSPITAL. ESCAPE. IN. DAYS.
I. AM. FREED. SIMON.
I. WILL. HAUNT. YOU. FOR. THE. REST. OF. MY. LIFE.
ARREST. ME. LIKE. A. GOOD. BOY. ANOTHER. EVIL. DOER. PLACED. INTO. REHABILITATION. BY. YOUR. PURE MISSION.
I. MEAN. WHAT. ELSE. CAN. YOU. DO. QUESTION MARK.
SHOOT. A. PARALYSED. CRIPPLE. IN. HIS. WHEELCHAIR. QUESTION MARK.
WELL, YEAH.
WITH THE GUN YOU MADE.

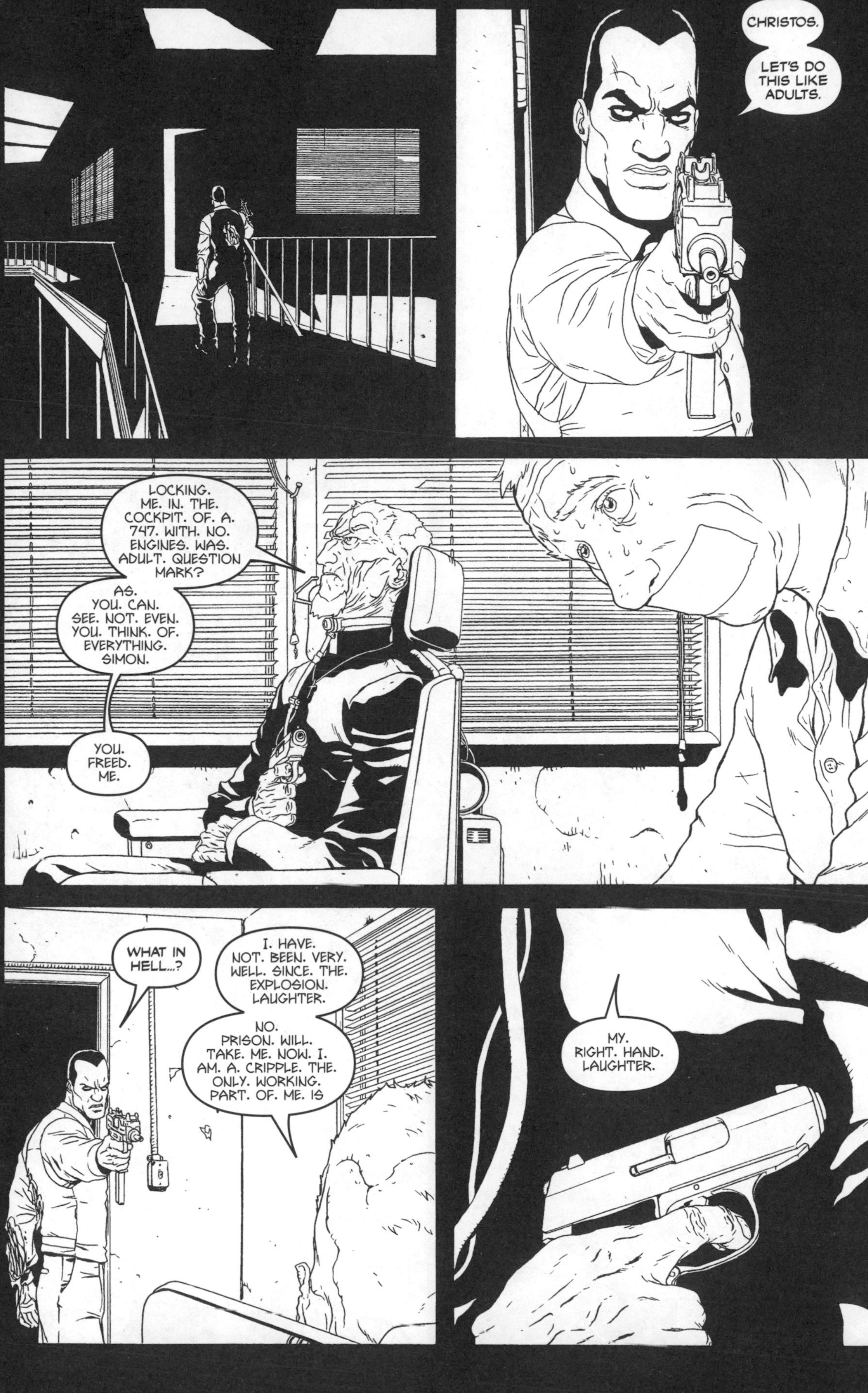
CHRISTOS.
LET'S DO THIS LIKE ADULTS.
LOCKING. ME. IN. THE. COCKPIT. OF. A. 747. WITH. NO. ENGINES. WAS. ADULT. QUESTION MARK?
AS. YOU. CAN. SEE. NOT. EVEN. YOU. THINK. OF. EVERYTHING. SIMON.
YOU. FREED. ME.
WHAT IN HELL...?
I. HAVE. NOT. BEEN. VERY. WELL. SINCE. THE. EXPLOSION. LAUGHTER.
NO. PRISON. WILL. TAKE. ME. NOW. I. AM. A. CRIPPLE. THE. ONLY. WORKING. PART. OF. ME. IS
MY. RIGHT. HAND. LAUGHTER.

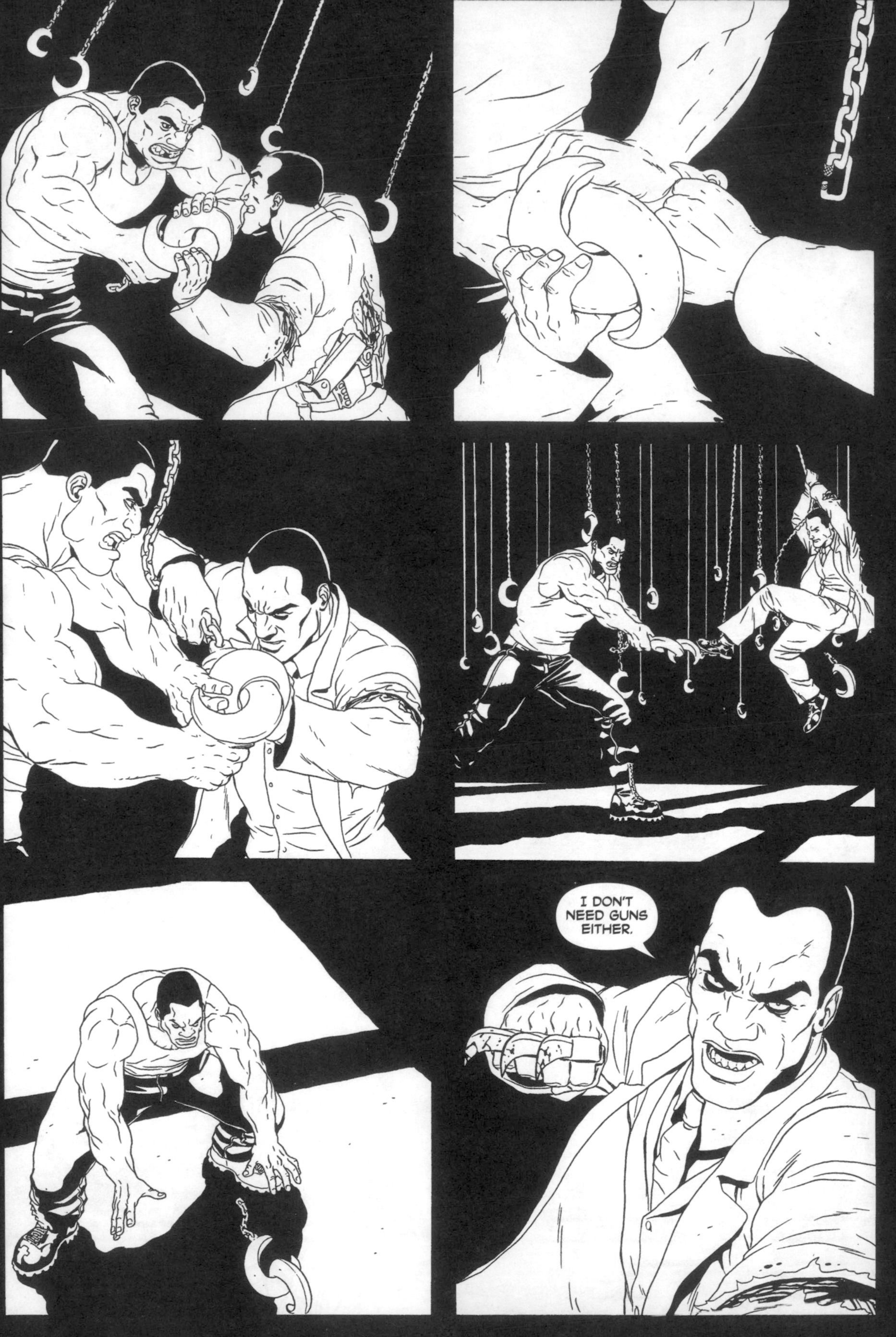
I DON'T NEED GUNS EITHER.

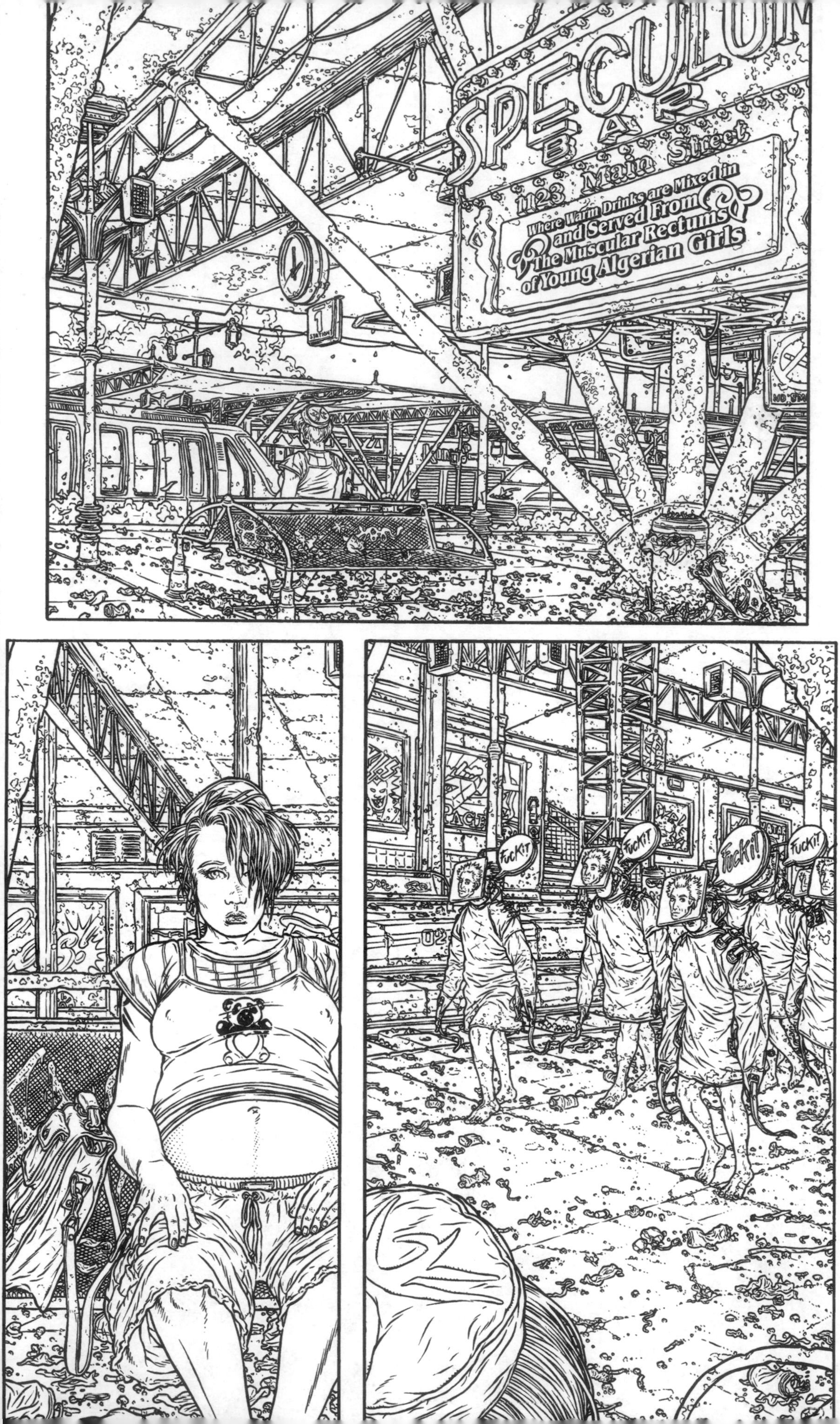
SPECULUM
1123 Main Street
Where Warm Drinks are Mixed in and Served From The Muscular Rectums of Young Algerian Girls
1 STATION
FUCKIT
FUCKIT
FUCKIT!
FUCKIT

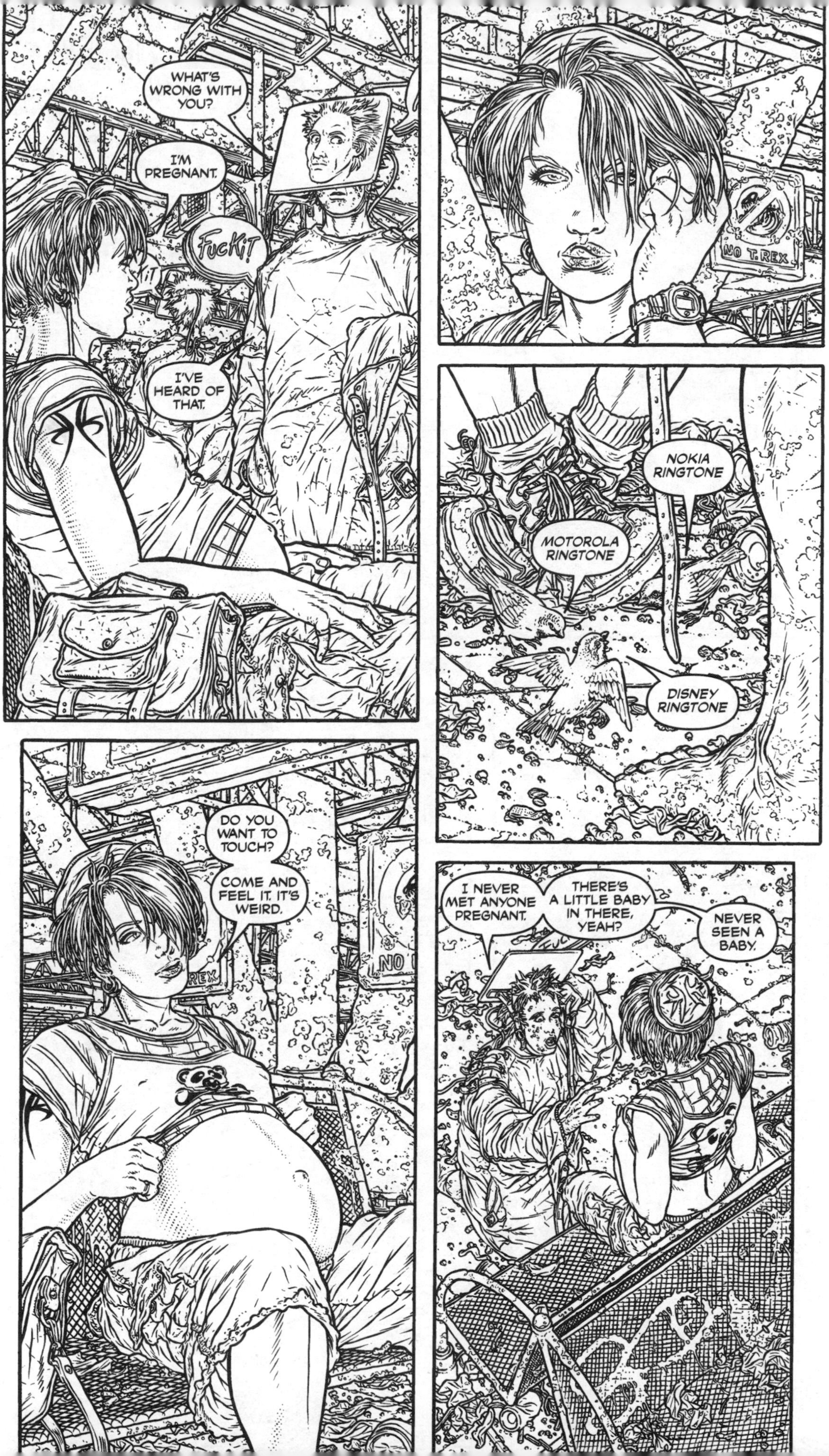
WHAT'S WRONG WITH YOU?
I'M PREGNANT.
FUCKIT!
I'VE HEARD OF THAT.
NO T. REX
NOKIA RINGTONE
MOTOROLA RINGTONE
DISNEY RINGTONE
DO YOU WANT TO TOUCH?
COME AND FEEL IT. IT'S WEIRD.
I NEVER MET ANYONE PREGNANT.
THERE'S A LITTLE BABY IN THERE, YEAH?
NEVER SEEN A BABY.

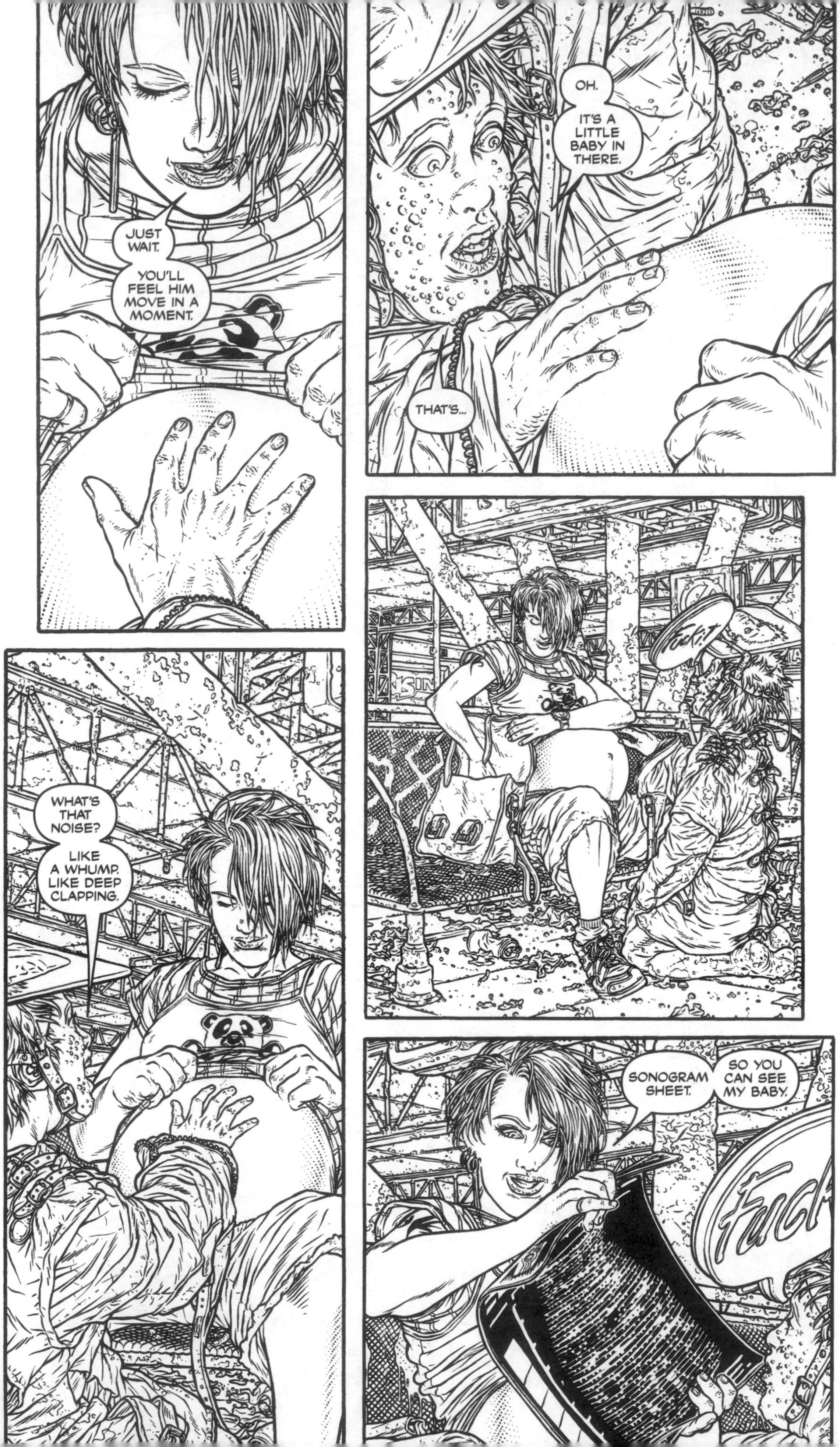

JUST WAIT.
YOU'LL FEEL HIM MOVE IN A MOMENT.
OH.
IT'S A LITTLE BABY IN THERE.
THAT'S...
WHAT'S THAT NOISE?
LIKE A WHUMP. LIKE DEEP CLAPPING.
SONOGRAM SHEET.
SO YOU CAN SEE MY BABY.

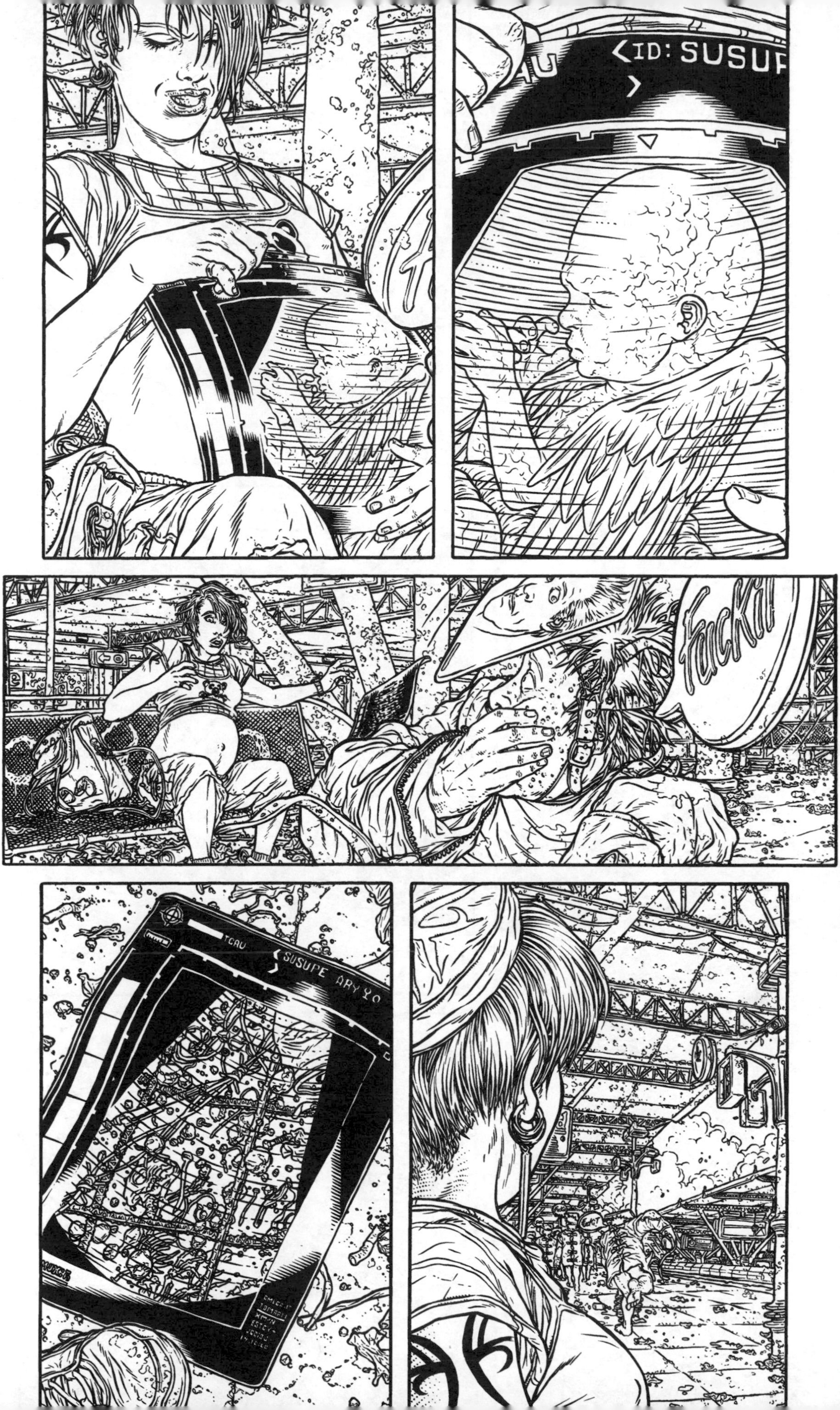

<ID: SUSUP
FucKit
TCAU
SUSUPE ARY

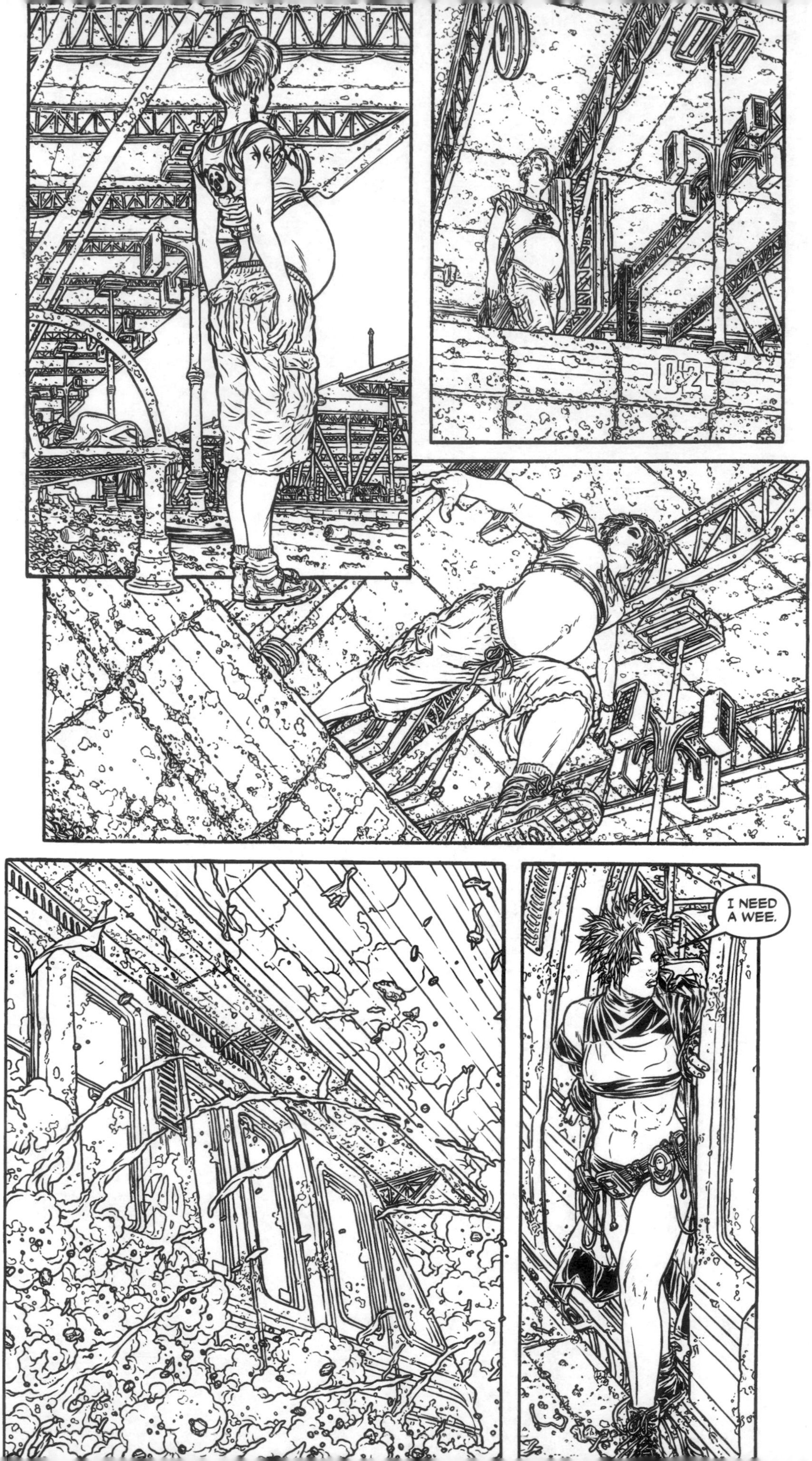
I NEED A WEE.

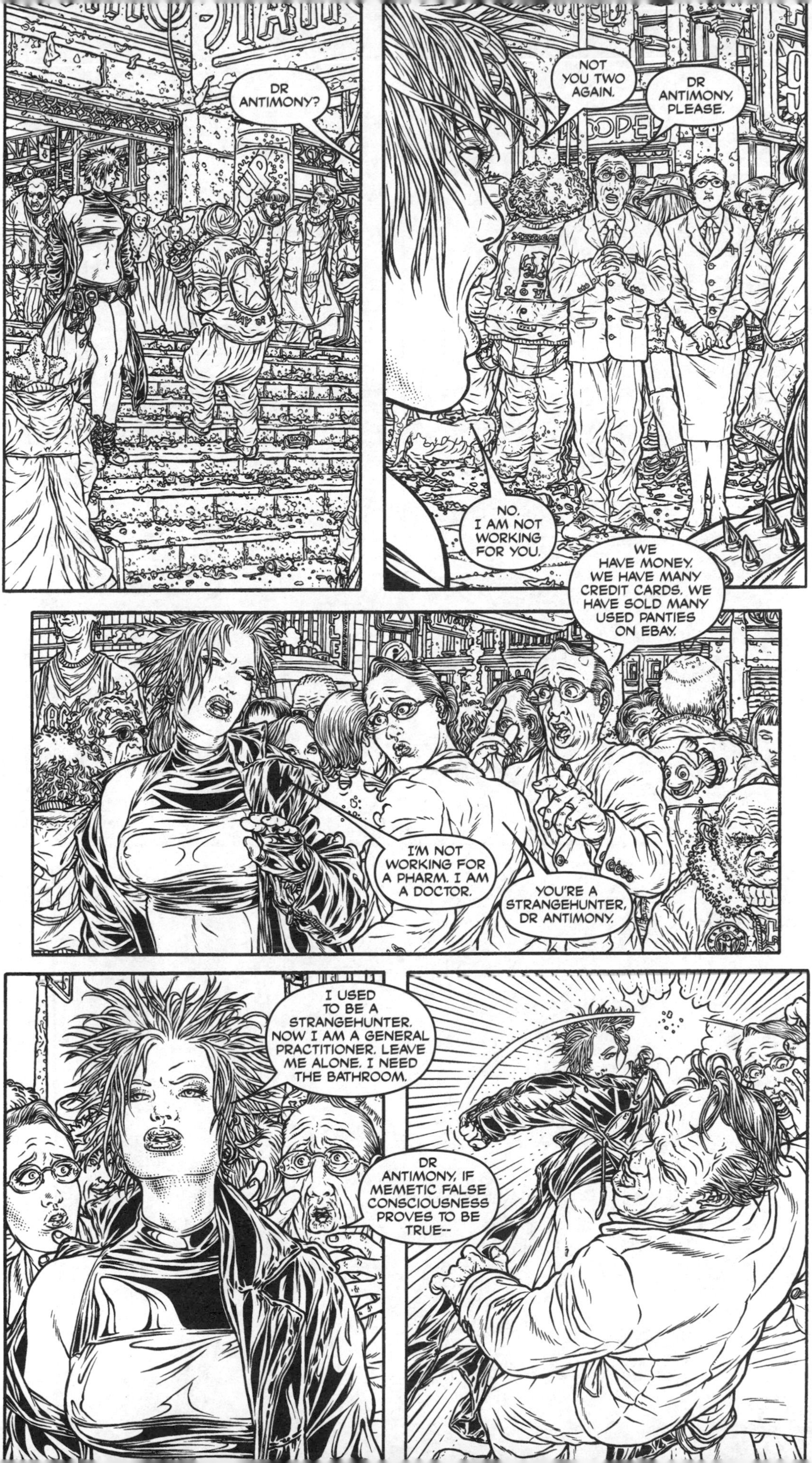
DR ANTIMONY?
NOT YOU TWO AGAIN.
DR ANTIMONY, PLEASE.
NO. I AM NOT WORKING FOR YOU.
WE HAVE MONEY. WE HAVE MANY CREDIT CARDS. WE HAVE SOLD MANY USED PANTIES ON EBAY.
I'M NOT WORKING FOR A PHARM. I AM A DOCTOR.
YOU'RE A STRANGEHUNTER, DR ANTIMONY.
I USED TO BE A STRANGEHUNTER. NOW I AM A GENERAL PRACTITIONER. LEAVE ME ALONE. I NEED THE BATHROOM.
DR ANTIMONY, IF MEMETIC FALSE CONSCIOUSNESS PROVES TO BE TRUE--

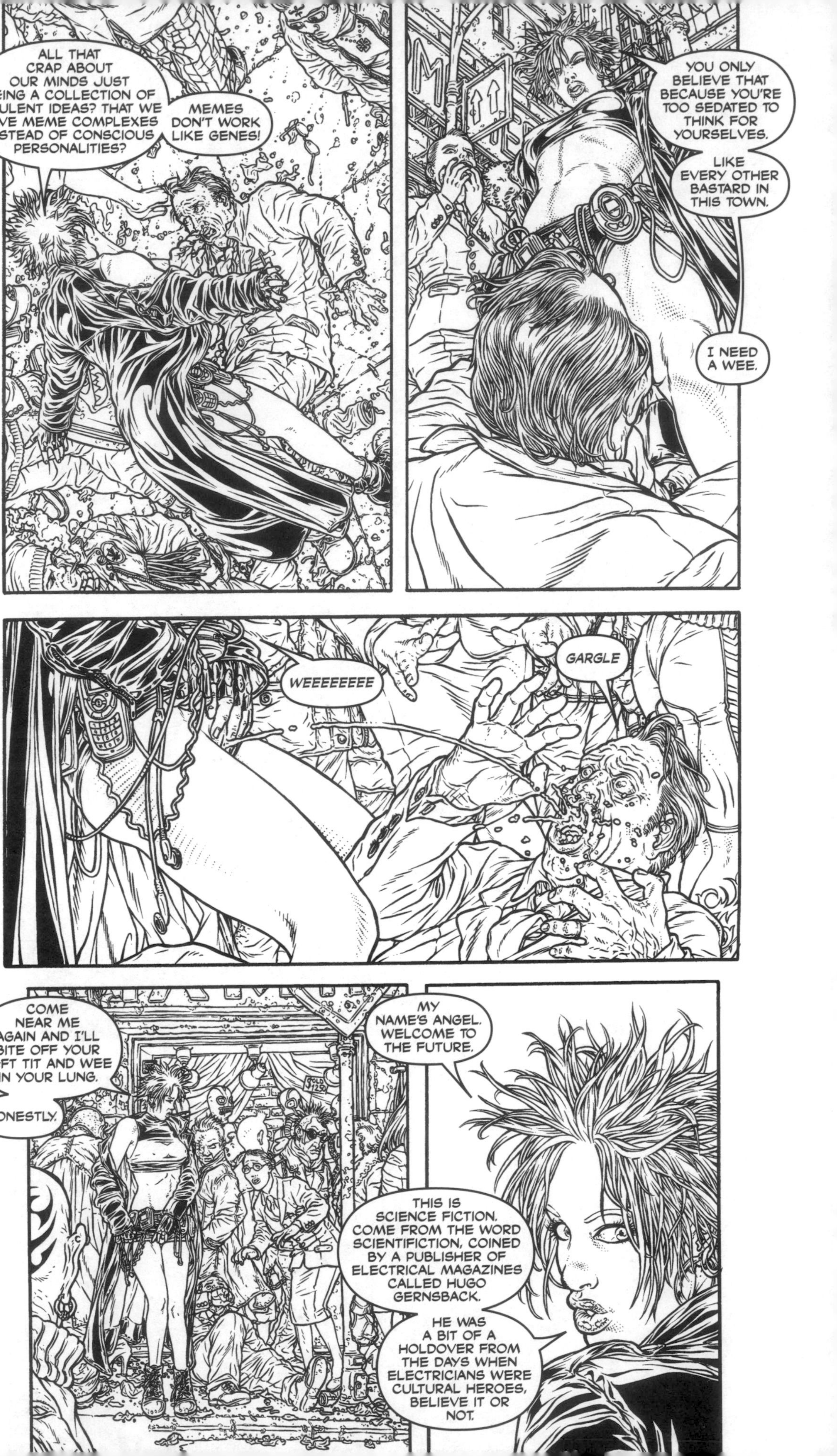
ALL THAT CRAP ABOUT OUR MINDS JUST BEING A COLLECTION OF VIRULENT IDEAS? THAT WE HAVE MEME COMPLEXES INSTEAD OF CONSCIOUS PERSONALITIES?
MEMES DON'T WORK LIKE GENES!
YOU ONLY BELIEVE THAT BECAUSE YOU'RE TOO SEDATED TO THINK FOR YOURSELVES.
LIKE EVERY OTHER BASTARD IN THIS TOWN.
I NEED A WEE.
WEEEEEEEE
GARGLE
COME NEAR ME AGAIN AND I'LL BITE OFF YOUR LEFT TIT AND WEE IN YOUR LUNG.
HONESTLY.
MY NAME'S ANGEL. WELCOME TO THE FUTURE.
THIS IS SCIENCE FICTION. COME FROM THE WORD SCIENTIFICTION, COINED BY A PUBLISHER OF ELECTRICAL MAGAZINES CALLED HUGO GERNSBACK.
HE WAS A BIT OF A HOLDOVER FROM THE DAYS WHEN ELECTRICIANS WERE CULTURAL HEROES, BELIEVE IT OR NOT.

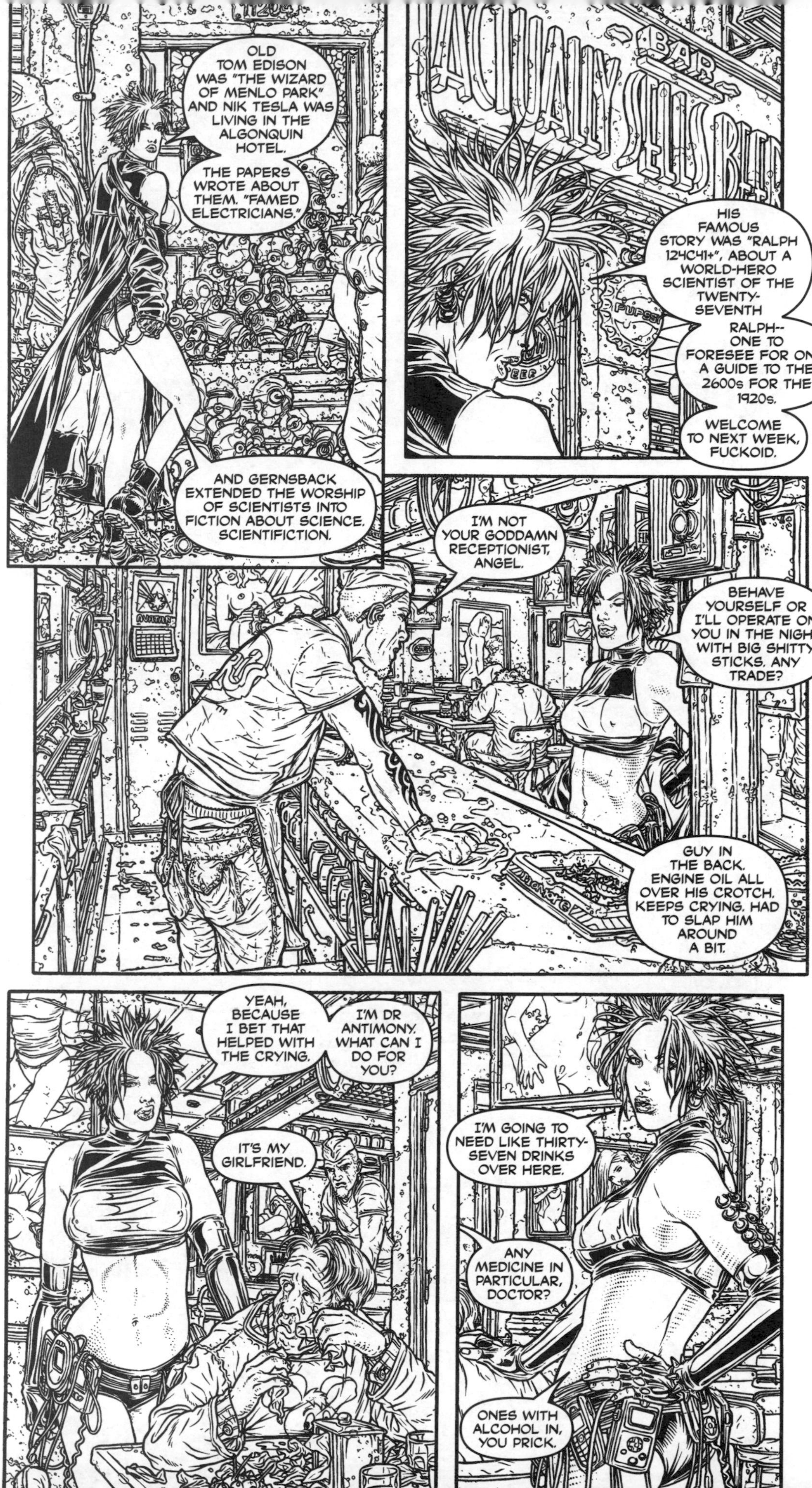
OLD TOM EDISON WAS "THE WIZARD OF MENLO PARK" AND NIK TESLA WAS LIVING IN THE ALGONQUIN HOTEL.
THE PAPERS WROTE ABOUT THEM. "FAMED ELECTRICIANS."
AND GERNSBACK EXTENDED THE WORSHIP OF SCIENTISTS INTO FICTION ABOUT SCIENCE. SCIENTIFICTION.
BAR
ACTUALLY SELLS
HIS FAMOUS STORY WAS "RALPH 124C41+", ABOUT A WORLD-HERO SCIENTIST OF THE TWENTY-SEVENTH
RALPH-- ONE TO FORESEE FOR ONE. A GUIDE TO THE 2600s FOR THE 1920s.
WELCOME TO NEXT WEEK, FUCKOID.
I'M NOT YOUR GODDAMN RECEPTIONIST, ANGEL.
BEHAVE YOURSELF OR I'LL OPERATE ON YOU IN THE NIGHT WITH BIG SHITTY STICKS. ANY TRADE?
GUY IN THE BACK. ENGINE OIL ALL OVER HIS CROTCH. KEEPS CRYING. HAD TO SLAP HIM AROUND A BIT.
YEAH, BECAUSE I BET THAT HELPED WITH THE CRYING.
I'M DR ANTIMONY. WHAT CAN I DO FOR YOU?
IT'S MY GIRLFRIEND.
I'M GOING TO NEED LIKE THIRTY-SEVEN DRINKS OVER HERE.
ANY MEDICINE IN PARTICULAR, DOCTOR?
ONES WITH ALCOHOL IN, YOU PRICK.

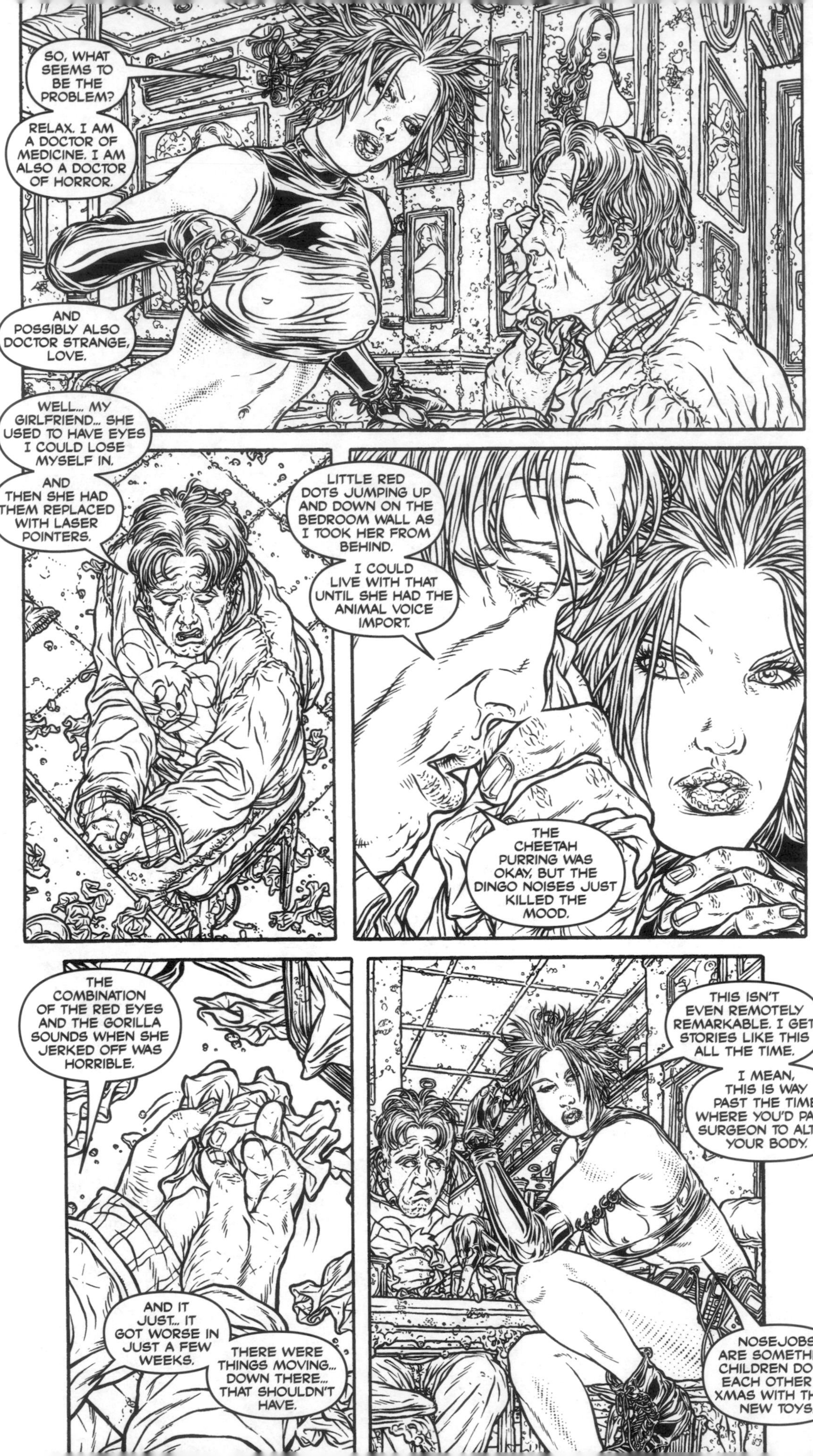
SO, WHAT SEEMS TO BE THE PROBLEM?
RELAX. I AM A DOCTOR OF MEDICINE. I AM ALSO A DOCTOR OF HORROR.
AND POSSIBLY ALSO DOCTOR STRANGE, LOVE.
WELL... MY GIRLFRIEND... SHE USED TO HAVE EYES I COULD LOSE MYSELF IN.
AND THEN SHE HAD THEM REPLACED WITH LASER POINTERS.
LITTLE RED DOTS JUMPING UP AND DOWN ON THE BEDROOM WALL AS I TOOK HER FROM BEHIND.
I COULD LIVE WITH THAT UNTIL SHE HAD THE ANIMAL VOICE IMPORT.
THE CHEETAH PURRING WAS OKAY, BUT THE DINGO NOISES JUST KILLED THE MOOD.
THE COMBINATION OF THE RED EYES AND THE GORILLA SOUNDS WHEN SHE JERKED OFF WAS HORRIBLE.
AND IT JUST... IT GOT WORSE IN JUST A FEW WEEKS.
THERE WERE THINGS MOVING... DOWN THERE... THAT SHOULDN'T HAVE.
THIS ISN'T EVEN REMOTELY REMARKABLE. I GET STORIES LIKE THIS ALL THE TIME.
I MEAN, THIS IS WAY PAST THE TIME WHERE YOU'D PAY A SURGEON TO ALTER YOUR BODY.
NOSEJOBS ARE SOMETHING CHILDREN DO TO EACH OTHER AT XMAS WITH THEIR NEW TOYS.

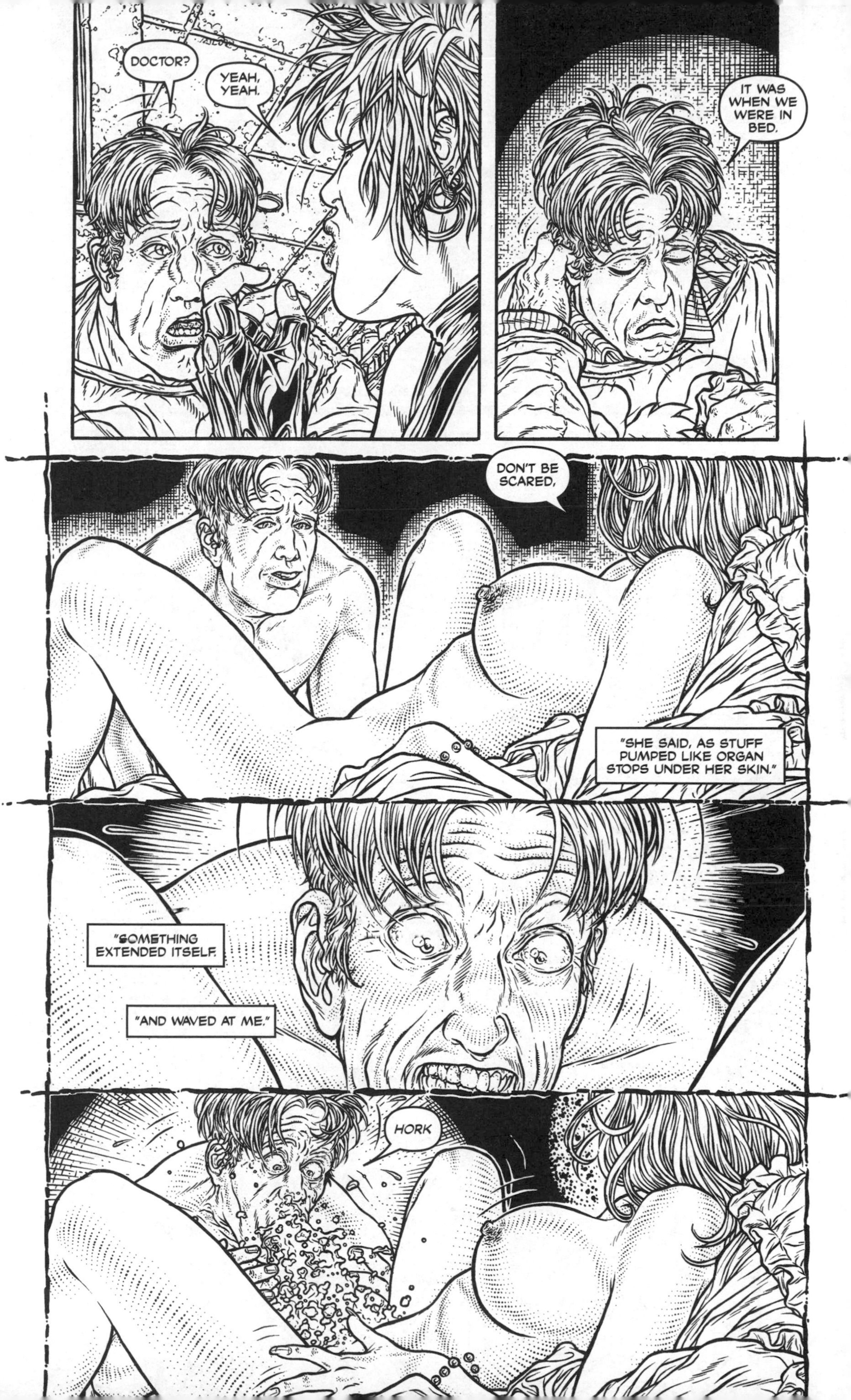
DOCTOR?
YEAH, YEAH.
IT WAS WHEN WE WERE IN BED.
DON'T BE SCARED,
"SHE SAID, AS STUFF PUMPED LIKE ORGAN STOPS UNDER HER SKIN."
"SOMETHING EXTENDED ITSELF.
"AND WAVED AT ME."
HORK

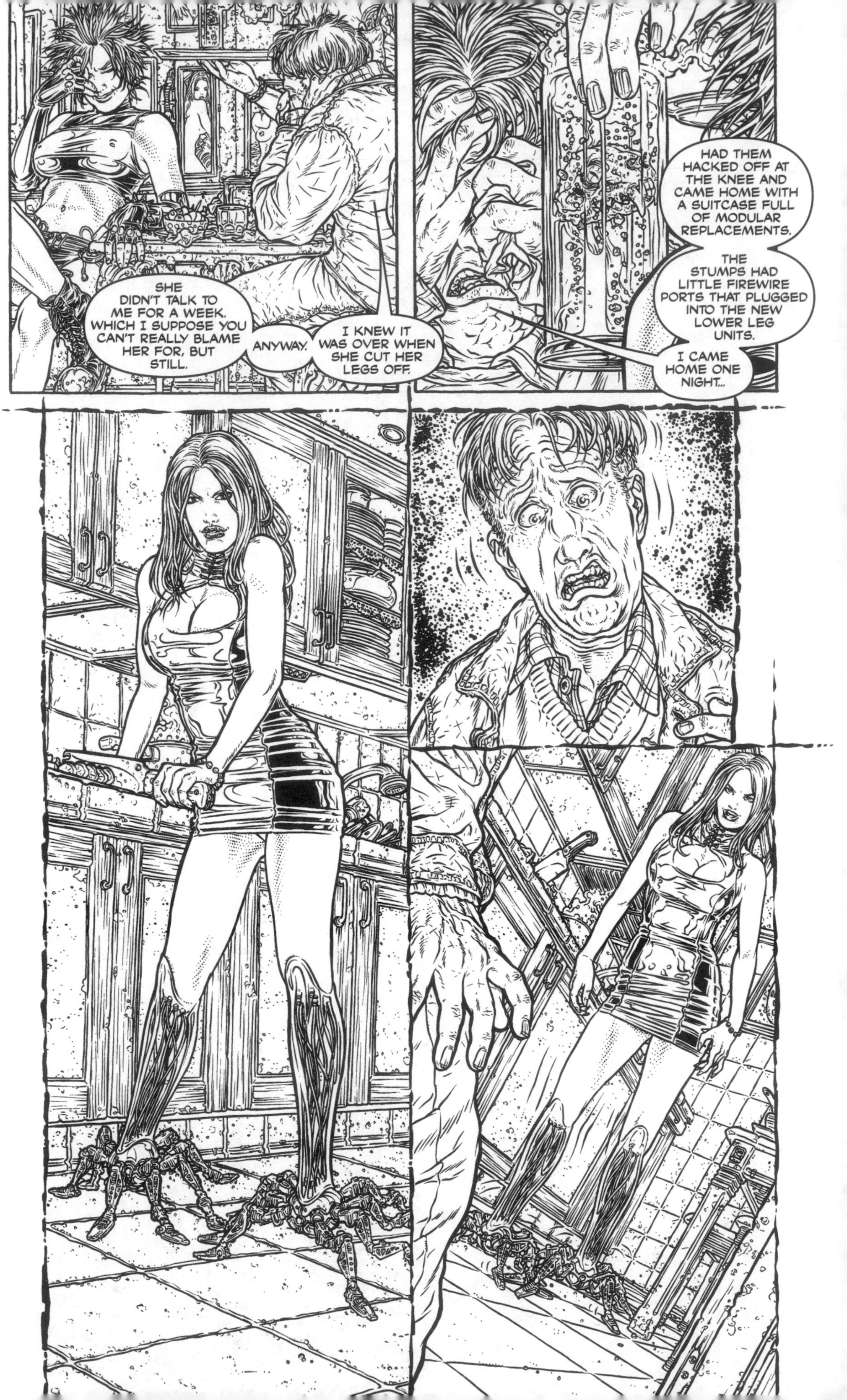
SHE DIDN'T TALK TO ME FOR A WEEK, WHICH I SUPPOSE YOU CAN'T REALLY BLAME HER FOR, BUT STILL.
ANYWAY.
I KNEW IT WAS OVER WHEN SHE CUT HER LEGS OFF.
HAD THEM HACKED OFF AT THE KNEE AND CAME HOME WITH A SUITCASE FULL OF MODULAR REPLACEMENTS.
THE STUMPS HAD LITTLE FIREWIRE PORTS THAT PLUGGED INTO THE NEW LOWER LEG UNITS.
I CAME HOME ONE NIGHT...

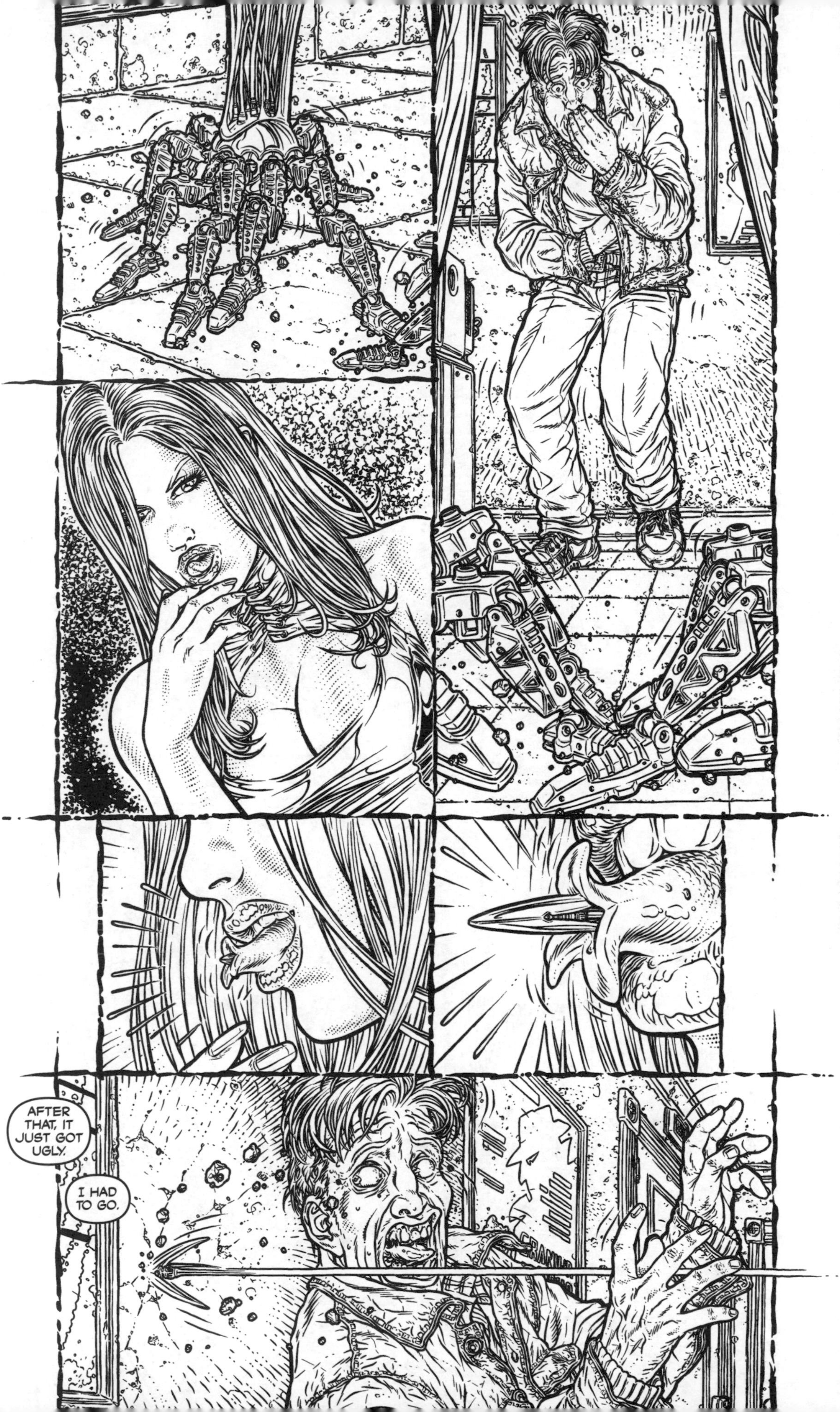
AFTER THAT, IT JUST GOT UGLY.
I HAD TO GO.

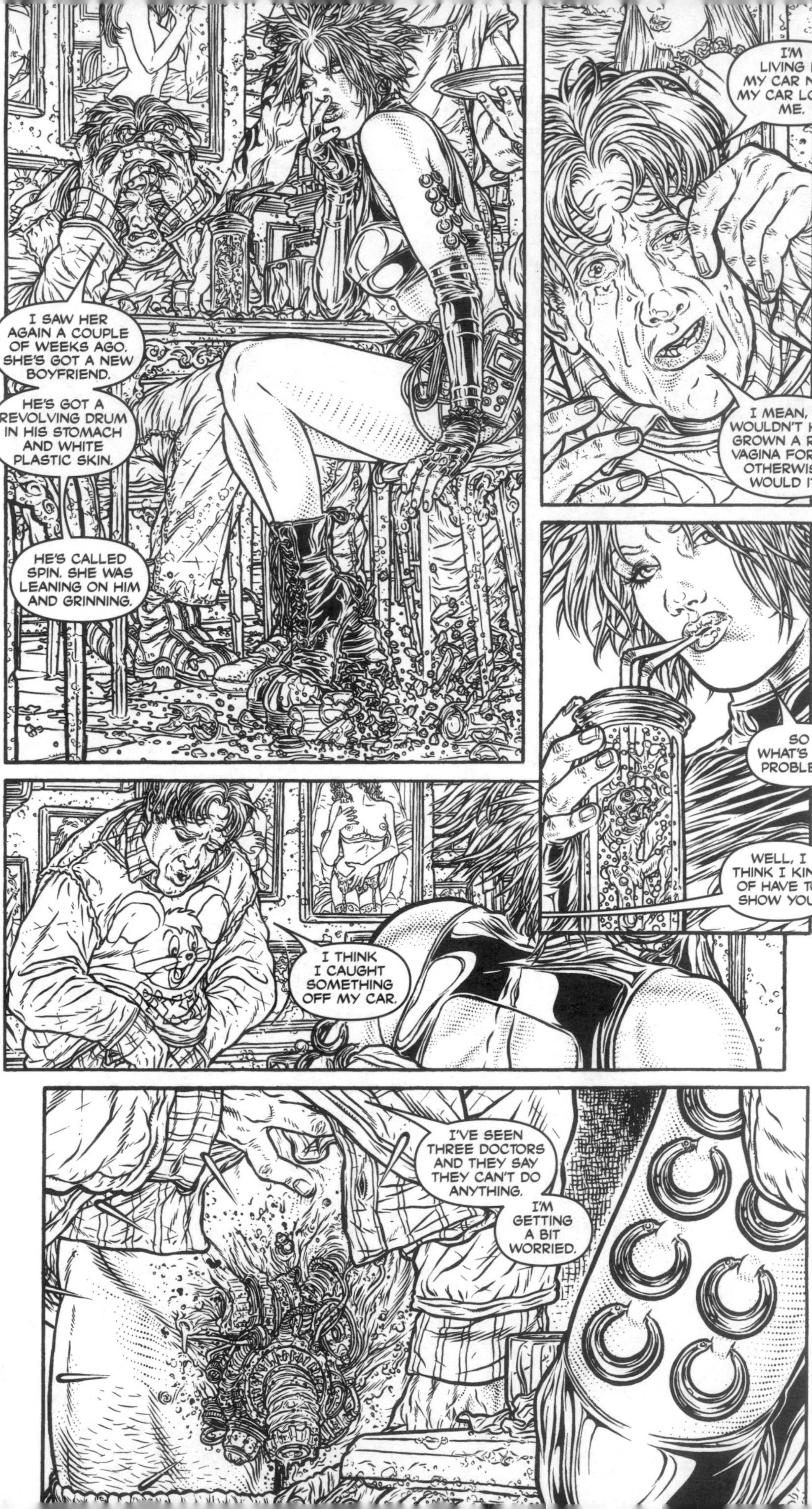
I SAW HER AGAIN A COUPLE OF WEEKS AGO. SHE'S GOT A NEW BOYFRIEND.
HE'S GOT A REVOLVING DRUM IN HIS STOMACH AND WHITE PLASTIC SKIN.
HE'S CALLED SPIN. SHE WAS LEANING ON HIM AND GRINNING.
I'M LIVING IN MY CAR NOW. MY CAR LOVES ME.
I MEAN, IT WOULDN'T HAVE GROWN A REAL VAGINA FOR ME OTHERWISE, WOULD IT?
SO WHAT'S THE PROBLEM?
WELL, I THINK I KIND OF HAVE TO SHOW YOU.
I THINK I CAUGHT SOMETHING OFF MY CAR.
I'VE SEEN THREE DOCTORS AND THEY SAY THEY CAN'T DO ANYTHING.
I'M GETTING A BIT WORRIED.

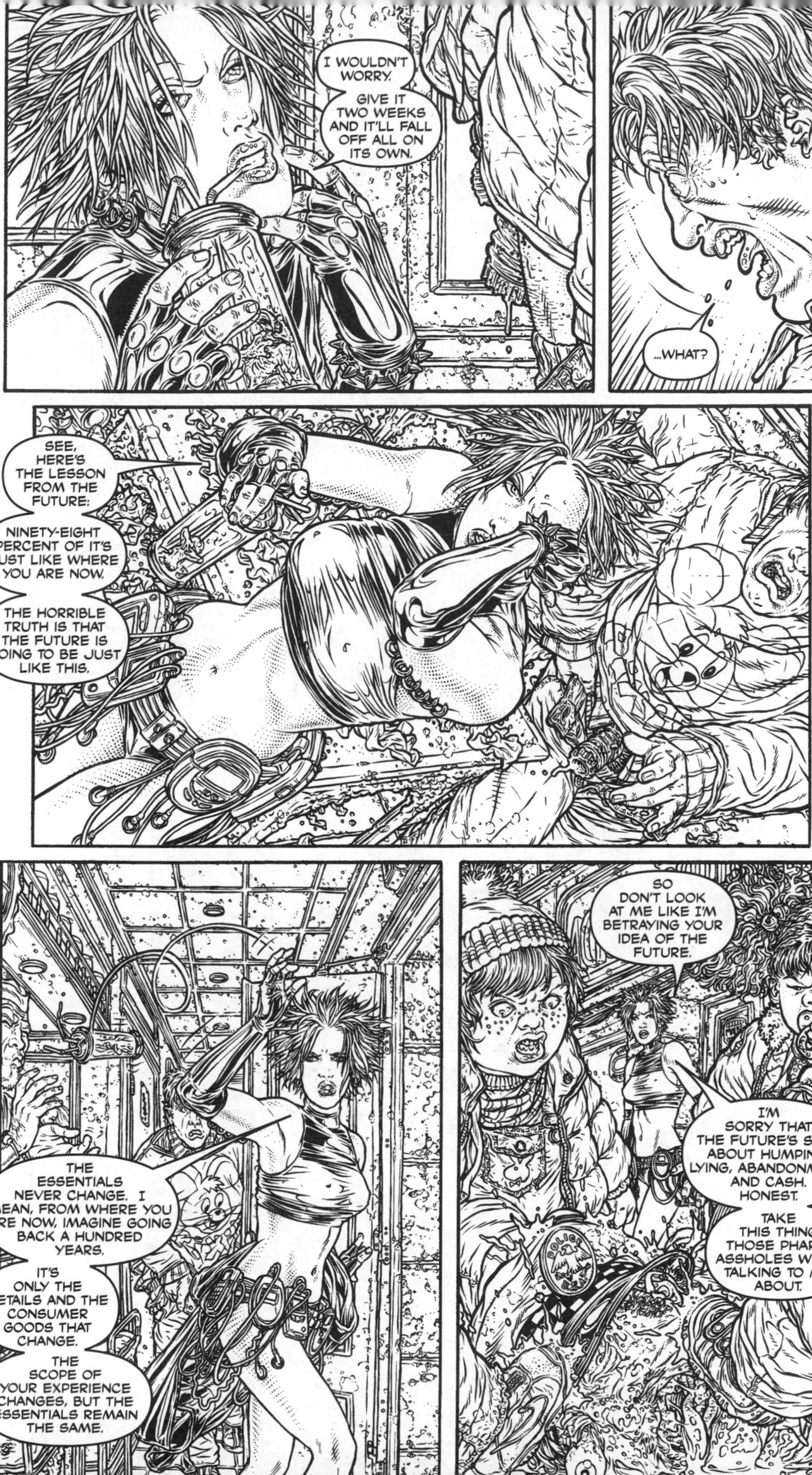
I WOULDN'T WORRY.
GIVE IT TWO WEEKS AND IT'LL FALL OFF ALL ON ITS OWN.
...WHAT?
SEE, HERE'S THE LESSON FROM THE FUTURE:
NINETY-EIGHT PERCENT OF IT'S JUST LIKE WHERE YOU ARE NOW.
THE HORRIBLE TRUTH IS THAT THE FUTURE IS GOING TO BE JUST LIKE THIS.
THE ESSENTIALS NEVER CHANGE. I MEAN, FROM WHERE YOU ARE NOW, IMAGINE GOING BACK A HUNDRED YEARS.
IT'S ONLY THE DETAILS AND THE CONSUMER GOODS THAT CHANGE.
THE SCOPE OF YOUR EXPERIENCE CHANGES, BUT THE ESSENTIALS REMAIN THE SAME.
SO DON'T LOOK AT ME LIKE I'M BETRAYING YOUR IDEA OF THE FUTURE.
I'M SORRY THAT THE FUTURE'S STILL ABOUT HUMPING, LYING, ABANDONMENT AND CASH. HONEST.
TAKE THIS THING THOSE PHARM ASSHOLES WERE TALKING TO ME ABOUT.

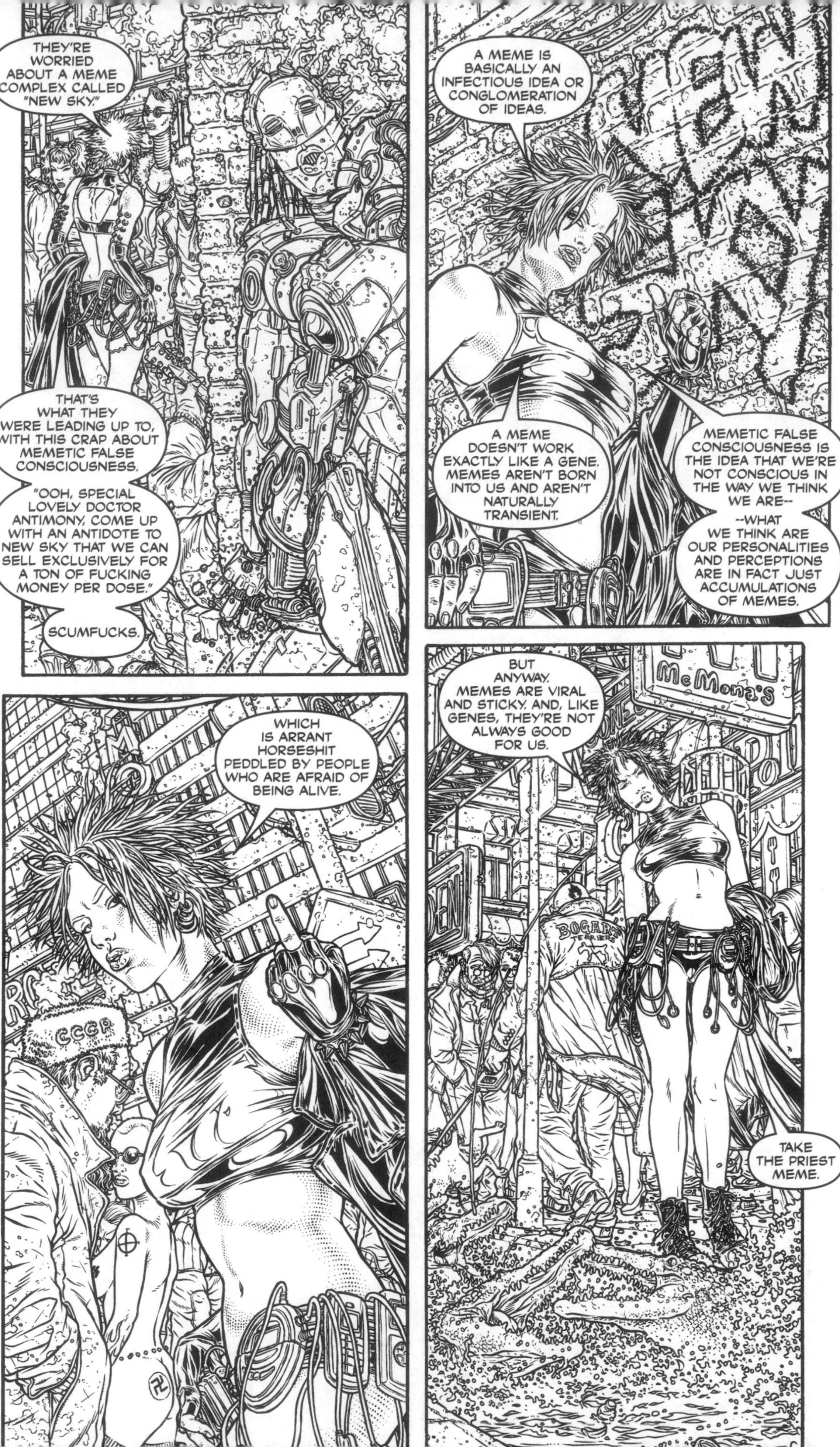
THEY'RE WORRIED ABOUT A MEME COMPLEX CALLED "NEW SKY."
THAT'S WHAT THEY WERE LEADING UP TO, WITH THIS CRAP ABOUT MEMETIC FALSE CONSCIOUSNESS.
"OOH, SPECIAL LOVELY DOCTOR ANTIMONY, COME UP WITH AN ANTIDOTE TO NEW SKY THAT WE CAN SELL EXCLUSIVELY FOR A TON OF FUCKING MONEY PER DOSE."
SCUMFUCKS.
A MEME IS BASICALLY AN INFECTIOUS IDEA OR CONGLOMERATION OF IDEAS.
A MEME DOESN'T WORK EXACTLY LIKE A GENE. MEMES AREN'T BORN INTO US AND AREN'T NATURALLY TRANSIENT.
MEMETIC FALSE CONSCIOUSNESS IS THE IDEA THAT WE'RE NOT CONSCIOUS IN THE WAY WE THINK WE ARE--
--WHAT WE THINK ARE OUR PERSONALITIES AND PERCEPTIONS ARE IN FACT JUST ACCUMULATIONS OF MEMES.
WHICH IS ARRANT HORSESHIT PEDDLED BY PEOPLE WHO ARE AFRAID OF BEING ALIVE.
BUT ANYWAY. MEMES ARE VIRAL AND STICKY. AND, LIKE GENES, THEY'RE NOT ALWAYS GOOD FOR US.
McMona's
TAKE THE PRIEST MEME.

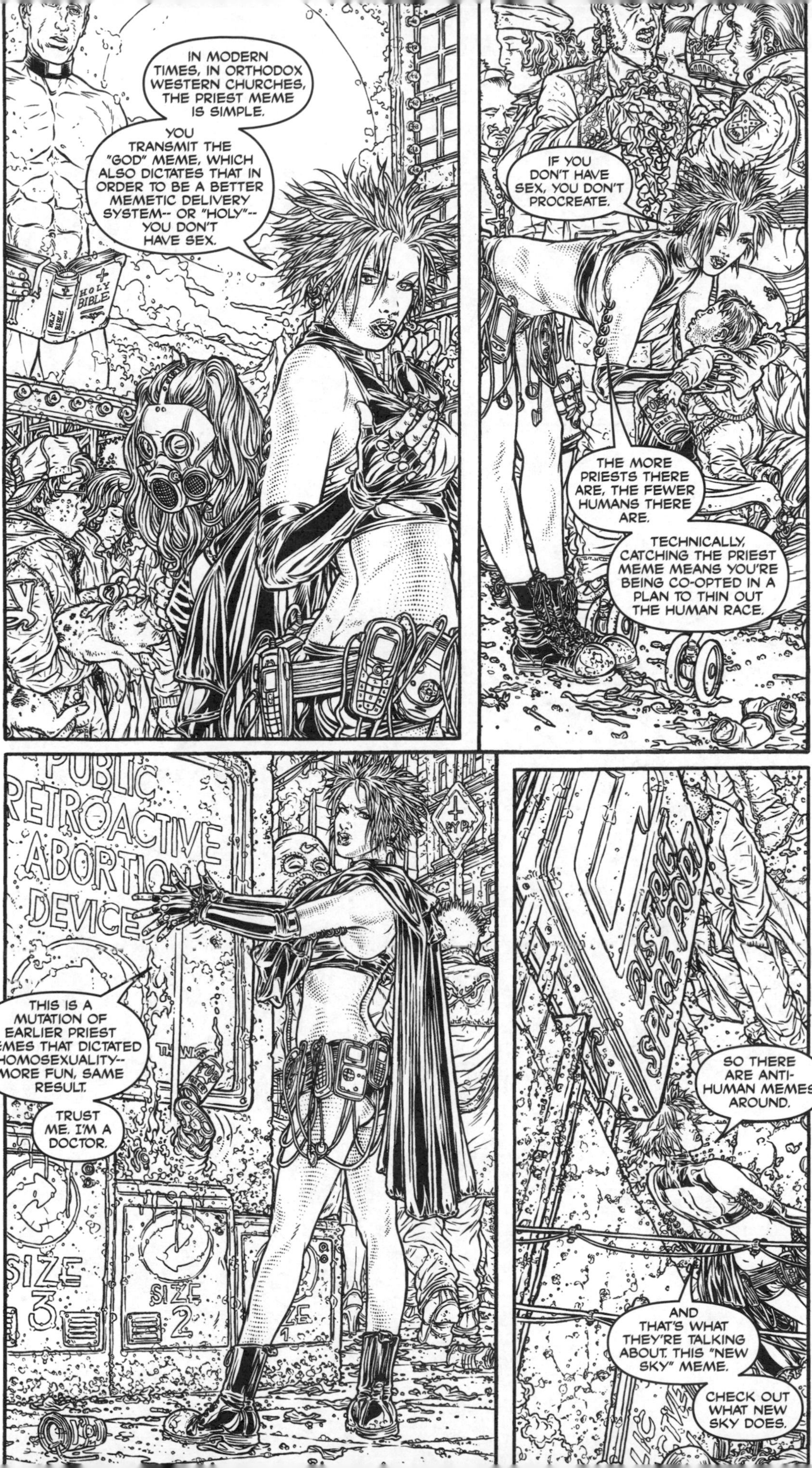
IN MODERN TIMES, IN ORTHODOX WESTERN CHURCHES, THE PRIEST MEME IS SIMPLE.
YOU TRANSMIT THE "GOD" MEME, WHICH ALSO DICTATES THAT IN ORDER TO BE A BETTER MEMETIC DELIVERY SYSTEM-- OR "HOLY"-- YOU DON'T HAVE SEX.
HOLY BIBLE
IF YOU DON'T HAVE SEX, YOU DON'T PROCREATE.
THE MORE PRIESTS THERE ARE, THE FEWER HUMANS THERE ARE.
TECHNICALLY, CATCHING THE PRIEST MEME MEANS YOU'RE BEING CO-OPTED IN A PLAN TO THIN OUT THE HUMAN RACE.
PUBLIC RETROACTIVE ABORTION DEVICE
THIS IS A MUTATION OF EARLIER PRIEST MEMES THAT DICTATED HOMOSEXUALITY-- MORE FUN, SAME RESULT.
TRUST ME. I'M A DOCTOR.
SIZE 3
SIZE 2
SO THERE ARE ANTI-HUMAN MEMES AROUND.
AND THAT'S WHAT THEY'RE TALKING ABOUT. THIS "NEW SKY" MEME.
CHECK OUT WHAT NEW SKY DOES.

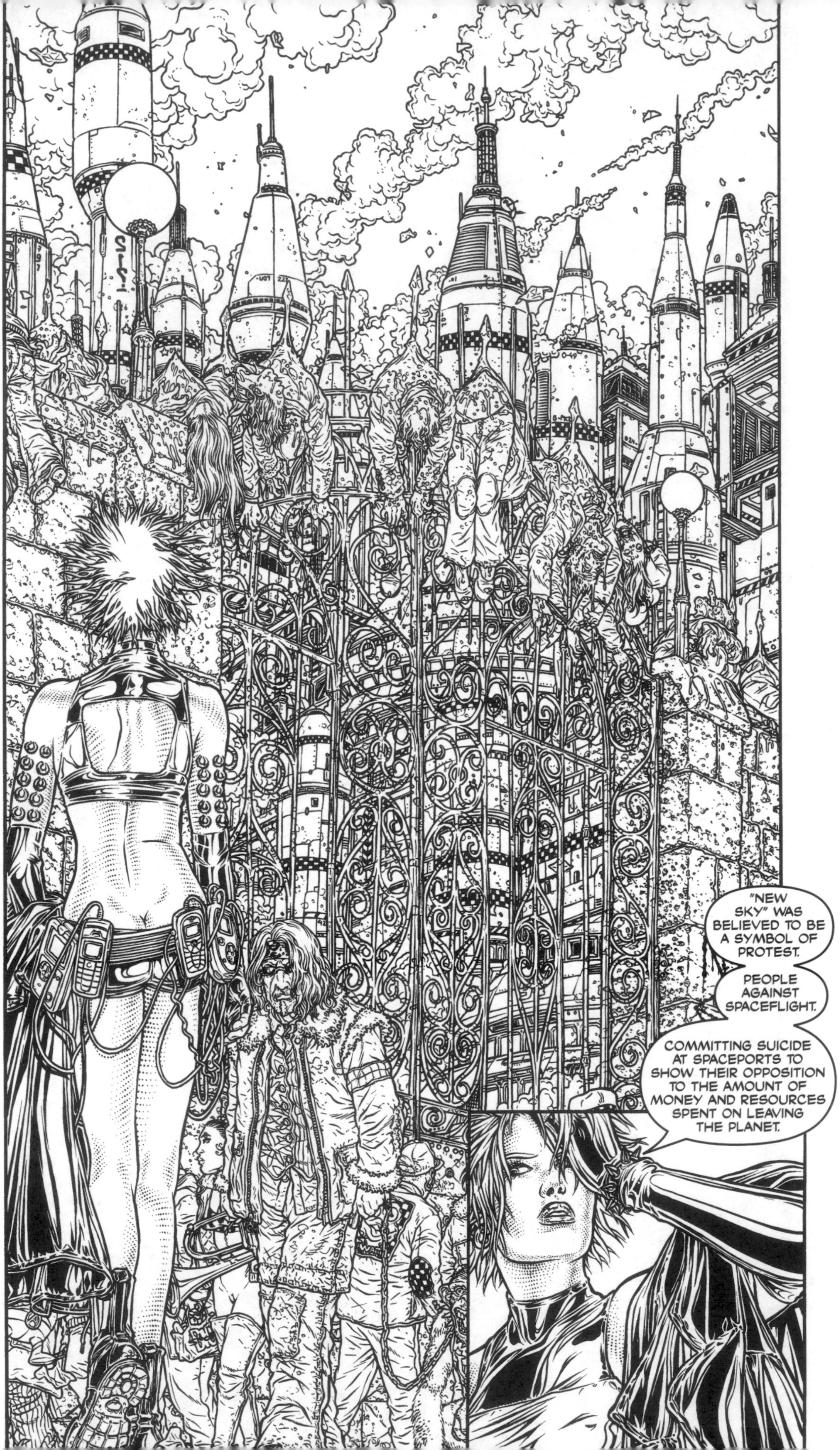
"NEW SKY" WAS BELIEVED TO BE A SYMBOL OF PROTEST.
PEOPLE AGAINST SPACEFLIGHT.
COMMITTING SUICIDE AT SPACEPORTS TO SHOW THEIR OPPOSITION TO THE AMOUNT OF MONEY AND RESOURCES SPENT ON LEAVING THE PLANET.

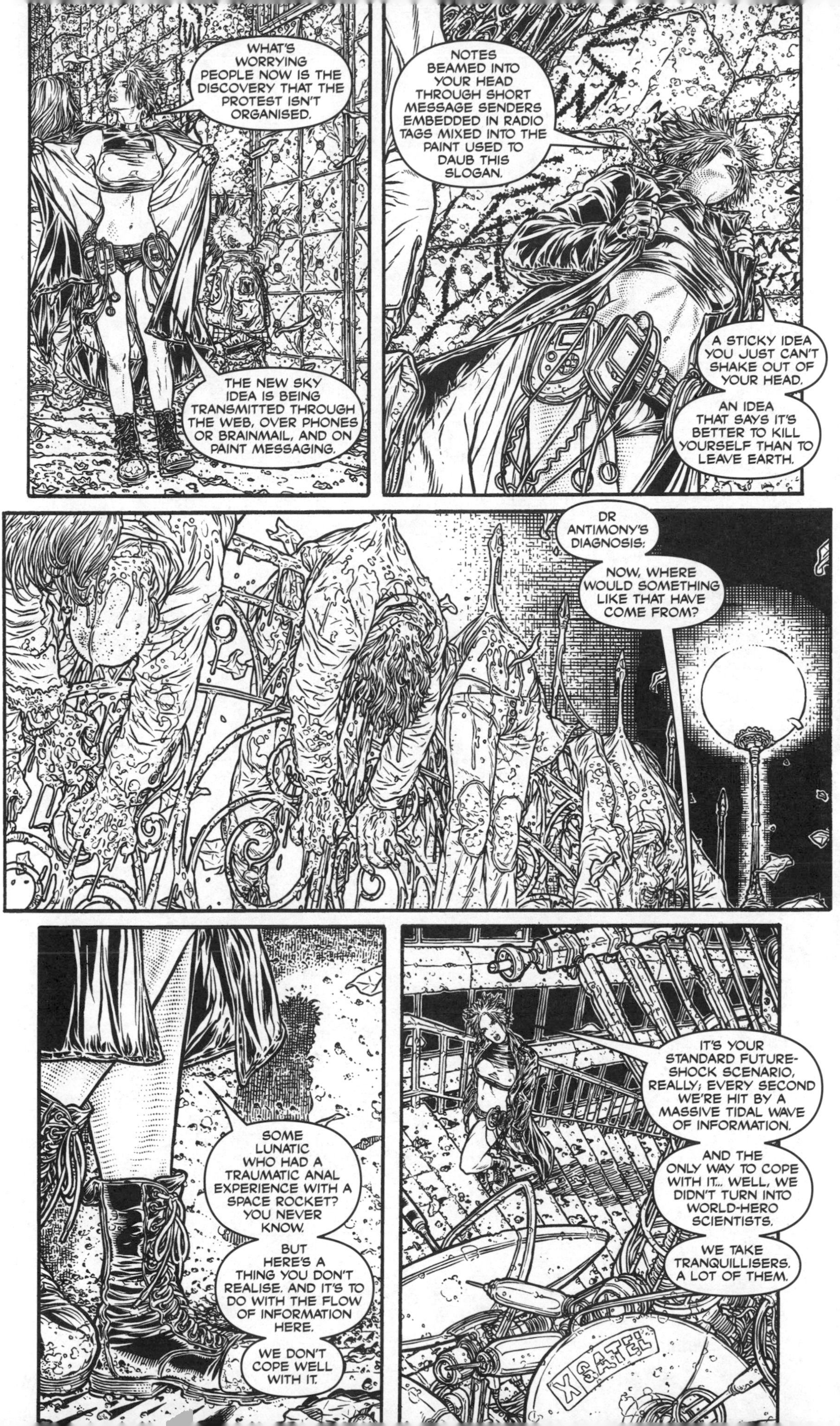

WHAT'S WORRYING PEOPLE NOW IS THE DISCOVERY THAT THE PROTEST ISN'T ORGANISED.
THE NEW SKY IDEA IS BEING TRANSMITTED THROUGH THE WEB, OVER PHONES OR BRAINMAIL, AND ON PAINT MESSAGING.
NOTES BEAMED INTO YOUR HEAD THROUGH SHORT MESSAGE SENDERS EMBEDDED IN RADIO TAGS MIXED INTO THE PAINT USED TO DAUB THIS SLOGAN.
A STICKY IDEA YOU JUST CAN'T SHAKE OUT OF YOUR HEAD.
AN IDEA THAT SAYS IT'S BETTER TO KILL YOURSELF THAN TO LEAVE EARTH.
DR ANTIMONY'S DIAGNOSIS:
NOW, WHERE WOULD SOMETHING LIKE THAT HAVE COME FROM?
SOME LUNATIC WHO HAD A TRAUMATIC ANAL EXPERIENCE WITH A SPACE ROCKET? YOU NEVER KNOW.
BUT HERE'S A THING YOU DON'T REALISE. AND IT'S TO DO WITH THE FLOW OF INFORMATION HERE.
WE DON'T COPE WELL WITH IT.
IT'S YOUR STANDARD FUTURE-SHOCK SCENARIO, REALLY; EVERY SECOND WE'RE HIT BY A MASSIVE TIDAL WAVE OF INFORMATION.
AND THE ONLY WAY TO COPE WITH IT... WELL, WE DIDN'T TURN INTO WORLD-HERO SCIENTISTS.
WE TAKE TRANQUILLISERS. A LOT OF THEM.

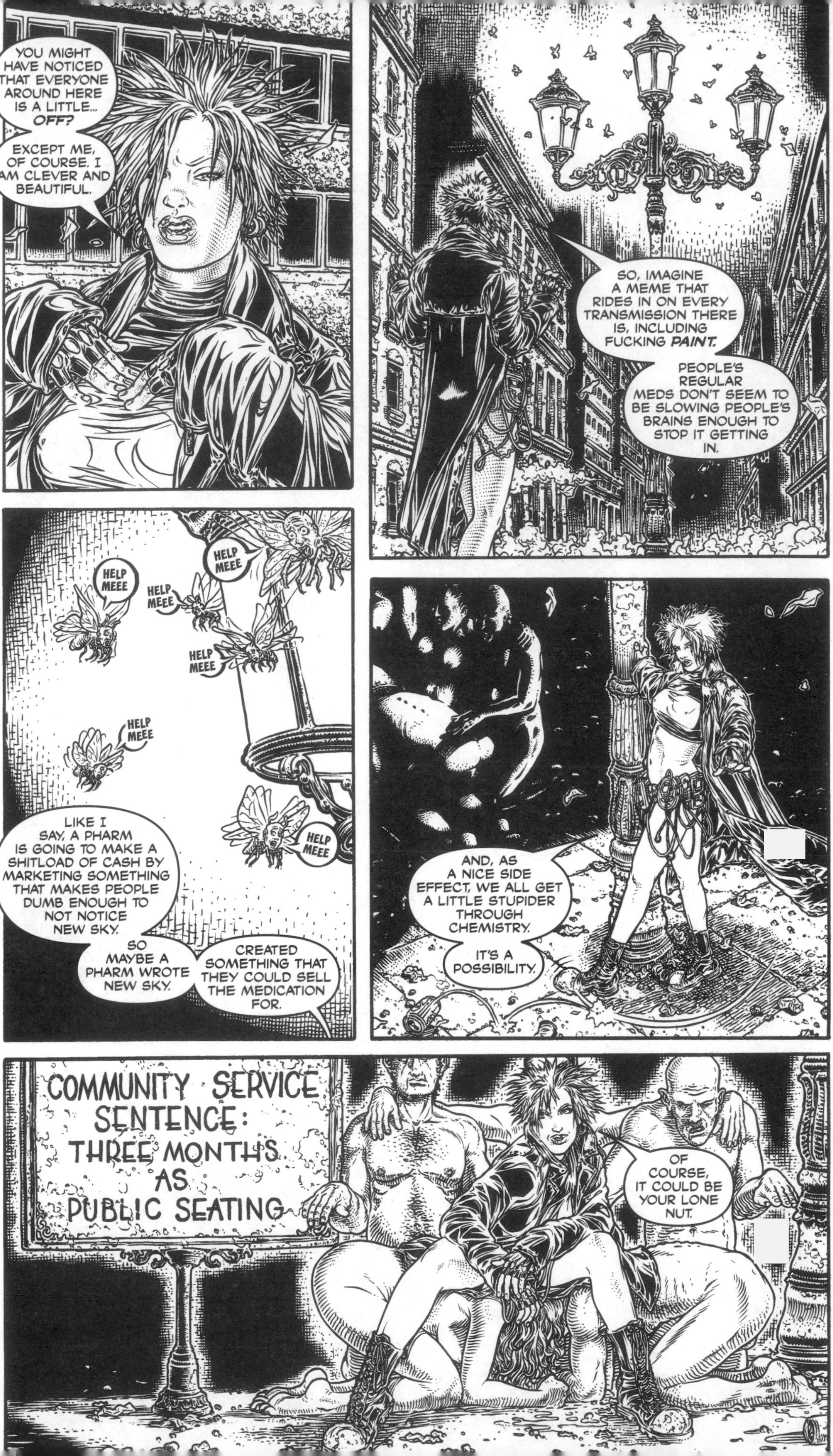
YOU MIGHT HAVE NOTICED THAT EVERYONE AROUND HERE IS A LITTLE... OFF?
EXCEPT ME, OF COURSE. I AM CLEVER AND BEAUTIFUL.
SO, IMAGINE A MEME THAT RIDES IN ON EVERY TRANSMISSION THERE IS, INCLUDING FUCKING PAINT.
PEOPLE'S REGULAR MEDS DON'T SEEM TO BE SLOWING PEOPLE'S BRAINS ENOUGH TO STOP IT GETTING IN.
HELP MEEE
HELP MEEE
HELP MEEE
HELP MEEE
HELP MEEE
HELP MEEE
LIKE I SAY, A PHARM IS GOING TO MAKE A SHITLOAD OF CASH BY MARKETING SOMETHING THAT MAKES PEOPLE DUMB ENOUGH TO NOT NOTICE NEW SKY.
SO MAYBE A PHARM WROTE NEW SKY.
CREATED SOMETHING THAT THEY COULD SELL THE MEDICATION FOR.
AND, AS A NICE SIDE EFFECT, WE ALL GET A LITTLE STUPIDER THROUGH CHEMISTRY.
IT'S A POSSIBILITY.
COMMUNITY SERVICE SENTENCE: THREE MONTHS AS PUBLIC SEATING
OF COURSE, IT COULD BE YOUR LONE NUT.

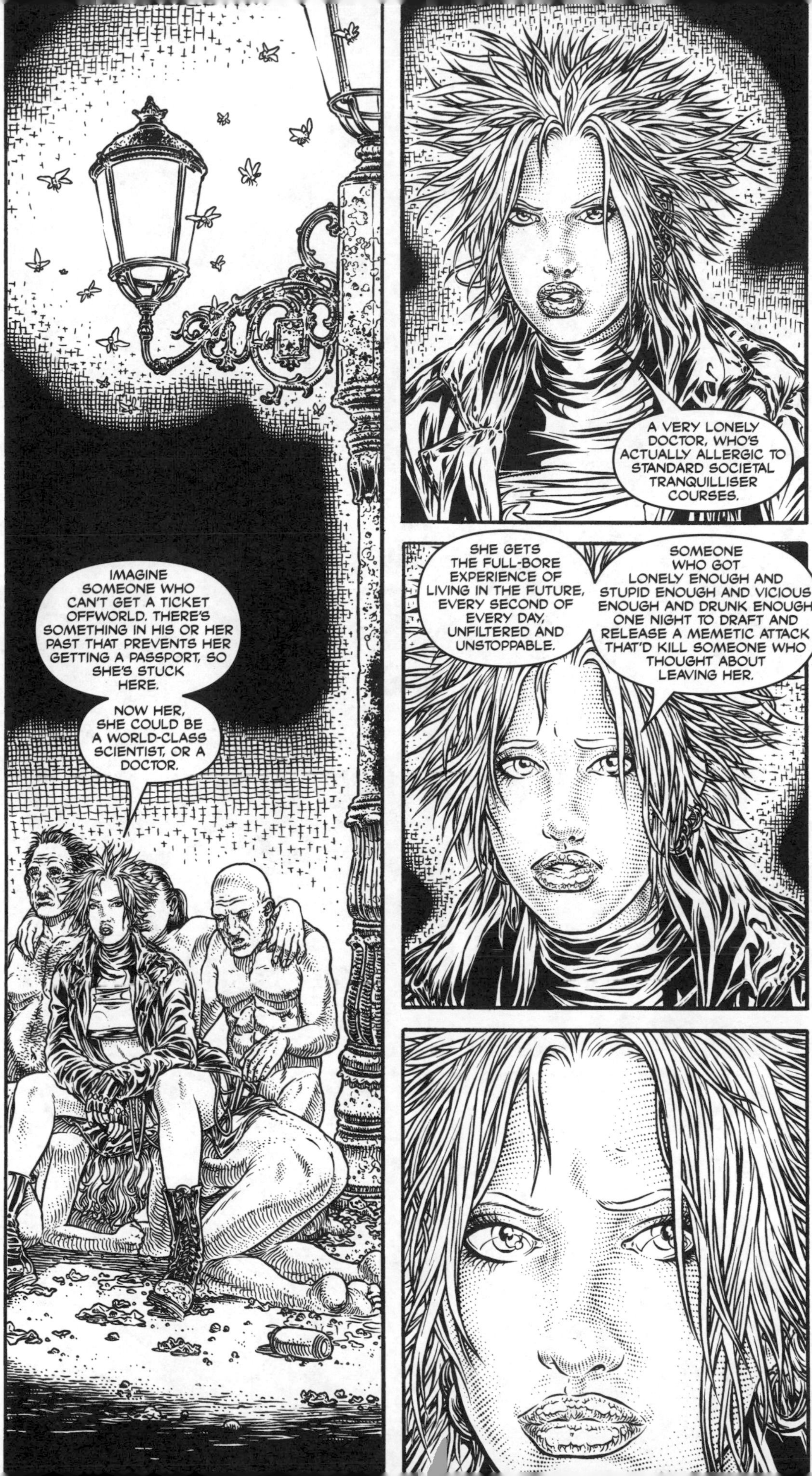
IMAGINE SOMEONE WHO CAN'T GET A TICKET OFFWORLD. THERE'S SOMETHING IN HIS OR HER PAST THAT PREVENTS HER GETTING A PASSPORT, SO SHE'S STUCK HERE.
NOW HER, SHE COULD BE A WORLD-CLASS SCIENTIST, OR A DOCTOR.
A VERY LONELY DOCTOR, WHO'S ACTUALLY ALLERGIC TO STANDARD SOCIETAL TRANQUILLISER COURSES.
SHE GETS THE FULL-BORE EXPERIENCE OF LIVING IN THE FUTURE, EVERY SECOND OF EVERY DAY, UNFILTERED AND UNSTOPPABLE.
SOMEONE WHO GOT LONELY ENOUGH AND STUPID ENOUGH AND VICIOUS ENOUGH AND DRUNK ENOUGH ONE NIGHT TO DRAFT AND RELEASE A MEMETIC ATTACK THAT'D KILL SOMEONE WHO THOUGHT ABOUT LEAVING HER.

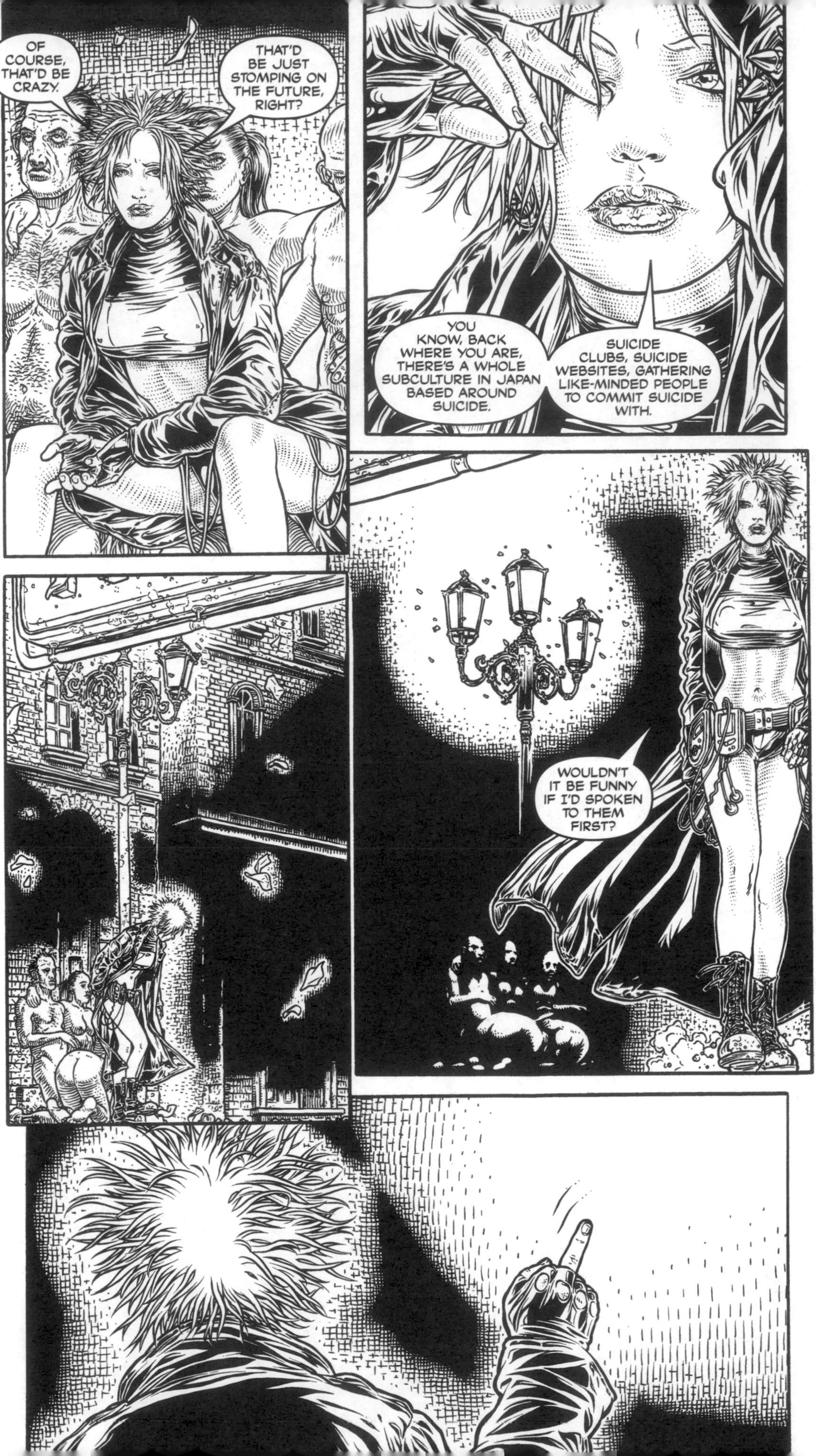
OF COURSE, THAT'D BE CRAZY.
THAT'D BE JUST STOMPING ON THE FUTURE, RIGHT?
YOU KNOW, BACK WHERE YOU ARE, THERE'S A WHOLE SUBCULTURE IN JAPAN BASED AROUND SUICIDE.
SUICIDE CLUBS, SUICIDE WEBSITES, GATHERING LIKE-MINDED PEOPLE TO COMMIT SUICIDE WITH.
WOULDN'T IT BE FUNNY IF I'D SPOKEN TO THEM FIRST?

WHAT THE FUCK ARE YOU LOOKING AT?

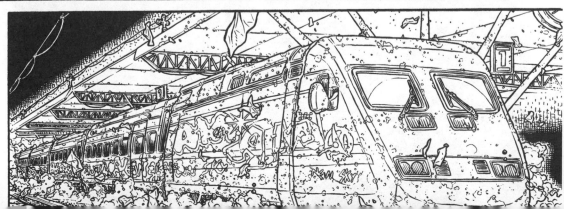

angel stomp future

YEARS AGO, I SAT DOWN AND THOUGHT ABOUT WHAT adventure comics might've looked like today if superhero comics hadn't have happened. If, in fact, the pulp tradition of Weird Thrillers had jumped straight into comics form without mutating into the superhero subgenre we know today. If you took away preconceptions about design and the dominant single form.

And then, a couple of years later, Alan Moore went ahead and did some of it with the America's Best Comics line. And Dan Jurgens did the rest with the Tangent line at DC.

The other day, I was thinking about response songs. Rappers taking shots at each other, covers that answer something in the original, art made in reaction to art. Which, you kind of hope, is not the same as being reactionary.

The small music labels 555 Recordings and Dark Beloved Cloud have singles clubs. People play down the importance of singles these days—they don't sell the way they used to, downloads bother the music business—but I love them. Sometimes one song contained on one object is all you need to move the axis of the world. Self-contained and saying all that needs to be said.

Singles and Tangent and ABC all kind of stuck together in my head, and I began conceiving of a response. The Apparat Singles Group. An imaginary line of comics singles. Four imaginary first issues of imaginary series from an imaginary line of comics, even.

This is what I think adventure comics would look like today if you blanked out the last sixty years of superhero comics. Yes, there would still be elements of great strangeness, because that's what the pulps traded on. There would be sf and high adventure and weird thrillers and occult journeys. But they would be of their time. The term "adventure" itself would have a dozen different definitions.

4C

The first comic I was ever given was a science fiction comic. That's how it started.

I love science fiction. It's where I can let rip. I have the actual scientific education of a mollusc, mind you. I am crap at science. I mean, I was the kid at school who

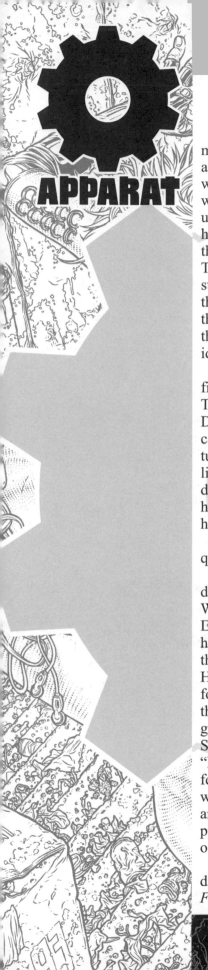

managed to set water on fire, you know? My greatest achievement in science, according to one of my teachers, was climbing up on a table and kicking the shit out of a guy who'd been bugging me for a month. (Said teacher came up afterwards and told me this, and also that he wished he'd done it.) But I read science news obsessively. I love the way science *sounds*. I love the ideas for their art. There's a crazy beauty about a theory of dimensional structure that assembles itself into a snowflake, or the idea that reality is a two-dimensional plane of information and the 3-D universe is a hologrammatic side-effect. And that's how I write science fiction. I use the sound of the ideas and then make it all up.

And then it all comes true anyway. The years since I finished *Transmetropolitan* have been a litany of horror. That book is *coming true*. Right down to the stupid details Darick Robertson and I threw in like two-headed cats and cameras in shades. Every time I invent something, lately, it turns up in the news six months later (including but not limited to space shuttles blowing up and, in a script I decided not to finish, snipers terrorising cities). And then I have to open up the throttle some more and let more horrible shit out from the back of my head.

It's possible that I'm actually driving humanity quickly towards total apocalypse.

I love the science fiction pulps. Always have. I own dozens of sf pulps from the 30s, and books of their covers. When I was a kid, I got bought the original edition of the Encyclopedia Of Science Fiction for Xmas, and spent hours poring over the black-and-white reproductions of the covers that illustrated the entries on magazines. Hoovered up information about them in the years that followed. Sf had a peculiar hold on the practitioners of those times. It wasn't just an interest, a useful and fun genre to write in, the way it often was for the crime writers. Sf was a *movement*. It was a *shared vision*, right from "Ralph 124C41+", something with the savour of religious fervour to it. The sf writers preached to their audiences with fire and brimstone, created leagues and societies among themselves, even seemed to gather into *ur*-nerd proto-communes where they lived on cheap soup and talk of The Future.

The sf pulps still survive today, in the shape of monthly digest-size magazines—*Asimov's, Fantasy & Science Fiction, Analog* and the like. (And, in the name of God,

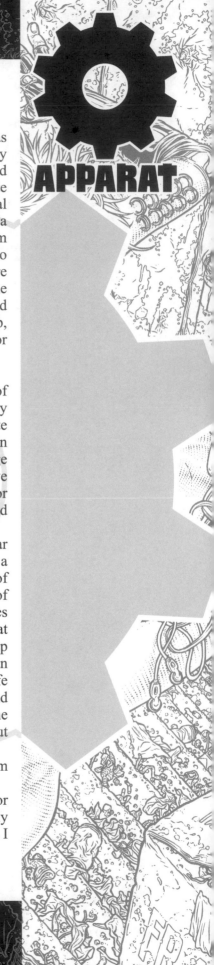

APPARAT

how does *Analog* sound science-fictional now? May as well call the thing *Clockwork,* or *Coal Scuttle.*) But they don't have the true spark of madness in their covers, and rarely in their content. Sf, in print, just doesn't excite people the way it used to. (You used to find the occasional exception in *Interzone,* which is also the best name for a science fiction magazine there is. Good old William Burroughs, eh?) Very few people put the lighted taper to the blue touch paper in the back of their brain and just fire big flaming chunks of it all over you anymore. Not the way they used to. You could look at those old covers and see people opening up the throttle and just letting rip, getting as crazy as possible, just for the hell of it, just for the art and the sound of it.

Which brings you to Juan Jose Ryp.

The artist group I'm working with is a weird kind of graph of my life, really. Laurenn McCubbin is one of my best friends and I've never worked with her, but a website I co-founded commissioned work from her. I've known Carla Speed McNeil for years, and produced a two-page piece with her a few years back on a *Transmet* book. I've never met Jacen Burrows, but have worked with him for years. And Juan Jose Ryp? Never met him, never worked with him.

I've wanted to, for a couple of years, ever since Avatar publisher William Christensen showed me his art in a London pub one afternoon. Ryp is the spiritual heir of those early sf pulp artists—working at the upper limit of imagination and endurance, filling every inch of his pages with exquisitely-illuminated insanity and producing it at almost impossible speeds. You have to work hard to keep up with Ryp, to feed enough ideas into him so that he can continue to cram those panels with the awful details of life in the future. As I write this, I haven't seen the pages, and it's entirely possible that forcing him to pull back, in the penultimate scene, may have caused his brain to jerk out of its casing and explode like an abused car engine.

Which I guess means I won't be working with him again.

I figure this could well be an introduction to Ryp for some people. I wrote this book for him, directly specifically to his style, to try and showcase him for you. I hope you enjoy meeting him. And Angel.

—Warren Ellis

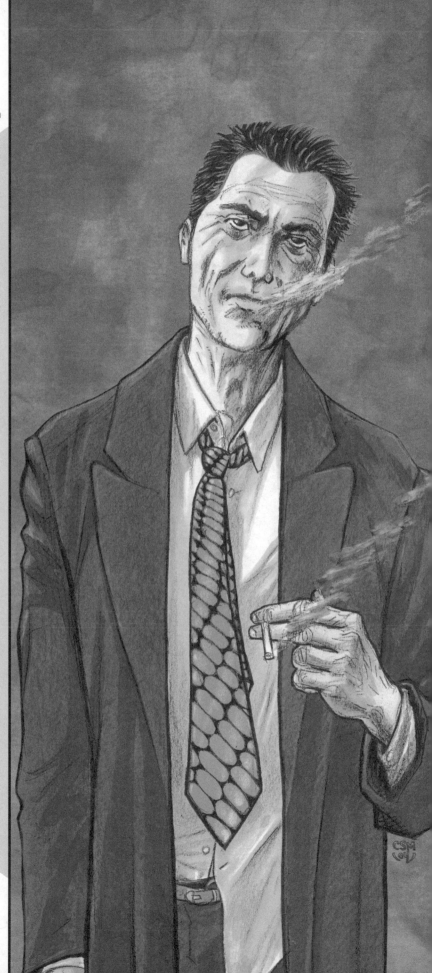

FRANK
IRONWINE™

APPARAT™

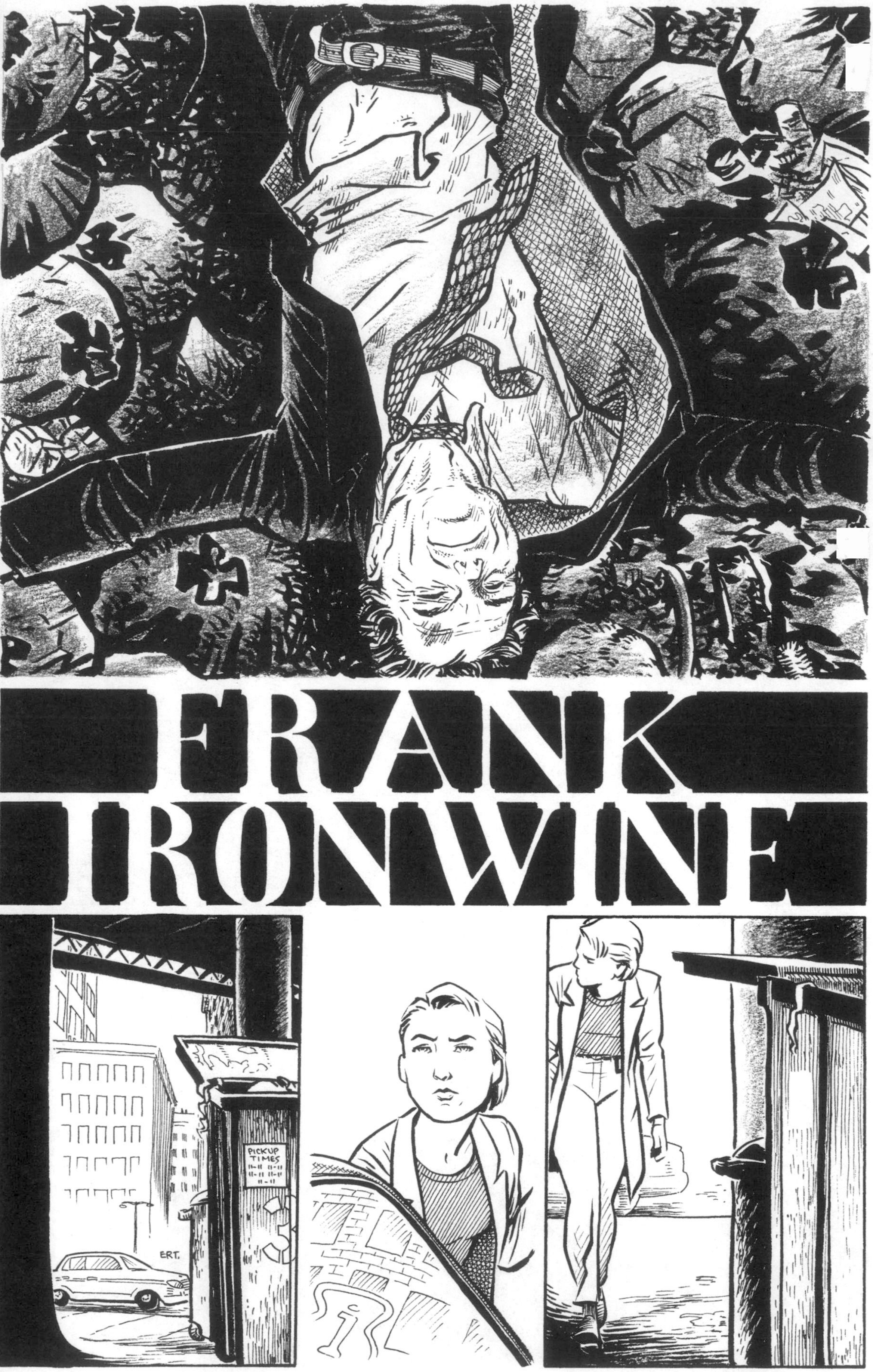
FRANK
IRONWINE
PICKUP TIMES
ERT.

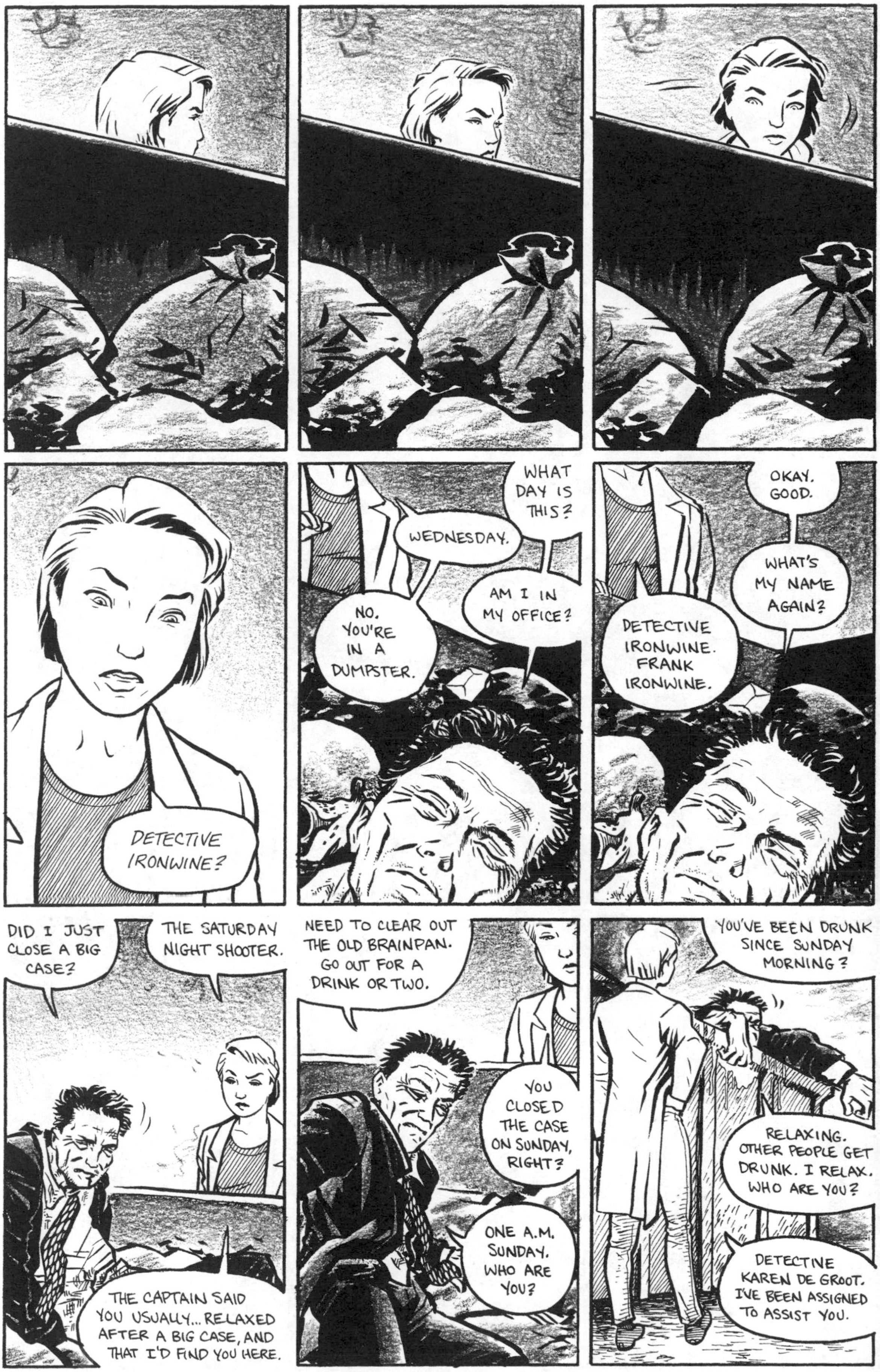
DETECTIVE IRONWINE?
WHAT DAY IS THIS?
WEDNESDAY.
AM I IN MY OFFICE?
NO. YOU'RE IN A DUMPSTER.
OKAY. GOOD.
WHAT'S MY NAME AGAIN?
DETECTIVE IRONWINE. FRANK IRONWINE.
DID I JUST CLOSE A BIG CASE?
THE SATURDAY NIGHT SHOOTER.
THE CAPTAIN SAID YOU USUALLY... RELAXED AFTER A BIG CASE, AND THAT I'D FIND YOU HERE.
NEED TO CLEAR OUT THE OLD BRAINPAN. GO OUT FOR A DRINK OR TWO.
YOU CLOSED THE CASE ON SUNDAY, RIGHT?
ONE A.M. SUNDAY. WHO ARE YOU?
YOU'VE BEEN DRUNK SINCE SUNDAY MORNING?
RELAXING. OTHER PEOPLE GET DRUNK. I RELAX. WHO ARE YOU?
DETECTIVE KAREN DE GROOT. I'VE BEEN ASSIGNED TO ASSIST YOU.

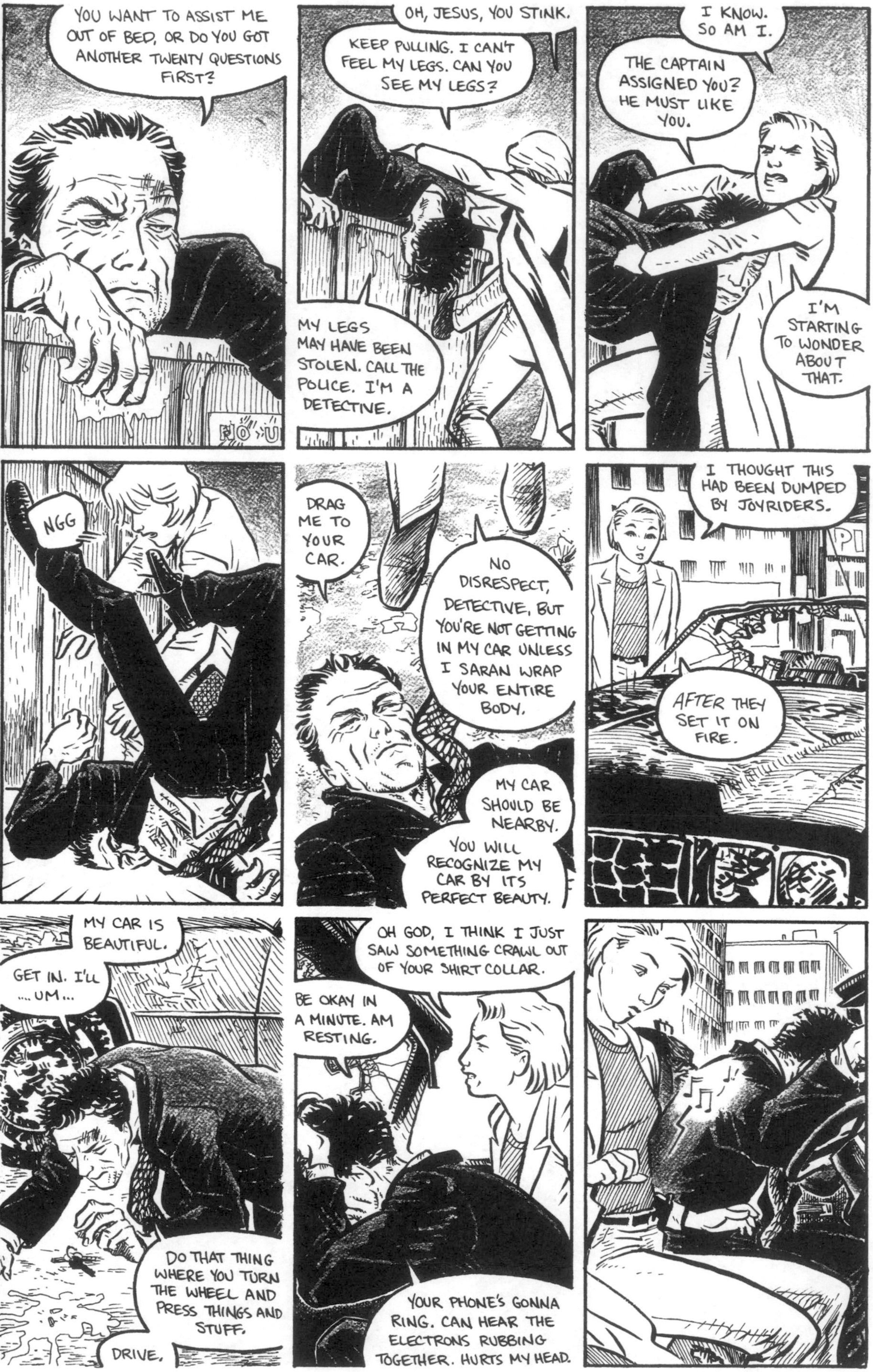
YOU WANT TO ASSIST ME OUT OF BED, OR DO YOU GOT ANOTHER TWENTY QUESTIONS FIRST?
NO U
OH, JESUS, YOU STINK.
KEEP PULLING. I CAN'T FEEL MY LEGS. CAN YOU SEE MY LEGS?
MY LEGS MAY HAVE BEEN STOLEN. CALL THE POLICE. I'M A DETECTIVE.
I KNOW. SO AM I.
THE CAPTAIN ASSIGNED YOU? HE MUST LIKE YOU.
I'M STARTING TO WONDER ABOUT THAT.
NGG
DRAG ME TO YOUR CAR.
NO DISRESPECT, DETECTIVE, BUT YOU'RE NOT GETTING IN MY CAR UNLESS I SARAN WRAP YOUR ENTIRE BODY.
MY CAR SHOULD BE NEARBY.
YOU WILL RECOGNIZE MY CAR BY ITS PERFECT BEAUTY.
I THOUGHT THIS HAD BEEN DUMPED BY JOYRIDERS.
AFTER THEY SET IT ON FIRE.
MY CAR IS BEAUTIFUL.
GET IN. I'LL ....UM...
DO THAT THING WHERE YOU TURN THE WHEEL AND PRESS THINGS AND STUFF.
DRIVE.
OH GOD, I THINK I JUST SAW SOMETHING CRAWL OUT OF YOUR SHIRT COLLAR.
BE OKAY IN A MINUTE. AM RESTING.
YOUR PHONE'S GONNA RING. CAN HEAR THE ELECTRONS RUBBING TOGETHER. HURTS MY HEAD.

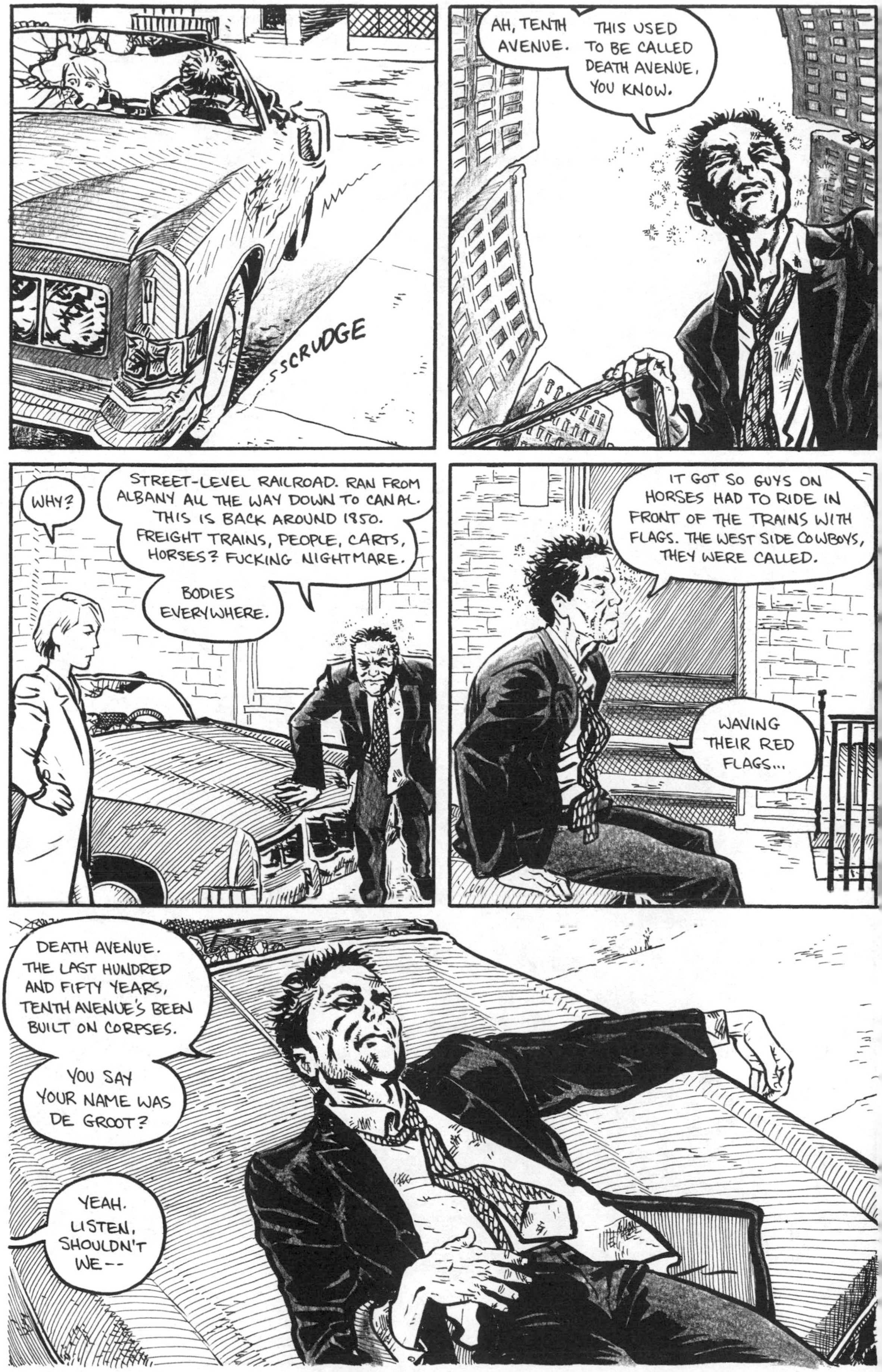
S-SCRUDGE
AH, TENTH AVENUE.
THIS USED TO BE CALLED DEATH AVENUE, YOU KNOW.
WHY?
STREET-LEVEL RAILROAD. RAN FROM ALBANY ALL THE WAY DOWN TO CANAL. THIS IS BACK AROUND 1850. FREIGHT TRAINS, PEOPLE, CARTS, HORSES? FUCKING NIGHTMARE.
BODIES EVERYWHERE.
IT GOT SO GUYS ON HORSES HAD TO RIDE IN FRONT OF THE TRAINS WITH FLAGS. THE WEST SIDE COWBOYS, THEY WERE CALLED.
WAVING THEIR RED FLAGS...
DEATH AVENUE. THE LAST HUNDRED AND FIFTY YEARS, TENTH AVENUE'S BEEN BUILT ON CORPSES.
YOU SAY YOUR NAME WAS DE GROOT?
YEAH. LISTEN, SHOULDN'T WE--

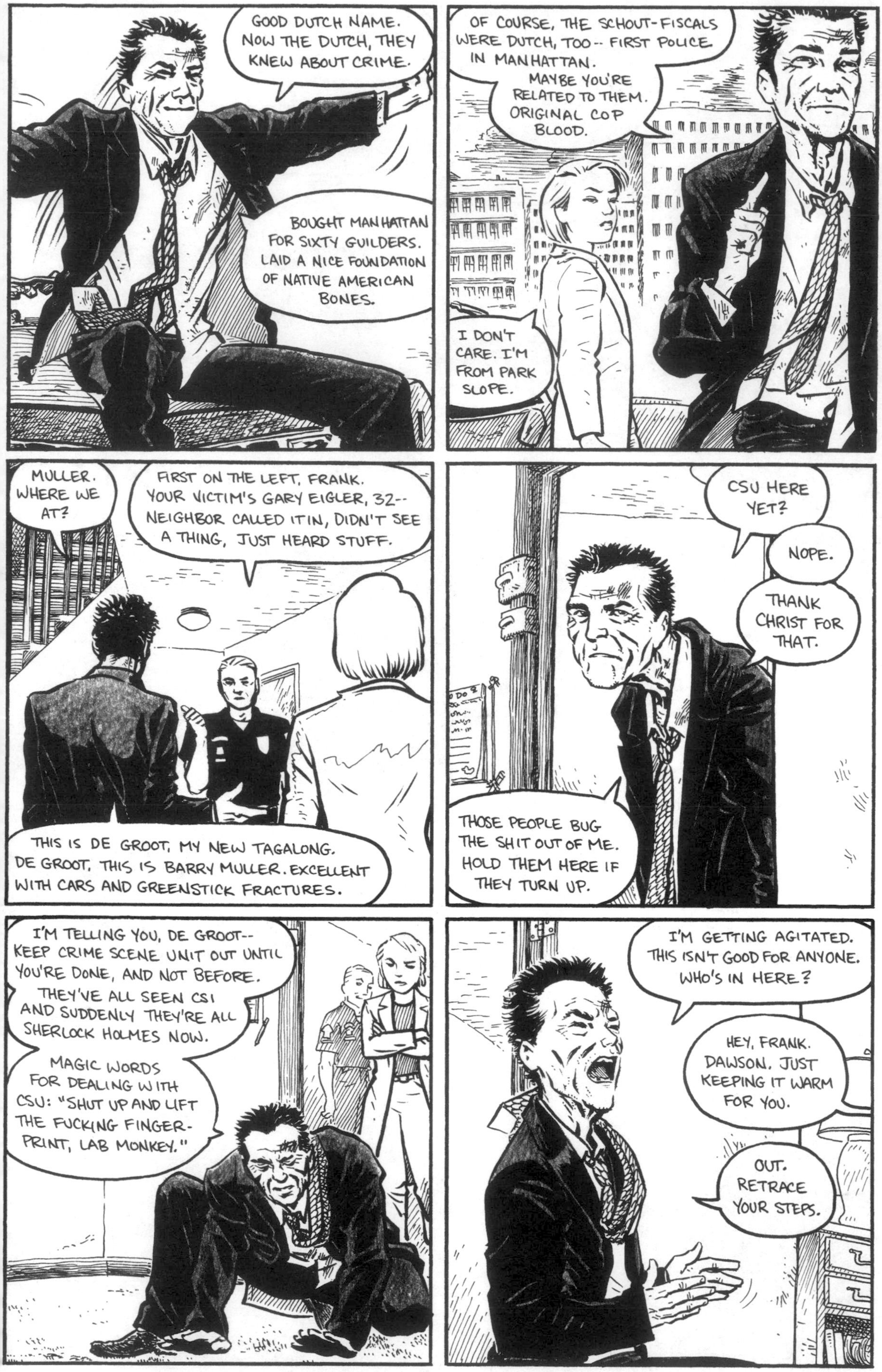
GOOD DUTCH NAME. NOW THE DUTCH, THEY KNEW ABOUT CRIME.
BOUGHT MANHATTAN FOR SIXTY GUILDERS. LAID A NICE FOUNDATION OF NATIVE AMERICAN BONES.
OF COURSE, THE SCHOUT-FISCALS WERE DUTCH, TOO-- FIRST POLICE IN MANHATTAN.
MAYBE YOU'RE RELATED TO THEM. ORIGINAL COP BLOOD.
I DON'T CARE. I'M FROM PARK SLOPE.
MULLER. WHERE WE AT?
FIRST ON THE LEFT, FRANK. YOUR VICTIM'S GARY EIGLER, 32-- NEIGHBOR CALLED IT IN, DIDN'T SEE A THING, JUST HEARD STUFF.
THIS IS DE GROOT, MY NEW TAGALONG. DE GROOT, THIS IS BARRY MULLER. EXCELLENT WITH CARS AND GREENSTICK FRACTURES.
CSU HERE YET?
NOPE.
THANK CHRIST FOR THAT.
THOSE PEOPLE BUG THE SHIT OUT OF ME. HOLD THEM HERE IF THEY TURN UP.
I'M TELLING YOU, DE GROOT-- KEEP CRIME SCENE UNIT OUT UNTIL YOU'RE DONE, AND NOT BEFORE.
THEY'VE ALL SEEN CSI AND SUDDENLY THEY'RE ALL SHERLOCK HOLMES NOW.
MAGIC WORDS FOR DEALING WITH CSU: "SHUT UP AND LIFT THE FUCKING FINGER-PRINT, LAB MONKEY."
I'M GETTING AGITATED. THIS ISN'T GOOD FOR ANYONE. WHO'S IN HERE?
HEY, FRANK. DAWSON. JUST KEEPING IT WARM FOR YOU.
OUT. RETRACE YOUR STEPS.

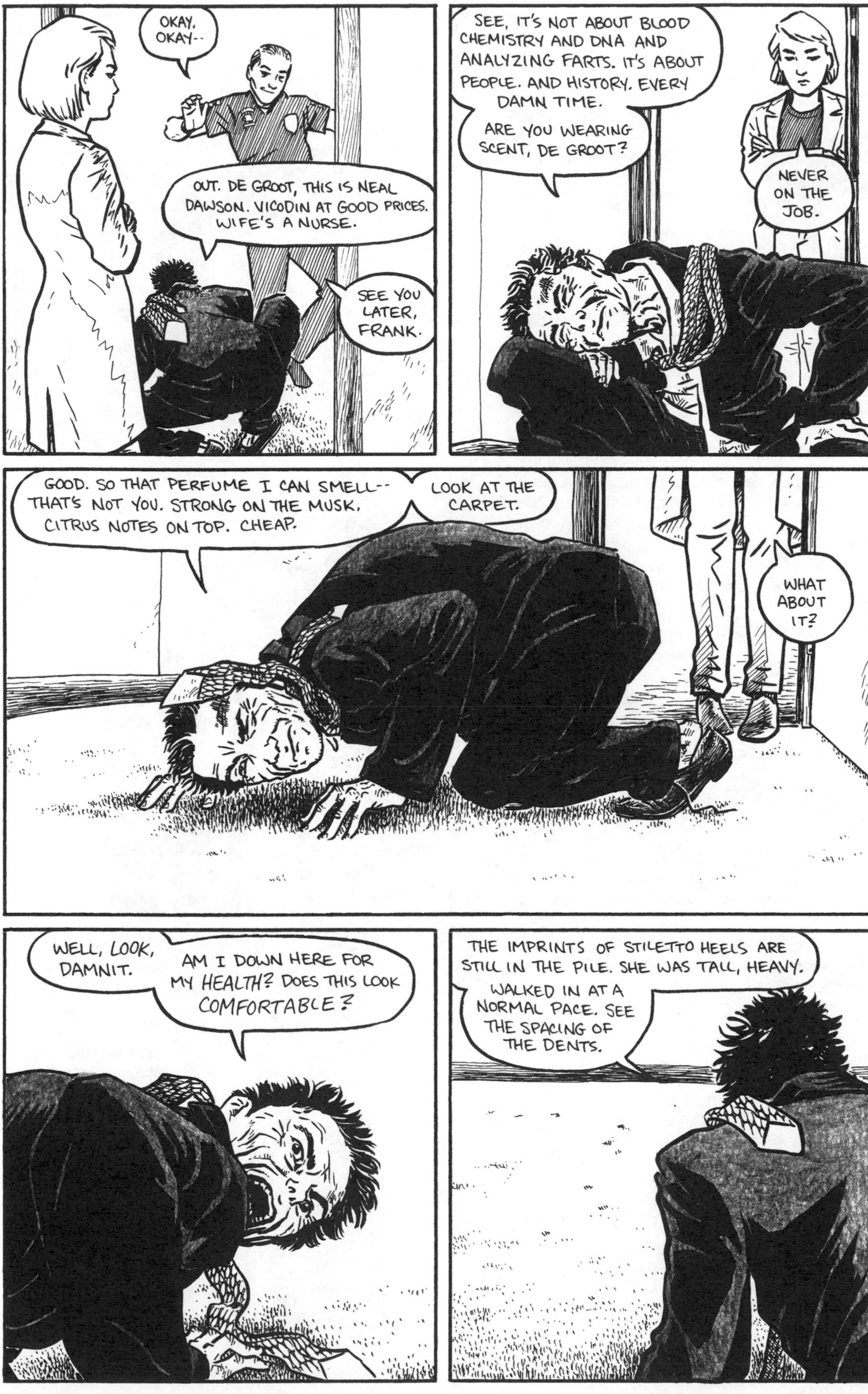
OKAY. OKAY--
OUT. DE GROOT, THIS IS NEAL DAWSON. VICODIN AT GOOD PRICES. WIFE'S A NURSE.
SEE YOU LATER, FRANK.
SEE, IT'S NOT ABOUT BLOOD CHEMISTRY AND DNA AND ANALYZING FARTS. IT'S ABOUT PEOPLE. AND HISTORY. EVERY DAMN TIME.
ARE YOU WEARING SCENT, DE GROOT?
NEVER ON THE JOB.
GOOD. SO THAT PERFUME I CAN SMELL-- THAT'S NOT YOU. STRONG ON THE MUSK. CITRUS NOTES ON TOP. CHEAP.
LOOK AT THE CARPET.
WHAT ABOUT IT?
WELL, LOOK, DAMNIT.
AM I DOWN HERE FOR MY HEALTH? DOES THIS LOOK COMFORTABLE?
THE IMPRINTS OF STILETTO HEELS ARE STILL IN THE PILE. SHE WAS TALL, HEAVY.
WALKED IN AT A NORMAL PACE. SEE THE SPACING OF THE DENTS.

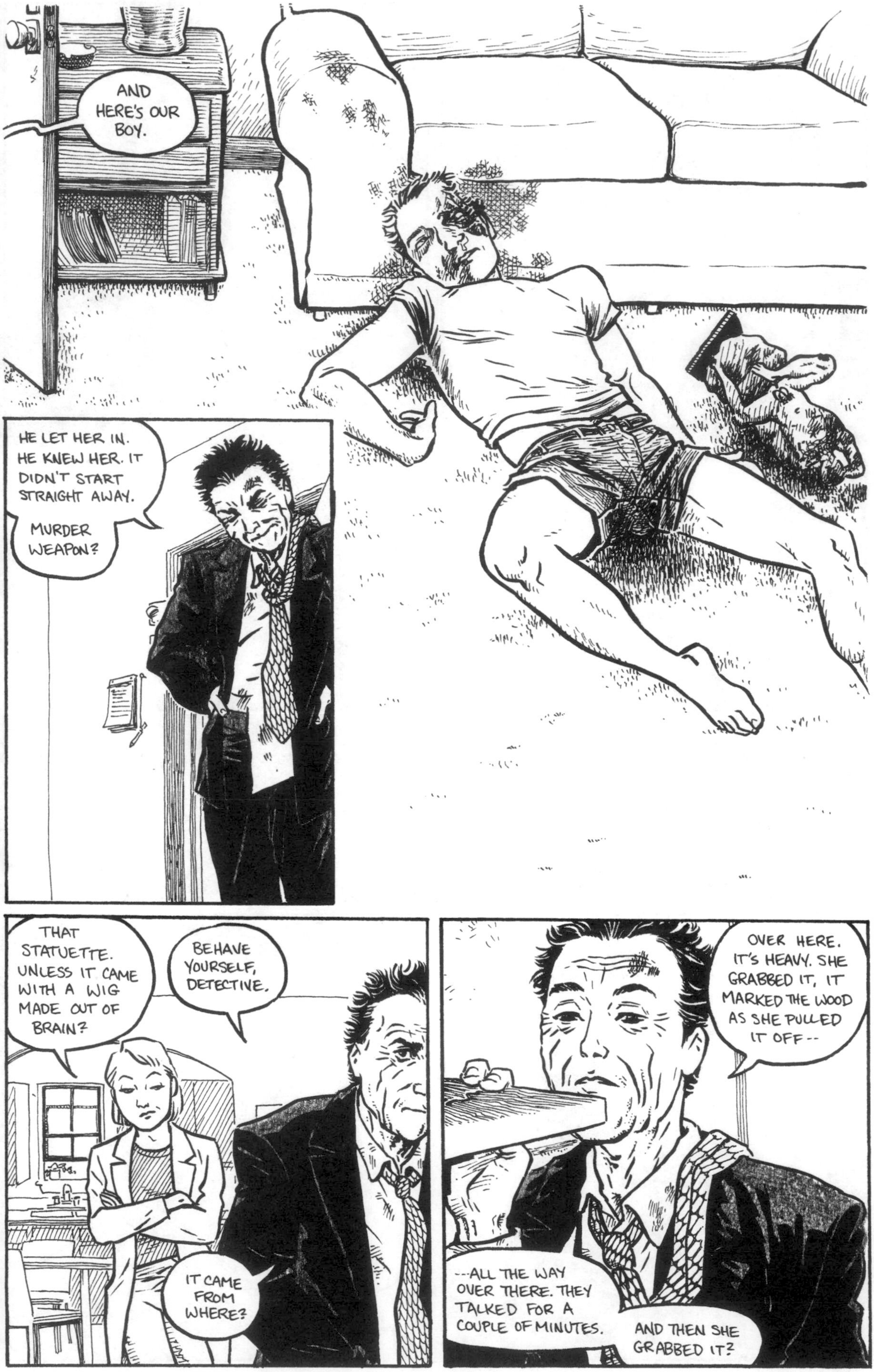
AND HERE'S OUR BOY.
HE LET HER IN. HE KNEW HER. IT DIDN'T START STRAIGHT AWAY.
MURDER WEAPON?
THAT STATUETTE. UNLESS IT CAME WITH A WIG MADE OUT OF BRAIN?
BEHAVE YOURSELF, DETECTIVE.
IT CAME FROM WHERE?
OVER HERE. IT'S HEAVY. SHE GRABBED IT, IT MARKED THE WOOD AS SHE PULLED IT OFF --
--ALL THE WAY OVER THERE. THEY TALKED FOR A COUPLE OF MINUTES.
AND THEN SHE GRABBED IT?

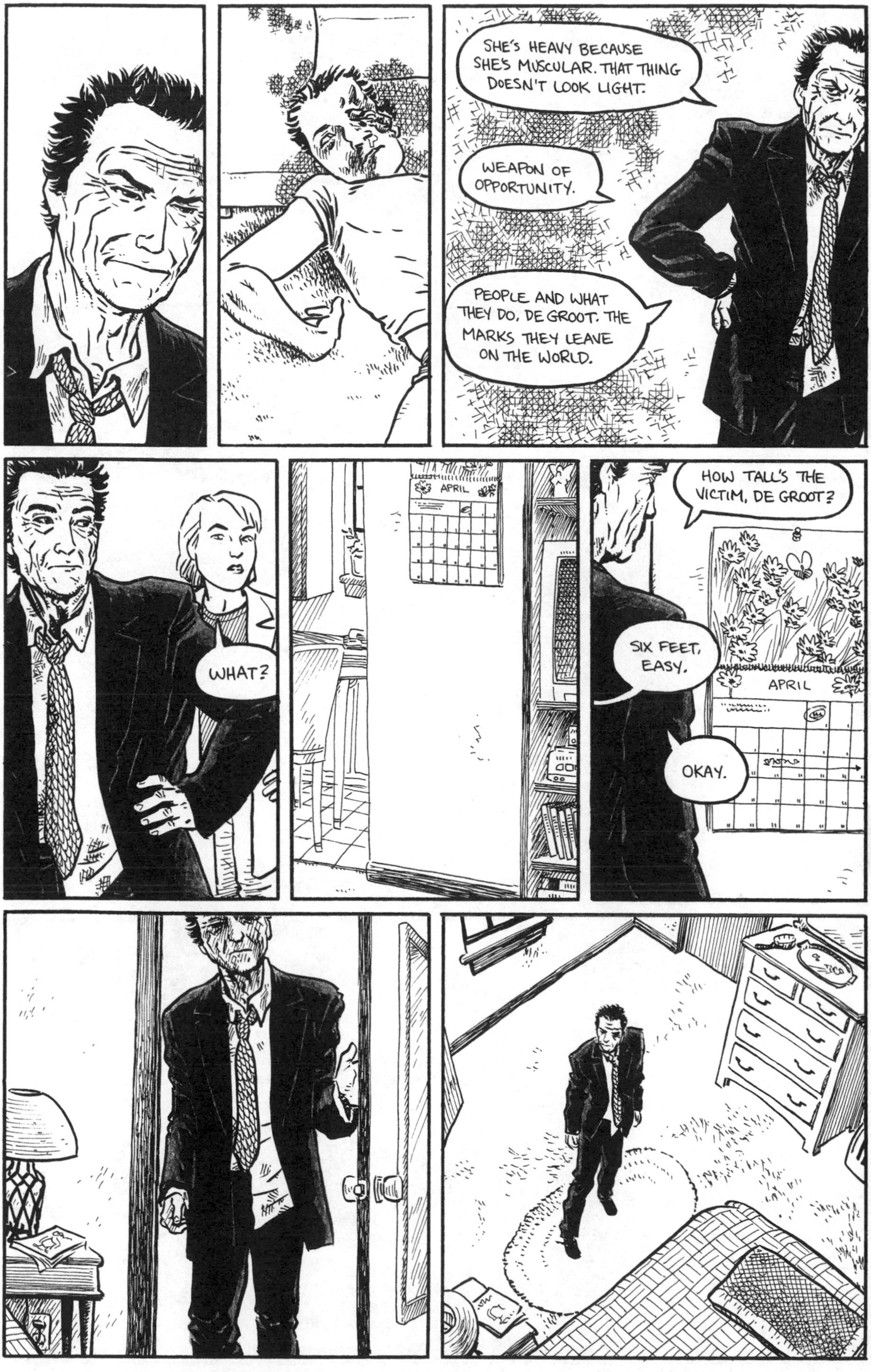
SHE'S HEAVY BECAUSE SHE'S MUSCULAR. THAT THING DOESN'T LOOK LIGHT.
WEAPON OF OPPORTUNITY.
PEOPLE AND WHAT THEY DO, DE GROOT. THE MARKS THEY LEAVE ON THE WORLD.
WHAT?
APRIL
HOW TALL'S THE VICTIM, DE GROOT?
SIX FEET, EASY.
APRIL
OKAY.

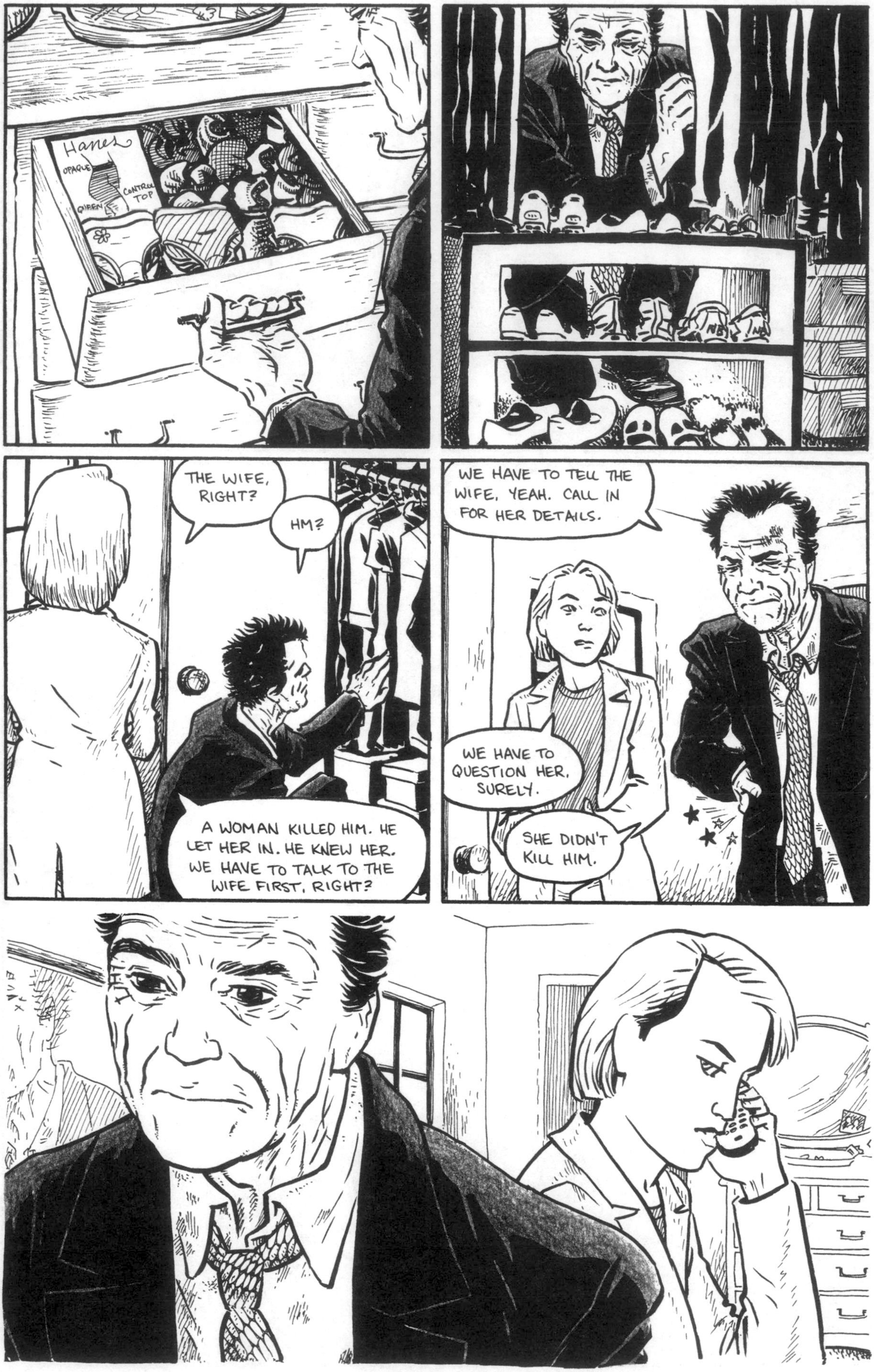
Hanes
OPAQUE
CONTROL TOP
QUEEN
THE WIFE, RIGHT?
HM?
A WOMAN KILLED HIM. HE LET HER IN. HE KNEW HER. WE HAVE TO TALK TO THE WIFE FIRST, RIGHT?
WE HAVE TO TELL THE WIFE, YEAH. CALL IN FOR HER DETAILS.
WE HAVE TO QUESTION HER, SURELY.
SHE DIDN'T KILL HIM.

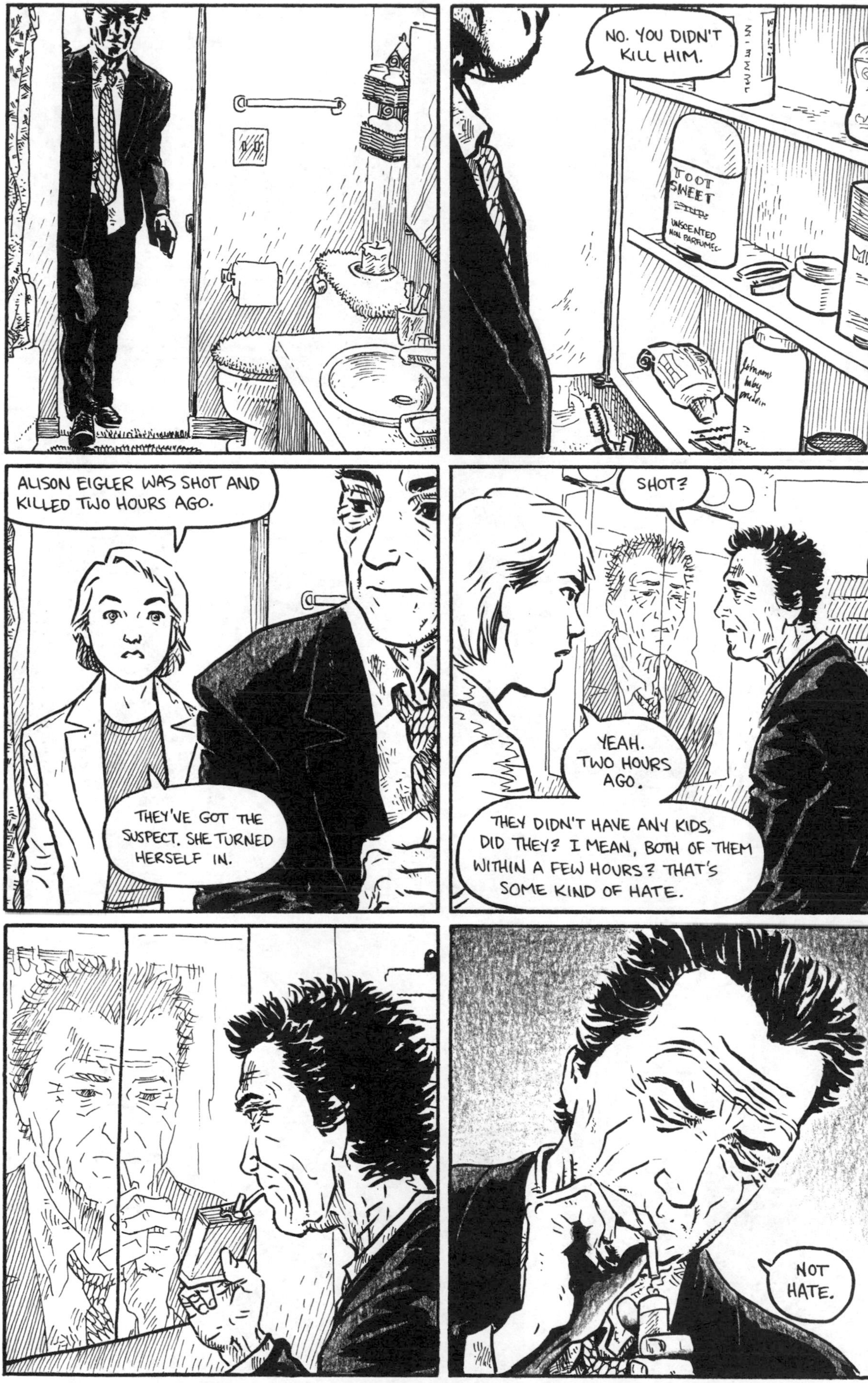
NO. YOU DIDN'T KILL HIM.
TOOT SWEET
UNSCENTED NON PARFUME
ALISON EIGLER WAS SHOT AND KILLED TWO HOURS AGO.
THEY'VE GOT THE SUSPECT. SHE TURNED HERSELF IN.
SHOT?
YEAH. TWO HOURS AGO.
THEY DIDN'T HAVE ANY KIDS, DID THEY? I MEAN, BOTH OF THEM WITHIN A FEW HOURS? THAT'S SOME KIND OF HATE.
NOT HATE.

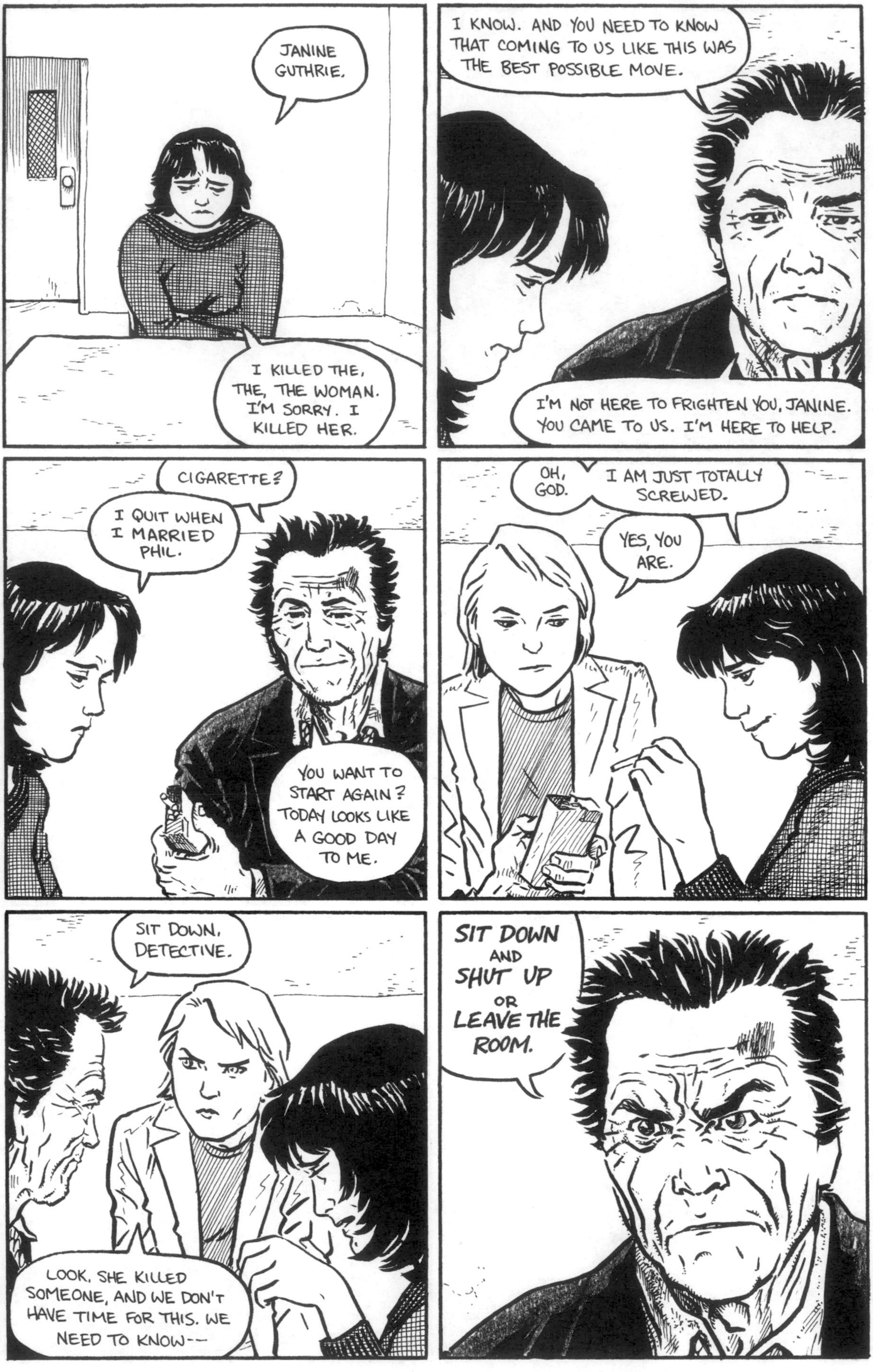
JANINE GUTHRIE.
I KILLED THE, THE, THE WOMAN. I'M SORRY. I KILLED HER.
I KNOW. AND YOU NEED TO KNOW THAT COMING TO US LIKE THIS WAS THE BEST POSSIBLE MOVE.
I'M NOT HERE TO FRIGHTEN YOU, JANINE. YOU CAME TO US. I'M HERE TO HELP.
CIGARETTE?
I QUIT WHEN I MARRIED PHIL.
YOU WANT TO START AGAIN? TODAY LOOKS LIKE A GOOD DAY TO ME.
OH, GOD.
I AM JUST TOTALLY SCREWED.
YES, YOU ARE.
SIT DOWN, DETECTIVE.
LOOK, SHE KILLED SOMEONE, AND WE DON'T HAVE TIME FOR THIS. WE NEED TO KNOW--
SIT DOWN AND SHUT UP OR LEAVE THE ROOM.

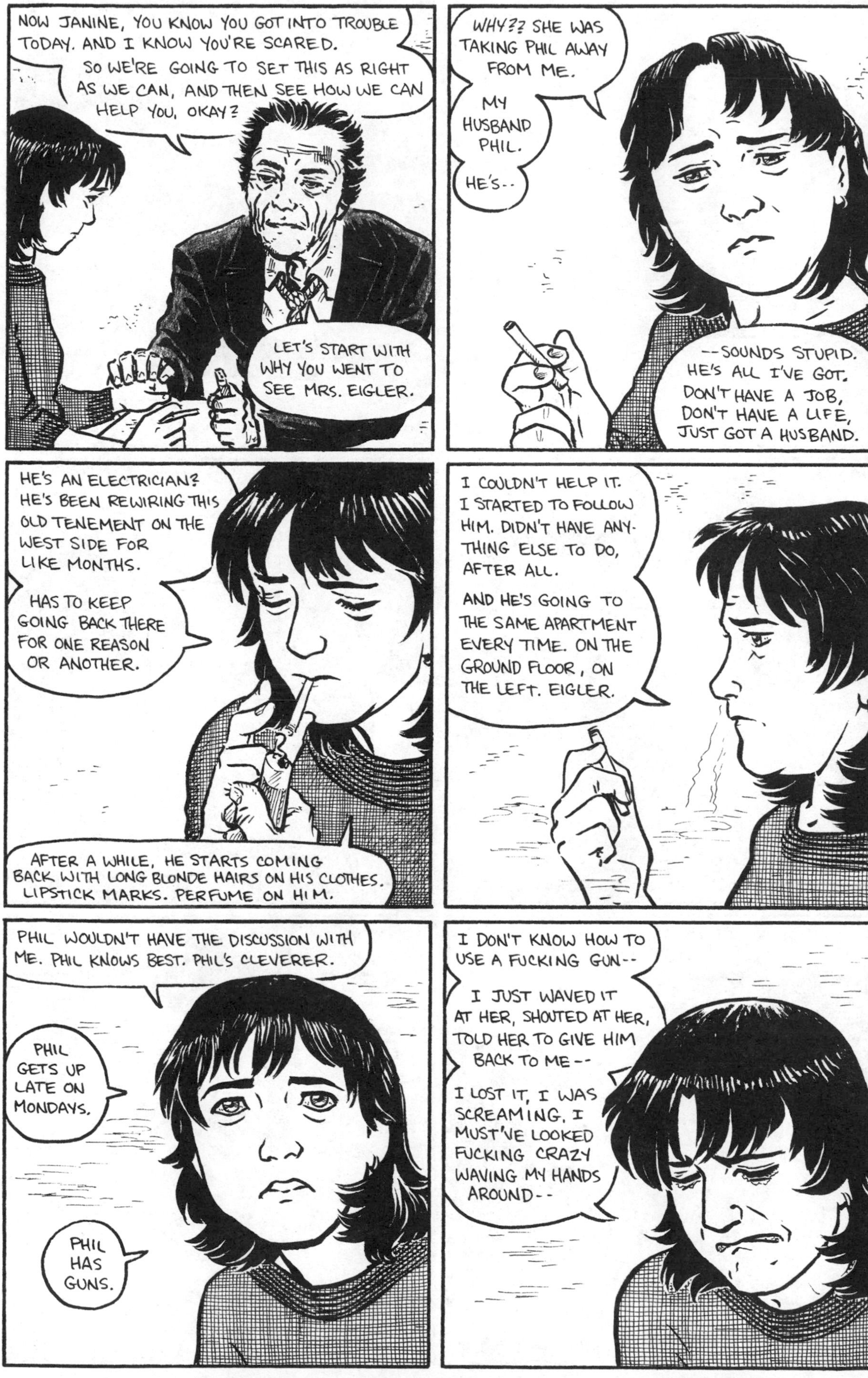
NOW JANINE, YOU KNOW YOU GOT INTO TROUBLE TODAY. AND I KNOW YOU'RE SCARED.
SO WE'RE GOING TO SET THIS AS RIGHT AS WE CAN, AND THEN SEE HOW WE CAN HELP YOU, OKAY?
LET'S START WITH WHY YOU WENT TO SEE MRS. EIGLER.
WHY?? SHE WAS TAKING PHIL AWAY FROM ME.
MY HUSBAND PHIL.
HE'S--
--SOUNDS STUPID. HE'S ALL I'VE GOT. DON'T HAVE A JOB, DON'T HAVE A LIFE, JUST GOT A HUSBAND.
HE'S AN ELECTRICIAN? HE'S BEEN REWIRING THIS OLD TENEMENT ON THE WEST SIDE FOR LIKE MONTHS.
HAS TO KEEP GOING BACK THERE FOR ONE REASON OR ANOTHER.
AFTER A WHILE, HE STARTS COMING BACK WITH LONG BLONDE HAIRS ON HIS CLOTHES. LIPSTICK MARKS. PERFUME ON HIM.
I COULDN'T HELP IT. I STARTED TO FOLLOW HIM. DIDN'T HAVE ANYTHING ELSE TO DO, AFTER ALL.
AND HE'S GOING TO THE SAME APARTMENT EVERY TIME. ON THE GROUND FLOOR, ON THE LEFT. EIGLER.
PHIL WOULDN'T HAVE THE DISCUSSION WITH ME. PHIL KNOWS BEST. PHIL'S CLEVERER.
PHIL GETS UP LATE ON MONDAYS.
PHIL HAS GUNS.
I DON'T KNOW HOW TO USE A FUCKING GUN--
I JUST WAVED IT AT HER, SHOUTED AT HER, TOLD HER TO GIVE HIM BACK TO ME--
I LOST IT, I WAS SCREAMING. I MUST'VE LOOKED FUCKING CRAZY WAVING MY HANDS AROUND--

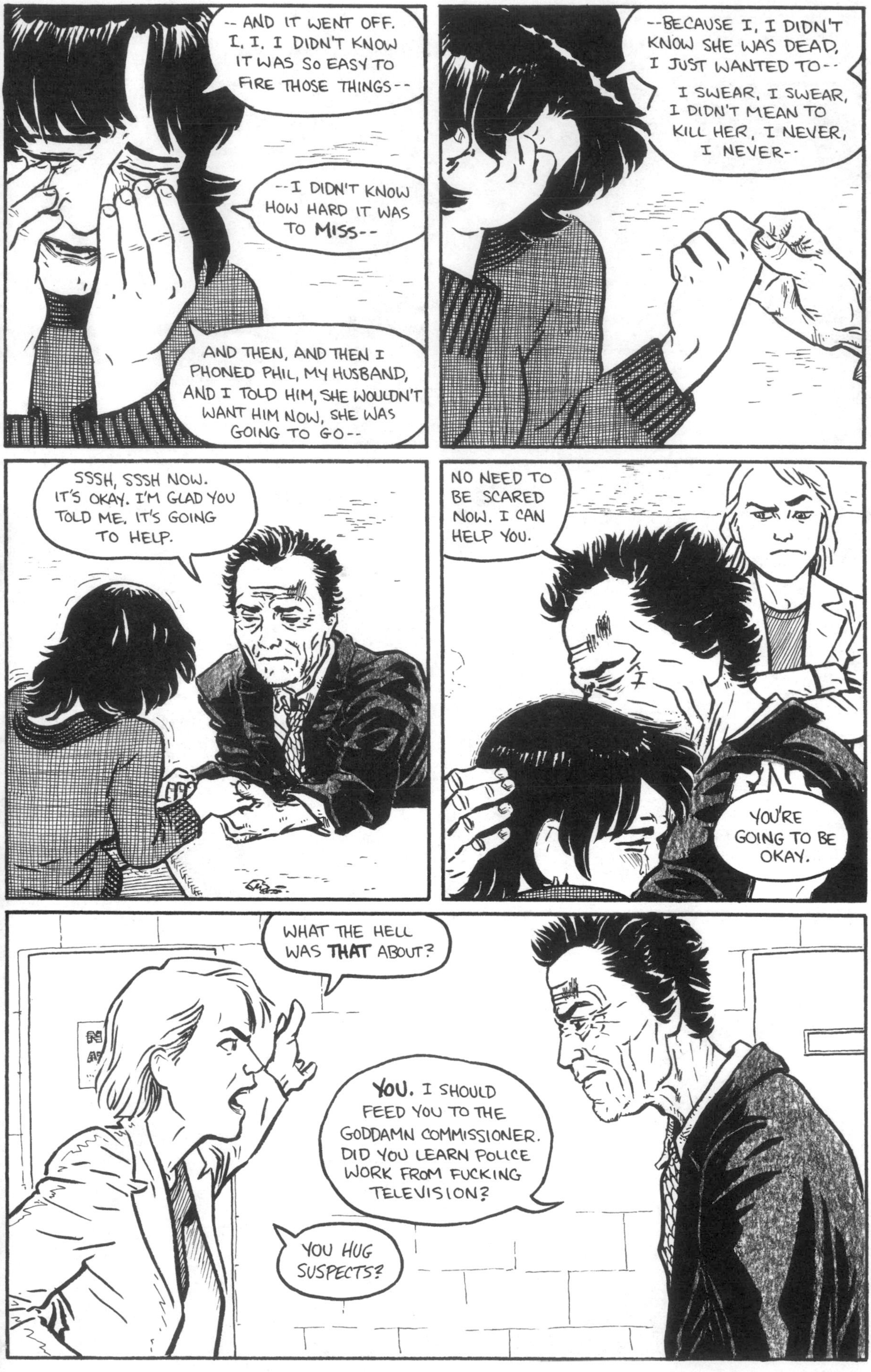
--AND IT WENT OFF. I, I, I DIDN'T KNOW IT WAS SO EASY TO FIRE THOSE THINGS--
--I DIDN'T KNOW HOW HARD IT WAS TO MISS--
AND THEN, AND THEN I PHONED PHIL, MY HUSBAND, AND I TOLD HIM, SHE WOULDN'T WANT HIM NOW, SHE WAS GOING TO GO--
--BECAUSE I, I DIDN'T KNOW SHE WAS DEAD, I JUST WANTED TO--
I SWEAR, I SWEAR, I DIDN'T MEAN TO KILL HER, I NEVER, I NEVER--
SSSH, SSSH NOW. IT'S OKAY. I'M GLAD YOU TOLD ME. IT'S GOING TO HELP.
NO NEED TO BE SCARED NOW. I CAN HELP YOU.
YOU'RE GOING TO BE OKAY.
WHAT THE HELL WAS THAT ABOUT?
YOU. I SHOULD FEED YOU TO THE GODDAMN COMMISSIONER. DID YOU LEARN POLICE WORK FROM FUCKING TELEVISION?
YOU HUG SUSPECTS?

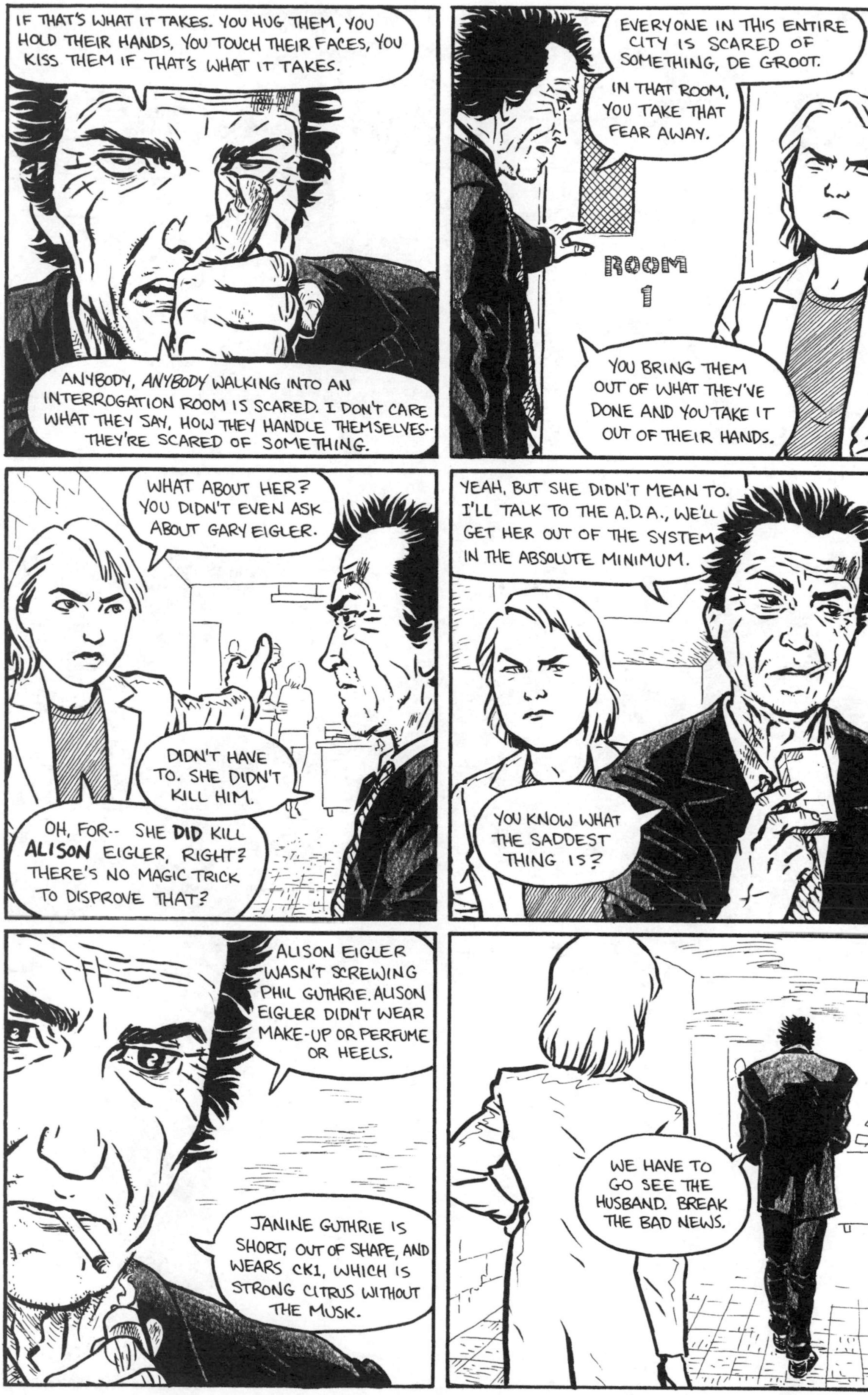
IF THAT'S WHAT IT TAKES. YOU HUG THEM, YOU HOLD THEIR HANDS, YOU TOUCH THEIR FACES, YOU KISS THEM IF THAT'S WHAT IT TAKES.
ANYBODY, *ANYBODY* WALKING INTO AN INTERROGATION ROOM IS SCARED. I DON'T CARE WHAT THEY SAY, HOW THEY HANDLE THEMSELVES-- THEY'RE SCARED OF SOMETHING.
EVERYONE IN THIS ENTIRE CITY IS SCARED OF SOMETHING, DE GROOT.
IN THAT ROOM, YOU TAKE THAT FEAR AWAY.
ROOM 1
YOU BRING THEM OUT OF WHAT THEY'VE DONE AND YOU TAKE IT OUT OF THEIR HANDS.
WHAT ABOUT HER? YOU DIDN'T EVEN ASK ABOUT GARY EIGLER.
DIDN'T HAVE TO. SHE DIDN'T KILL HIM.
OH, FOR-- SHE **DID** KILL **ALISON** EIGLER, RIGHT? THERE'S NO MAGIC TRICK TO DISPROVE THAT?
YEAH, BUT SHE DIDN'T MEAN TO. I'LL TALK TO THE A.D.A., WE'LL GET HER OUT OF THE SYSTEM IN THE ABSOLUTE MINIMUM.
YOU KNOW WHAT THE SADDEST THING IS?
ALISON EIGLER WASN'T SCREWING PHIL GUTHRIE. ALISON EIGLER DIDN'T WEAR MAKE-UP OR PERFUME OR HEELS.
JANINE GUTHRIE IS SHORT, OUT OF SHAPE, AND WEARS CK1, WHICH IS STRONG CITRUS WITHOUT THE MUSK.
WE HAVE TO GO SEE THE HUSBAND. BREAK THE BAD NEWS.

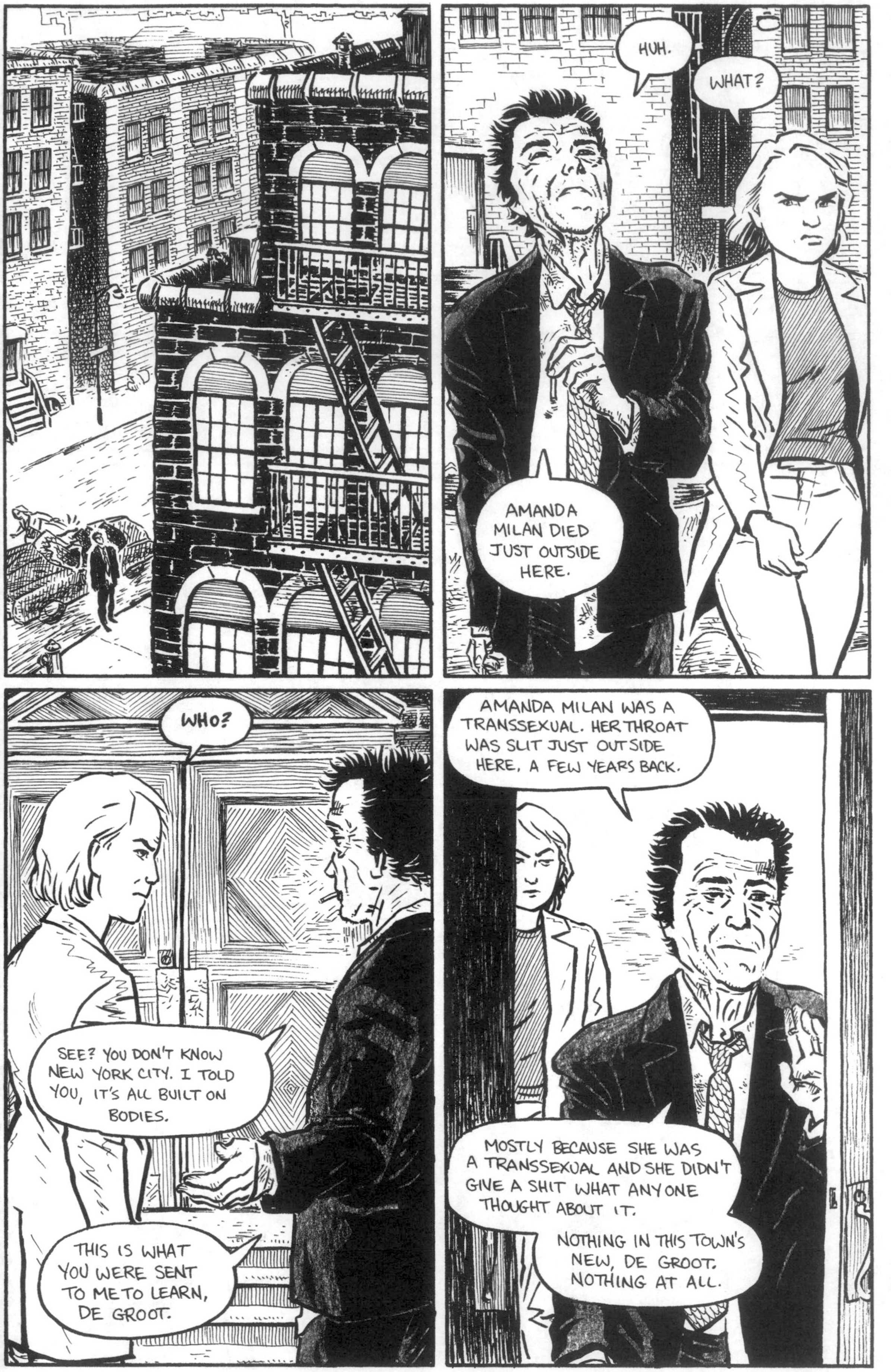
HUH.
WHAT?
AMANDA MILAN DIED JUST OUTSIDE HERE.
WHO?
SEE? YOU DON'T KNOW NEW YORK CITY. I TOLD YOU, IT'S ALL BUILT ON BODIES.
THIS IS WHAT YOU WERE SENT TO ME TO LEARN, DE GROOT.
AMANDA MILAN WAS A TRANSSEXUAL. HER THROAT WAS SLIT JUST OUTSIDE HERE, A FEW YEARS BACK.
MOSTLY BECAUSE SHE WAS A TRANSSEXUAL AND SHE DIDN'T GIVE A SHIT WHAT ANYONE THOUGHT ABOUT IT.
NOTHING IN THIS TOWN'S NEW, DE GROOT. NOTHING AT ALL.

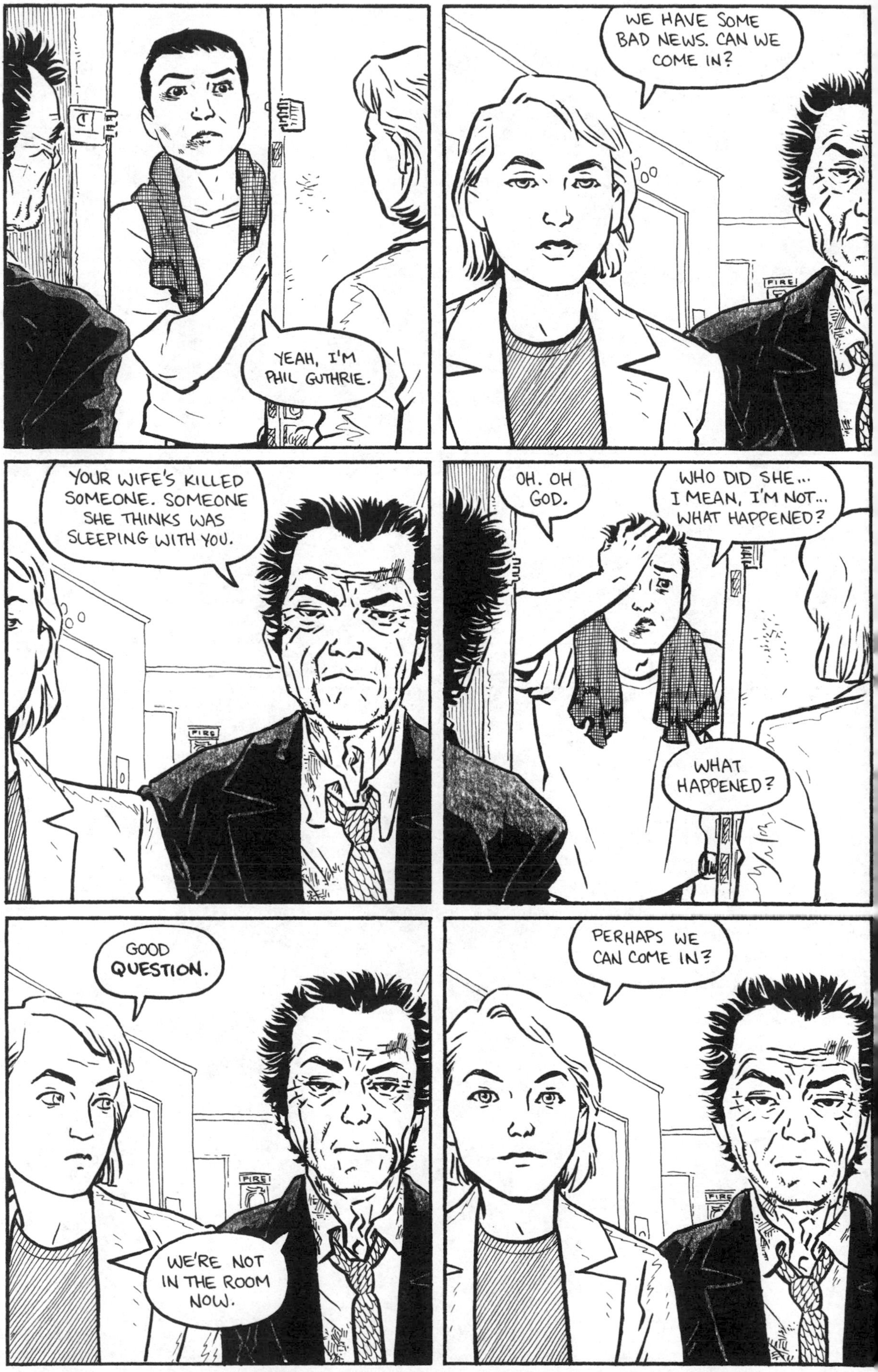
YEAH, I'M PHIL GUTHRIE.
WE HAVE SOME BAD NEWS. CAN WE COME IN?
YOUR WIFE'S KILLED SOMEONE. SOMEONE SHE THINKS WAS SLEEPING WITH YOU.
OH. OH GOD.
WHO DID SHE... I MEAN, I'M NOT... WHAT HAPPENED?
WHAT HAPPENED?
GOOD QUESTION.
WE'RE NOT IN THE ROOM NOW.
PERHAPS WE CAN COME IN?

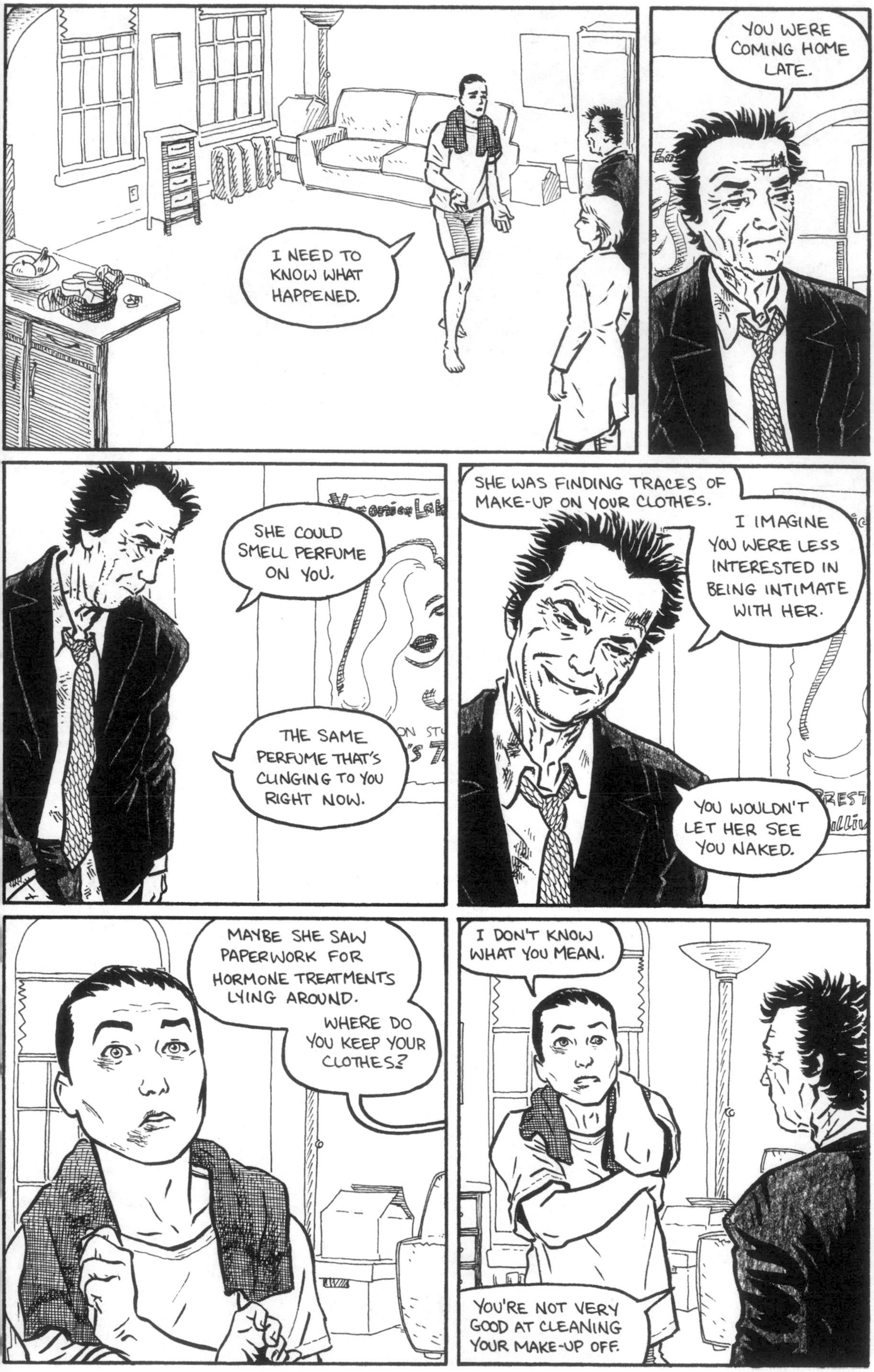
I NEED TO KNOW WHAT HAPPENED.
YOU WERE COMING HOME LATE.
SHE COULD SMELL PERFUME ON YOU.
THE SAME PERFUME THAT'S CLINGING TO YOU RIGHT NOW.
SHE WAS FINDING TRACES OF MAKE-UP ON YOUR CLOTHES.
I IMAGINE YOU WERE LESS INTERESTED IN BEING INTIMATE WITH HER.
YOU WOULDN'T LET HER SEE YOU NAKED.
MAYBE SHE SAW PAPERWORK FOR HORMONE TREATMENTS LYING AROUND.
WHERE DO YOU KEEP YOUR CLOTHES?
I DON'T KNOW WHAT YOU MEAN.
YOU'RE NOT VERY GOOD AT CLEANING YOUR MAKE-UP OFF.

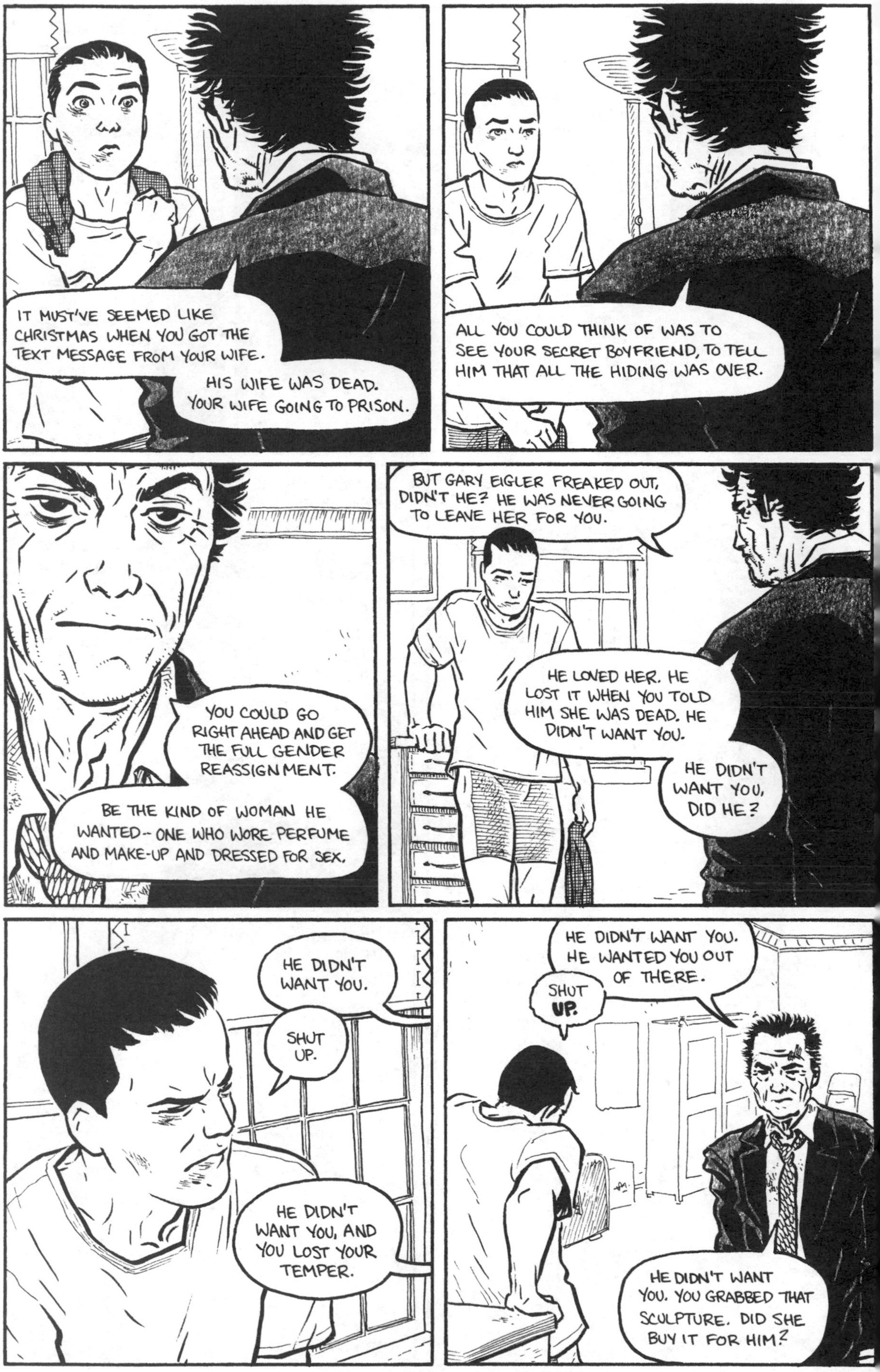
IT MUST'VE SEEMED LIKE CHRISTMAS WHEN YOU GOT THE TEXT MESSAGE FROM YOUR WIFE.
HIS WIFE WAS DEAD. YOUR WIFE GOING TO PRISON.
ALL YOU COULD THINK OF WAS TO SEE YOUR SECRET BOYFRIEND, TO TELL HIM THAT ALL THE HIDING WAS OVER.
YOU COULD GO RIGHT AHEAD AND GET THE FULL GENDER REASSIGNMENT.
BE THE KIND OF WOMAN HE WANTED-- ONE WHO WORE PERFUME AND MAKE-UP AND DRESSED FOR SEX.
BUT GARY EIGLER FREAKED OUT, DIDN'T HE? HE WAS NEVER GOING TO LEAVE HER FOR YOU.
HE LOVED HER. HE LOST IT WHEN YOU TOLD HIM SHE WAS DEAD. HE DIDN'T WANT YOU.
HE DIDN'T WANT YOU, DID HE?
HE DIDN'T WANT YOU.
SHUT UP.
HE DIDN'T WANT YOU, AND YOU LOST YOUR TEMPER.
HE DIDN'T WANT YOU. HE WANTED YOU OUT OF THERE.
SHUT UP.
HE DIDN'T WANT YOU. YOU GRABBED THAT SCULPTURE. DID SHE BUY IT FOR HIM?

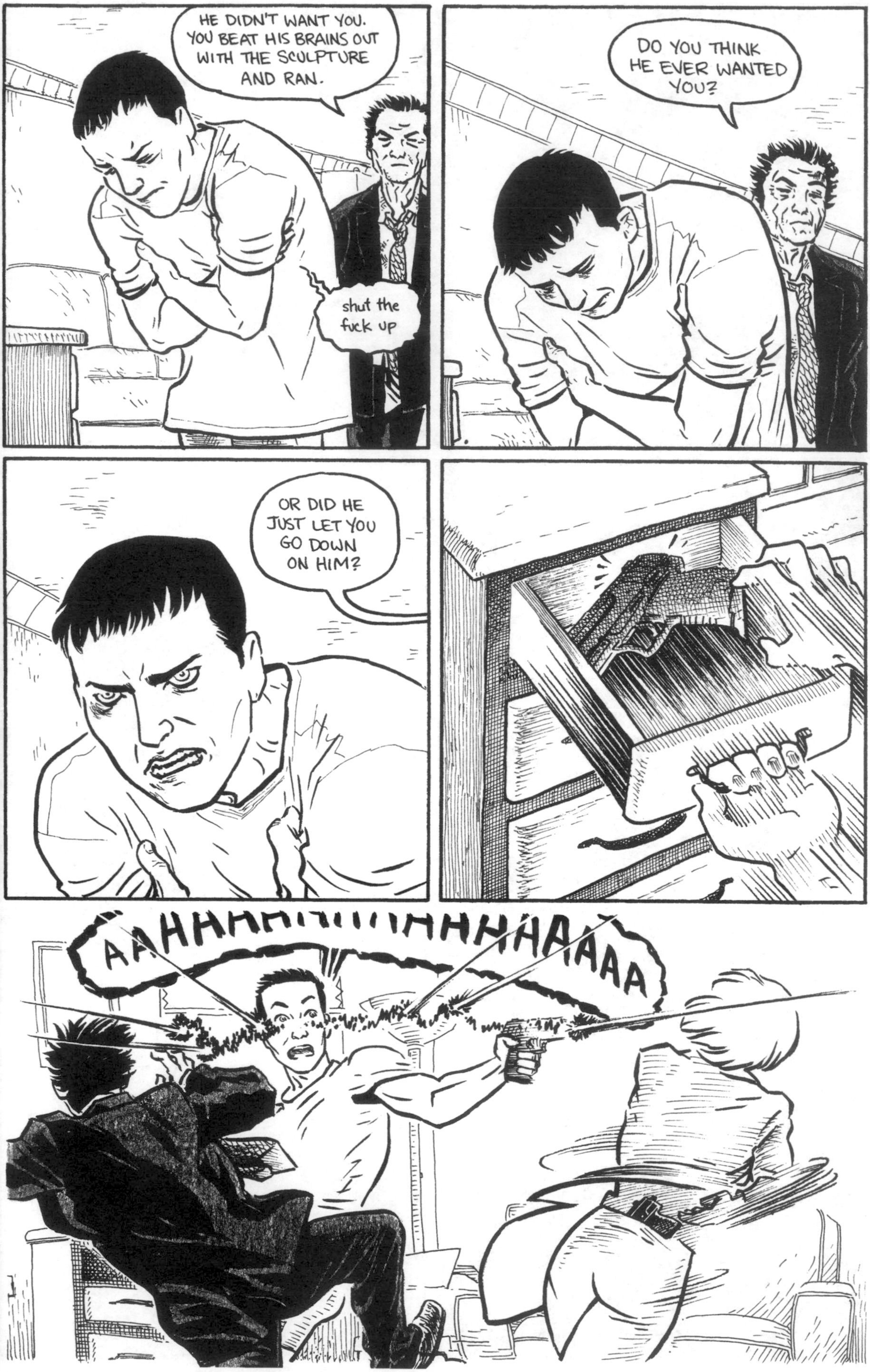
HE DIDN'T WANT YOU. YOU BEAT HIS BRAINS OUT WITH THE SCULPTURE AND RAN.
shut the fuck up
DO YOU THINK HE EVER WANTED YOU?
OR DID HE JUST LET YOU GO DOWN ON HIM?
AAHHHHHHHHHHAAAAA

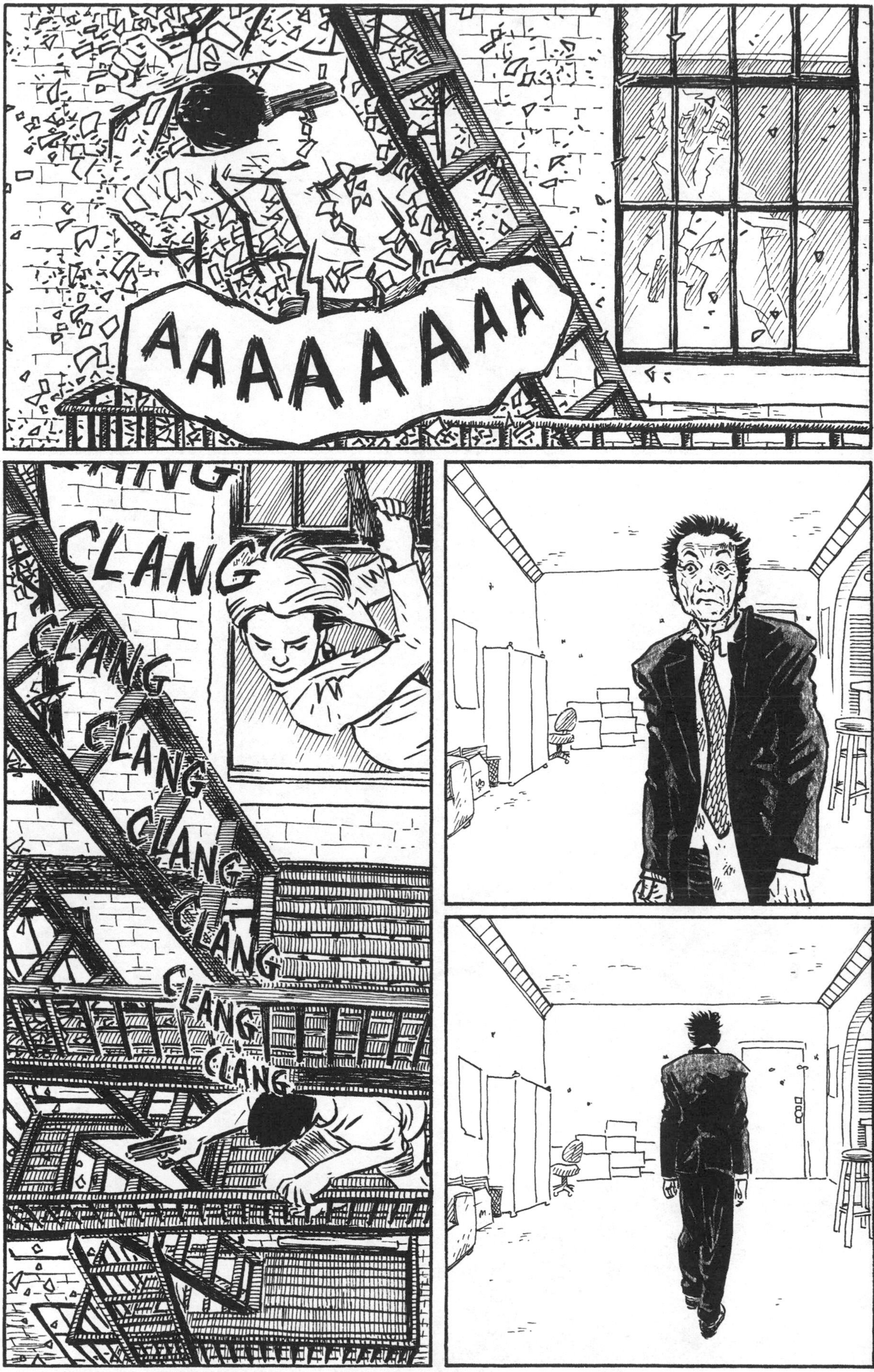
AAAAAAAA
CLANG
CLANG
CLANG
CLANG
CLANG
CLANG
CLANG
CLANG

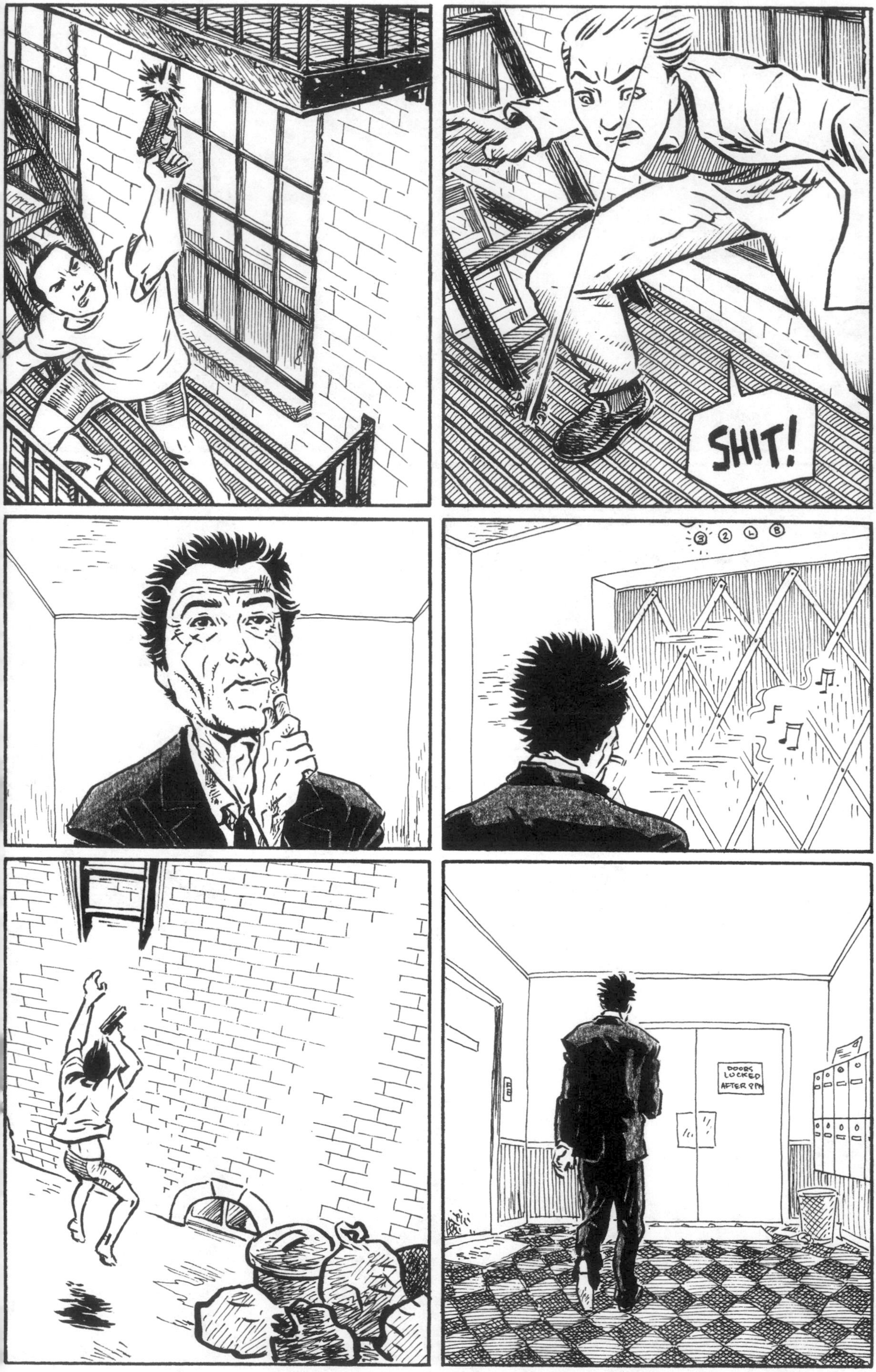
SHIT!
3 2 L B
DOORS LOCKED AFTER 8PM

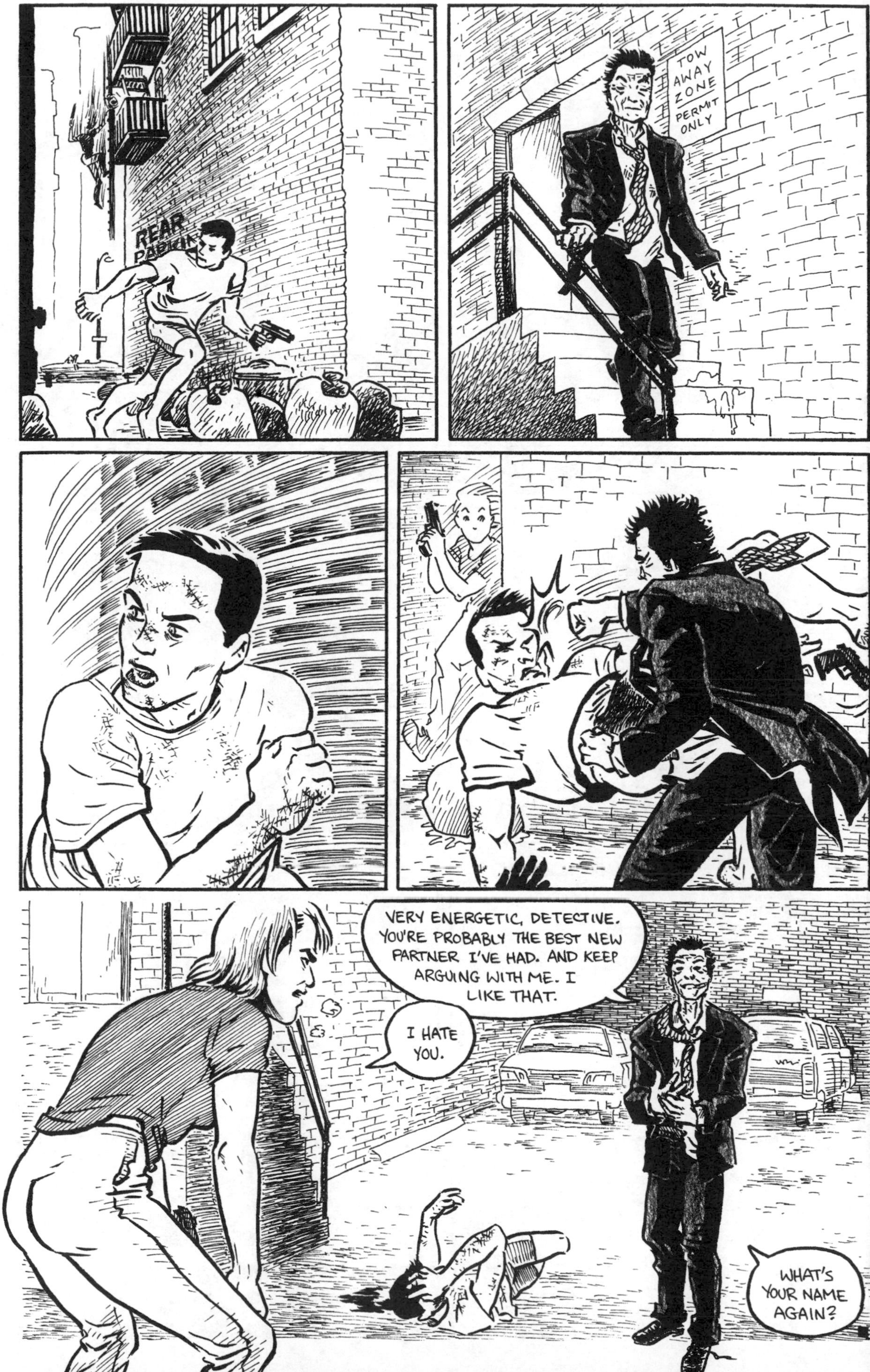
REAR PARKIN
TOW AWAY ZONE
PERMIT ONLY
VERY ENERGETIC, DETECTIVE. YOU'RE PROBABLY THE BEST NEW PARTNER I'VE HAD. AND KEEP ARGUING WITH ME. I LIKE THAT.
I HATE YOU.
WHAT'S YOUR NAME AGAIN?

frank ironwine

YEARS AGO, I SAT DOWN AND THOUGHT ABOUT WHAT ADVENTURE comics might've looked like today if superhero comics hadn't have happened. If, in fact, the pulp tradition of Weird Thrillers had jumped straight into comics form without mutating into the superhero subgenre we know today. If you took away preconceptions about design and the dominant single form.

And then, a couple of years later, Alan Moore went ahead and did some of it with the America's Best Comics line. And Dan Jurgens did the rest with the Tangent line at DC.

The other day, I was thinking about response songs. Rappers taking shots at each other, covers that answer something in the original, art made in reaction to art. Which, you kind of hope, is not the same as being reactionary.

The small music labels 555 Recordings and Dark Beloved Cloud have singles clubs. People play down the importance of singles these days—they don't sell the way they used to, downloads bother the music business—but I love them. Sometimes one song contained on one object is all you need to move the axis of the world. Self-contained and saying all that needs to be said.

Singles and Tangent and ABC all kind of stuck together in my head, and I began conceiving of a response. The Apparat Singles Group. An imaginary line of comics singles. Four imaginary first issues of imaginary series from an imaginary line of comics, even.

This is what I think adventure comics would look like today if you blanked out the last sixty years of superhero comics. Yes, there would still be elements of great strangeness, because that's what the pulps traded on. There would be sf and high adventure and weird thrillers and occult journeys. But they would be of their time. The term "adventure" itself would have a dozen different definitions.

CRIME AND THE CITY

The crime pulps were possibly the most influential of the whole pulp publishing movement. When you say "pulp", sure, you think of lurid thrillers and wild science fiction, the sort of thing that *Sky Captain* scraped off the top of the form. But *Black Mask* and its peers published Raymond Chandler and Dashiel Hammett. You can't underestimate the force with which Chandler, particularly,

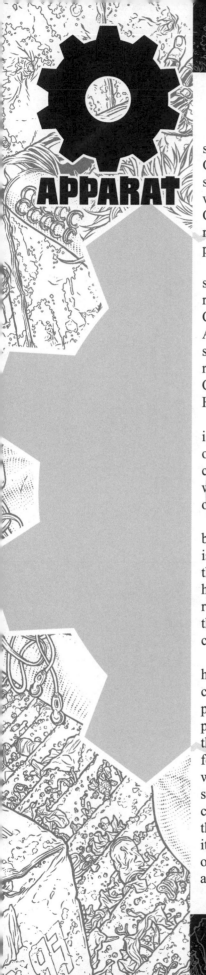

APPARAT

struck. From those who regarded genre work with disdain, Chandler was perceived to have elevated crime fiction into social fiction, contemporary mimetic fictions uniquely worthy of consideration. Genre-friendly readers heard Chandler make crime fiction rattle and sing with the sound of real streets like no-one else. Chandler and his more gifted peers changed the face of literature from the crime pulps.

As the pulps began to fade—and, perhaps, grew too small for those people—the crime writers moved to books rather than comics, and on from there to Hollywood. (Where Chandler worked pretty hard at drinking himself to death.) And crime fiction became perhaps the most commercially successful genre of the 20th century. Even modern-day TV ratings-eaters like *CSI* very clearly come out of both Chandler and Arthur Conan Doyle, the creator of Sherlock Holmes.

At the same time, doing straight crime fiction in comics is one of the Western medium's hardest dollars. Crime is one of the genres that got fused into superhero fiction, and comics readers today still like their crime gimmicked up with a pervert suit or a magic hand or something, to lift it out of the ordinary.

But crime, to me, is never ordinary. Crime is the map we build our houses around. Everything's based on crime. This is how Frank Ironwine sees the world. New York's built on the bones of the people who were murdered to make it happen. There are no new crimes in New York City, not really. They've all happened before, and understanding their patterns is a step towards understanding the city. But no crime is ordinary.

Sitting down to write *Frank Ironwine*, looking for a handle on how that particular strain of early 20th century crime fiction might have mutated through comics to the present day... I found I felt that TV, in particular, had lost the plot. The procedural has become all. I love *Quincy M.E.* in the same healthy platonic way as the next man, but the forensic crime show has become just freakish. The detective who makes a psychological and emotional connection with suspects, victims and landscapes is gone. It's all about the chill computation of the evidence. And when it transpires that evidence can lie, they simply throw more computers at it. Fractionating farts with lasers. And what is to me the core of crime fiction gets lost. It's about people. It's about people and their actions and emotions and patterns and places.

See, I liked *Colombo*. Horribly difficult shows to write.

The "open" detective story, which exposes the mystery at the start and makes the story about the dance between the detective and the criminal, attempting to outsmart and outplay each other. But it was about the people, and about the knowledge of people. I liked that. I miss that. Part of what made Philip Marlowe work was his understanding of the time and place he was living in, and his ability to read people based upon that.

I didn't want Frank to be a Dirty Harry figure, and I didn't want to make him a reactionary creation, but there was a sense of wanting to lead the pulp detective past both comics *and* the moving image towards my imaginary future. I've been fascinated since childhood with Sherlock Holmes—an archetype who survives into the present day in the form of Robert Goren in *Law & Order: Criminal Intent*—and wanted something like Holmes' gift in Frank. Similar, but warmer. Holmes is the true father of *CSI,* in his insistence that the solution of mysteries be utterly emotionless and logical (although, when not pursuing the game, Holmes himself is a wriggly figure of arch pleasure, best captured onscreen by Jeremy Brett in the Eighties). Frank had to come at it from the other direction—that minds and feelings were the way into crimes. That and maps. Throw away the mass spectrometers, lasers and crime-lights. Let it be about old things. About history. Every city you've ever heard of is built on bones.

Frank himself, obviously, is an old thing—a hangover from the days when all TV detectives were middle-aged white men, perhaps. Ironwine is an old Jewish name I found in an old book ten or eleven years ago.

Yeah... like most things in this Apparat stunt, this is wish-fulfilment. Wouldn't it be nice if there were real detectives again? With something approaching real personalities—as best as I could get it that week, anyway. In stories powered by people and knowledge rather than robots and laboratories.

Carla Speed McNeil has been one of my favourite artists since I first saw the early issues of her sf magnum opus *Finder.* She may be familiar to you as one of the illustrators of Greg Rucka's superior *Queen And Country* serial. Writing something that she agreed to draw is a personal highlight for me.

—Warren Ellis

APPARAT

quit city™

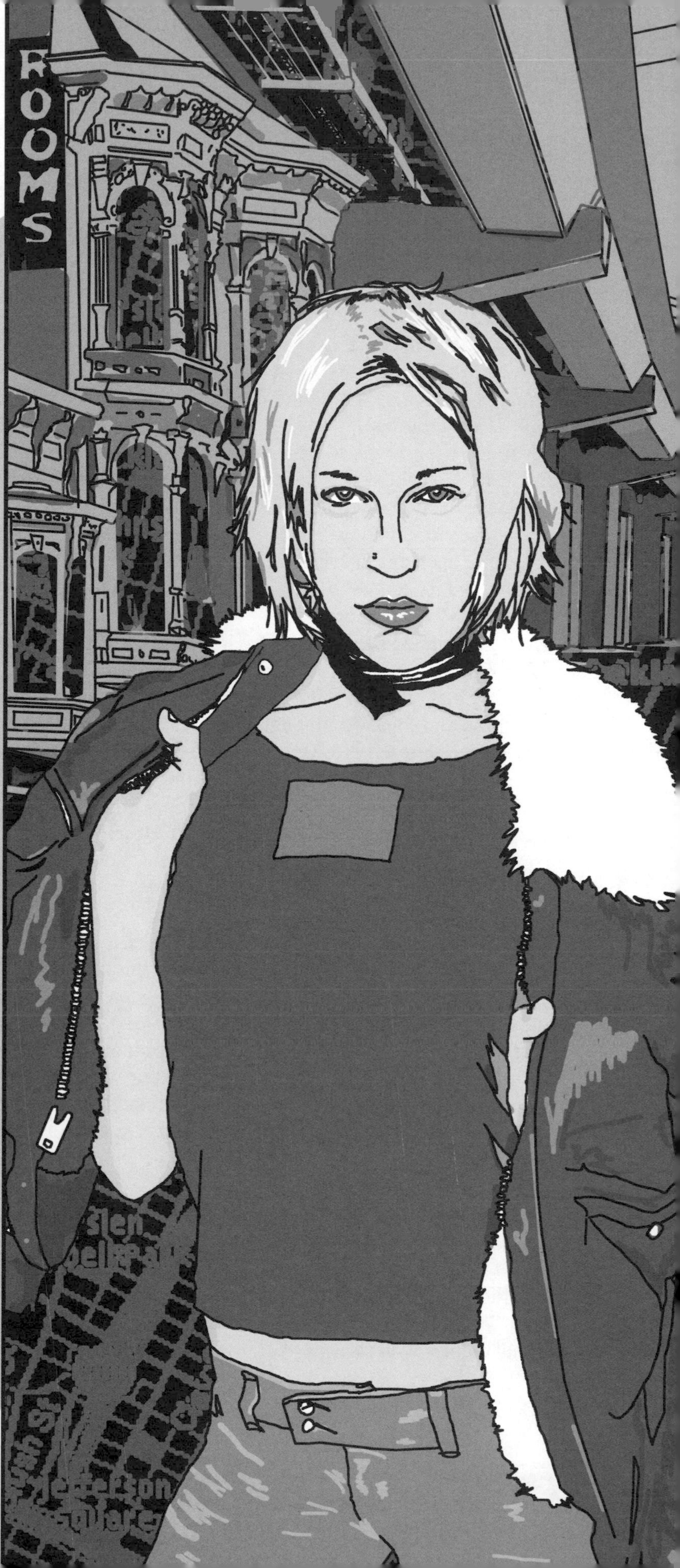
ROOMS

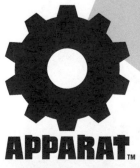

APPARAT™

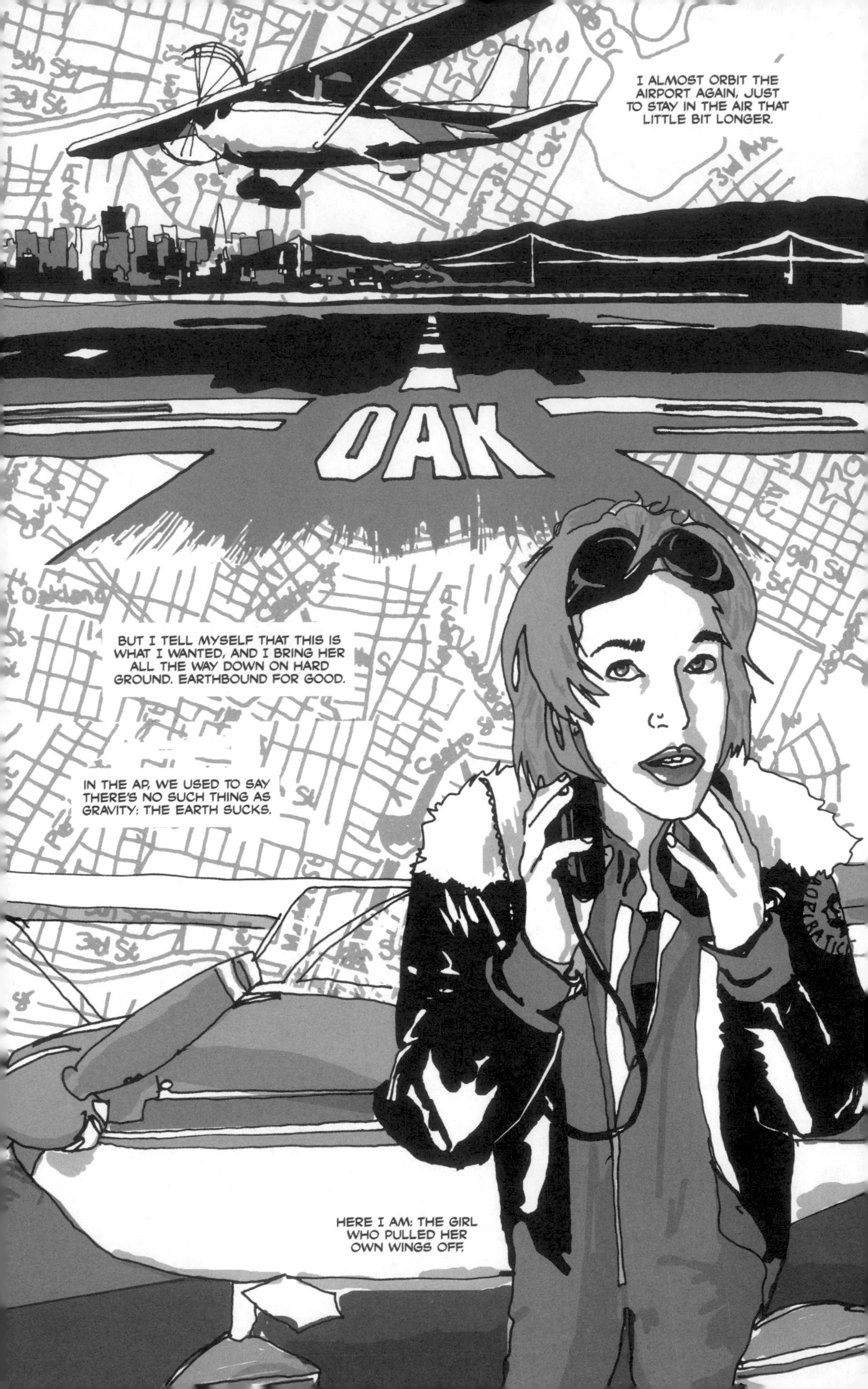

I ALMOST ORBIT THE AIRPORT AGAIN, JUST TO STAY IN THE AIR THAT LITTLE BIT LONGER.
OAK
BUT I TELL MYSELF THAT THIS IS WHAT I WANTED, AND I BRING HER ALL THE WAY DOWN ON HARD GROUND. EARTHBOUND FOR GOOD.
IN THE AP, WE USED TO SAY THERE'S NO SUCH THING AS GRAVITY: THE EARTH SUCKS.
HERE I AM: THE GIRL WHO PULLED HER OWN WINGS OFF.

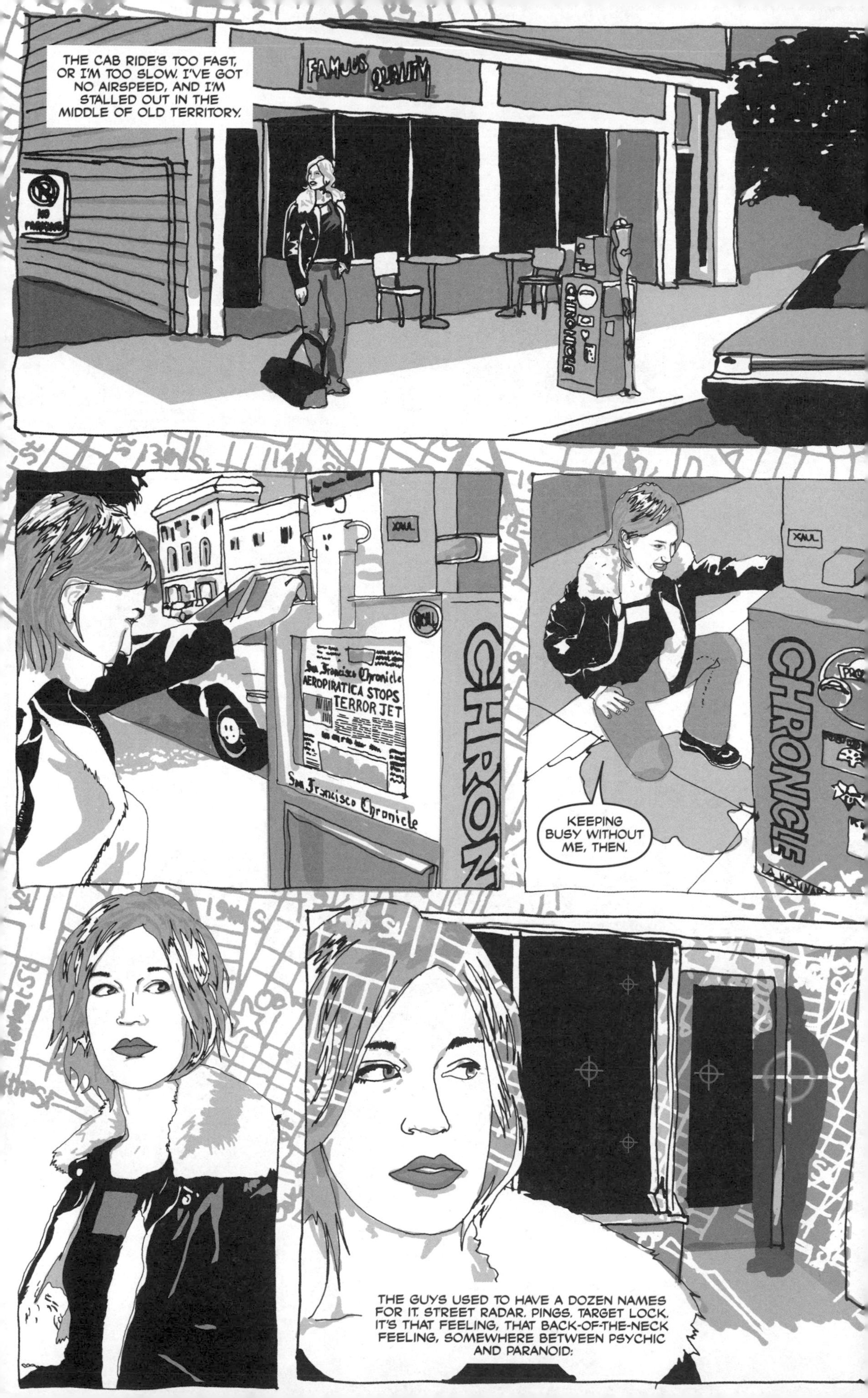
THE CAB RIDE'S TOO FAST, OR I'M TOO SLOW. I'VE GOT NO AIRSPEED, AND I'M STALLED OUT IN THE MIDDLE OF OLD TERRITORY.
CHRONICLE
San Francisco Chronicle
AEROPIRATICA STOPS TERROR JET
San Francisco Chronicle
CHRON
CHRONICLE
KEEPING BUSY WITHOUT ME, THEN.
THE GUYS USED TO HAVE A DOZEN NAMES FOR IT. STREET RADAR. PINGS. TARGET LOCK. IT'S THAT FEELING, THAT BACK-OF-THE-NECK FEELING, SOMEWHERE BETWEEN PSYCHIC AND PARANOID:

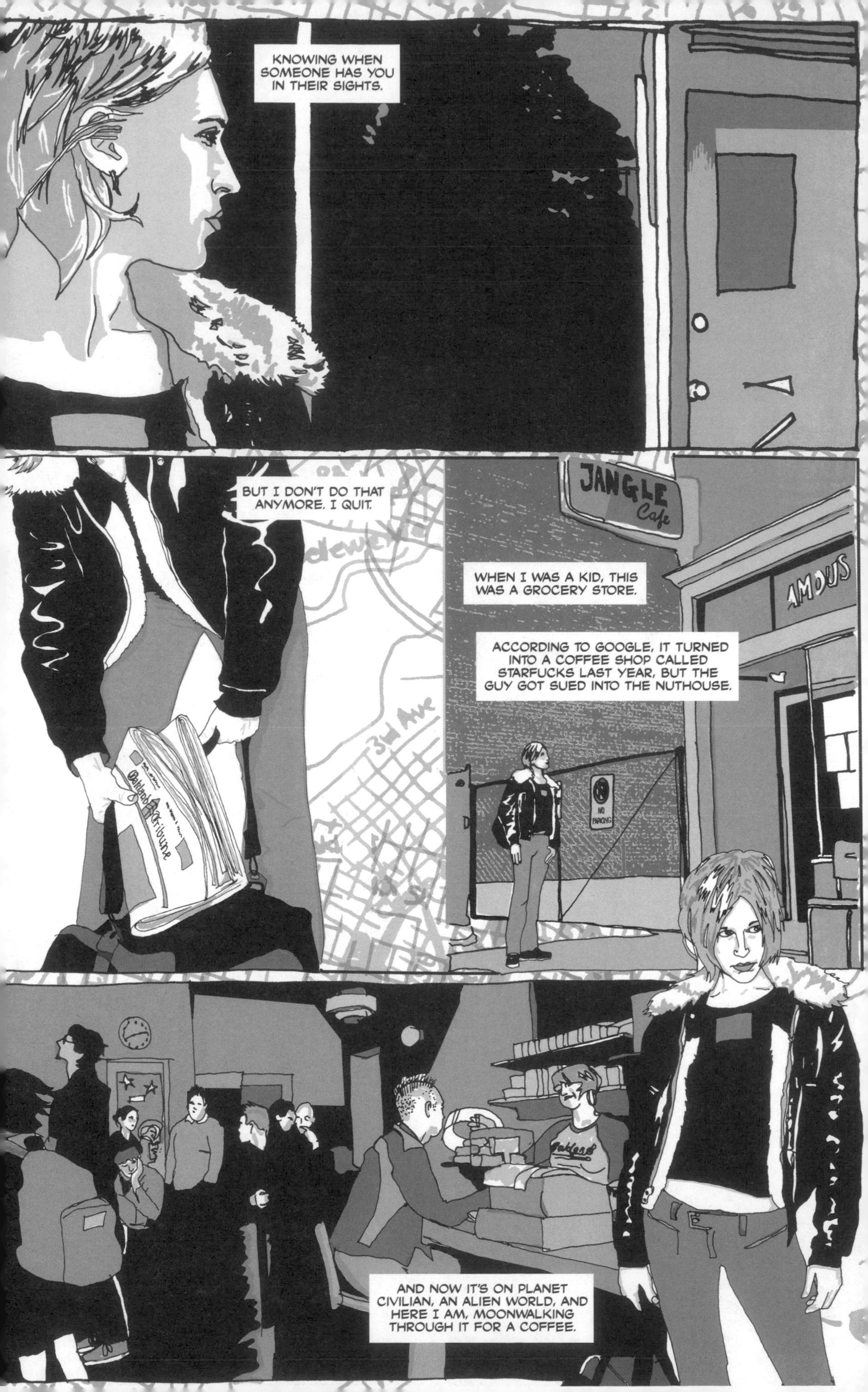
KNOWING WHEN SOMEONE HAS YOU IN THEIR SIGHTS.
BUT I DON'T DO THAT ANYMORE. I QUIT.
JANGLE Cafe
WHEN I WAS A KID, THIS WAS A GROCERY STORE.
ACCORDING TO GOOGLE, IT TURNED INTO A COFFEE SHOP CALLED STARFUCKS LAST YEAR, BUT THE GUY GOT SUED INTO THE NUTHOUSE.
NO PARKING
AND NOW IT'S ON PLANET CIVILIAN, AN ALIEN WORLD, AND HERE I AM, MOONWALKING THROUGH IT FOR A COFFEE.

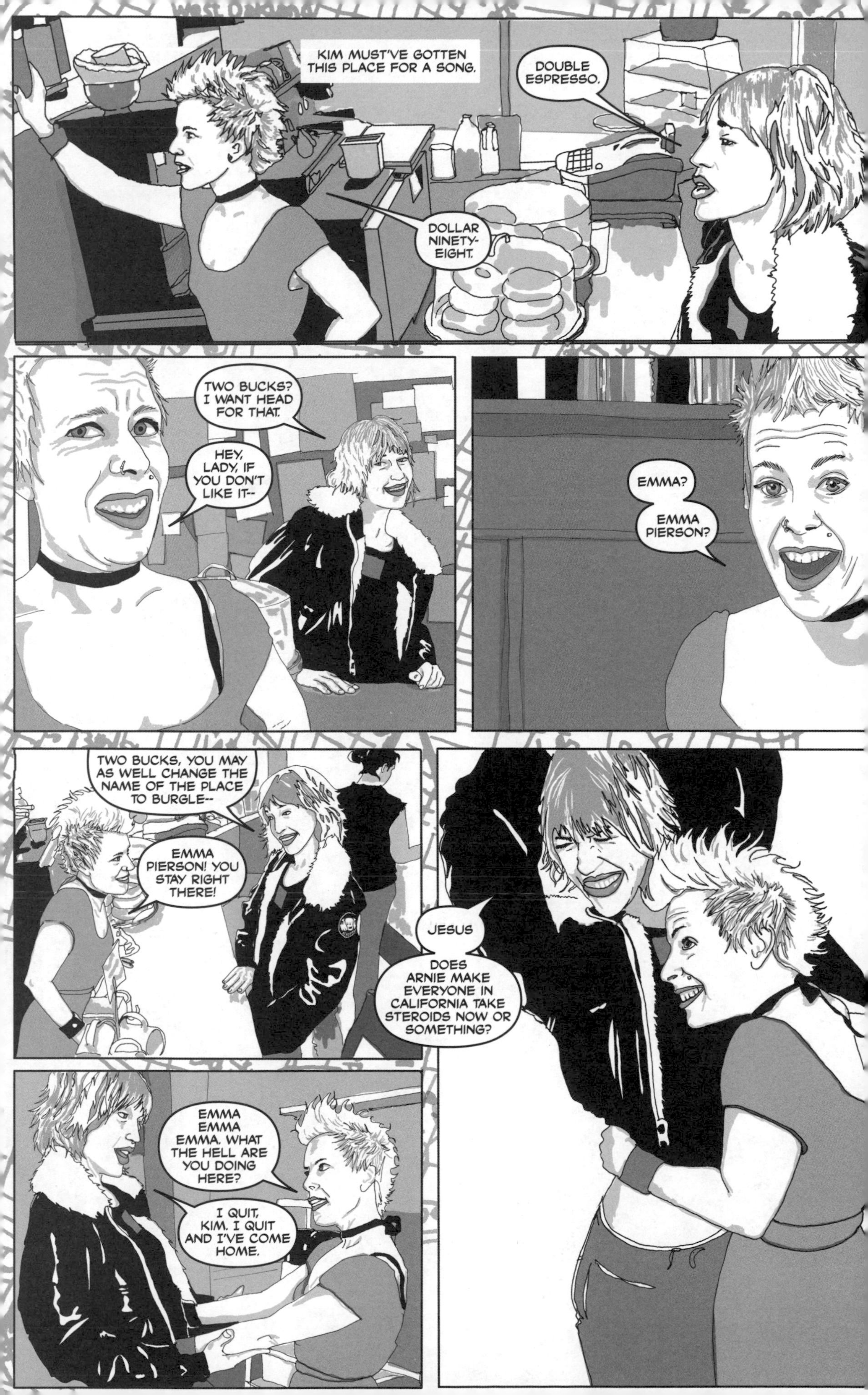
KIM MUST'VE GOTTEN THIS PLACE FOR A SONG.
DOUBLE ESPRESSO.
DOLLAR NINETY-EIGHT.
TWO BUCKS? I WANT HEAD FOR THAT.
HEY, LADY, IF YOU DON'T LIKE IT--
EMMA?
EMMA PIERSON?
TWO BUCKS, YOU MAY AS WELL CHANGE THE NAME OF THE PLACE TO BURGLE--
EMMA PIERSON! YOU STAY RIGHT THERE!
JESUS
DOES ARNIE MAKE EVERYONE IN CALIFORNIA TAKE STEROIDS NOW OR SOMETHING?
EMMA EMMA EMMA. WHAT THE HELL ARE YOU DOING HERE?
I QUIT, KIM. I QUIT AND I'VE COME HOME.

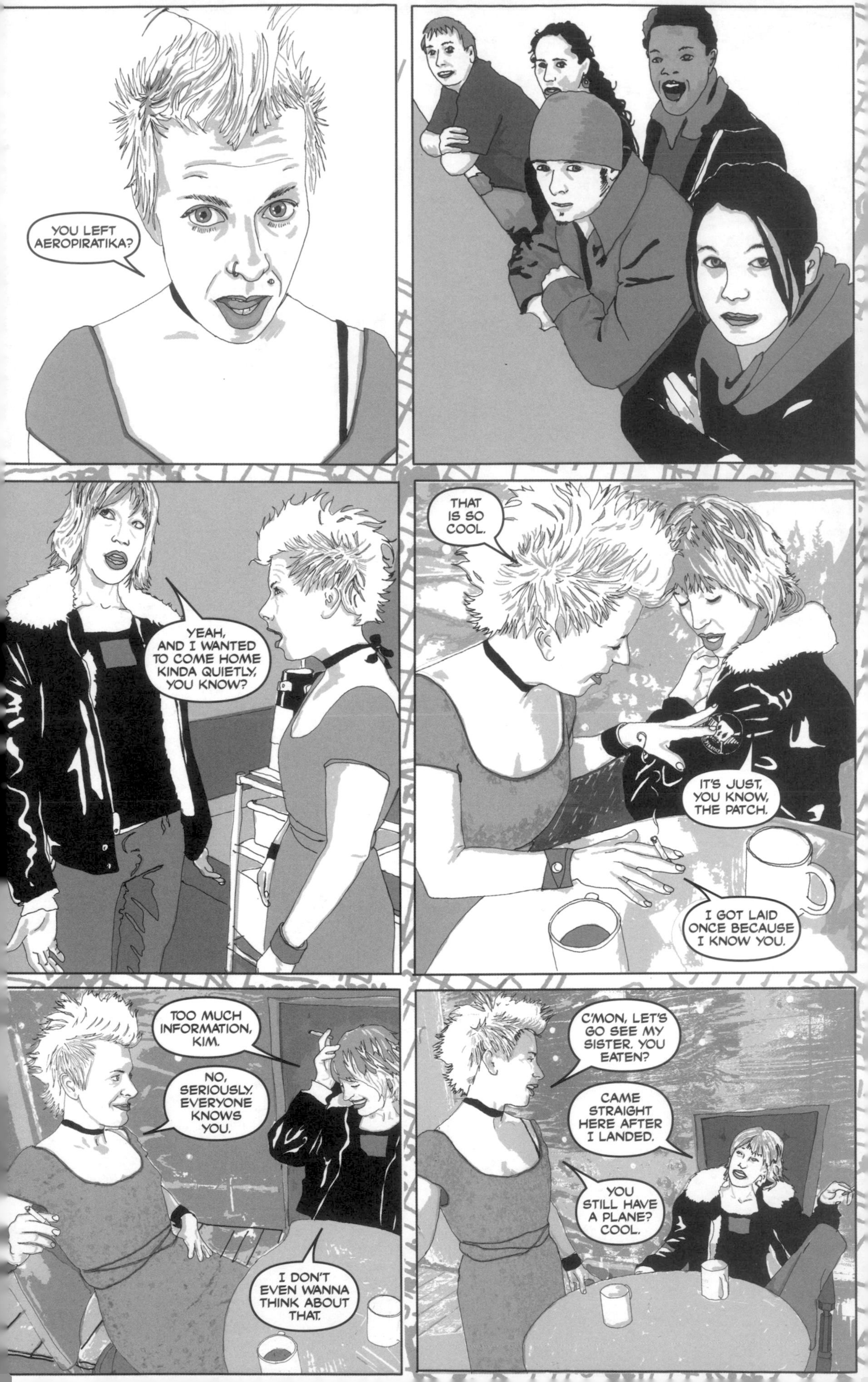
YOU LEFT AEROPIRATIKA?
YEAH, AND I WANTED TO COME HOME KINDA QUIETLY, YOU KNOW?
THAT IS SO COOL.
IT'S JUST, YOU KNOW, THE PATCH.
I GOT LAID ONCE BECAUSE I KNOW YOU.
TOO MUCH INFORMATION, KIM.
NO, SERIOUSLY. EVERYONE KNOWS YOU.
I DON'T EVEN WANNA THINK ABOUT THAT.
C'MON, LET'S GO SEE MY SISTER. YOU EATEN?
CAME STRAIGHT HERE AFTER I LANDED.
YOU STILL HAVE A PLANE? COOL.

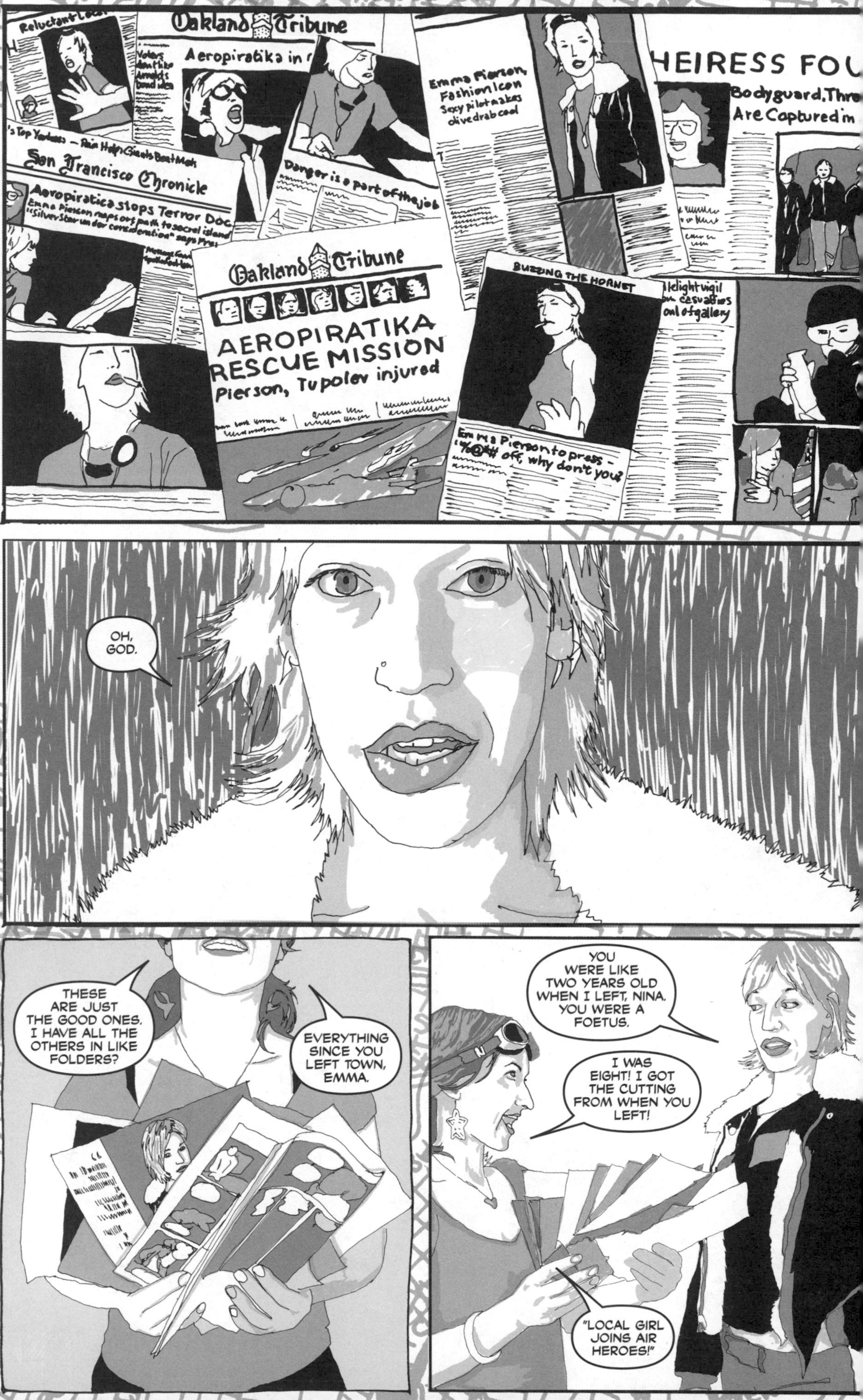

Oakland Tribune
Aeropiratika in
Emma Pierson, Fashion Icon
Sexy pilot makes olive drab cool
HEIRESS FOU
Bodyguard, Thre
Are Captured in
San Francisco Chronicle
Aeropiratica stops Terror Doc
Danger is a part of the job
Oakland Tribune
AEROPIRATIKA RESCUE MISSION
Pierson, Tupolev injured
BUZZING THE HORNET
Emma Pierson to press - '%@#! off, why don't you?
OH, GOD.
THESE ARE JUST THE GOOD ONES. I HAVE ALL THE OTHERS IN LIKE FOLDERS?
EVERYTHING SINCE YOU LEFT TOWN, EMMA.
YOU WERE LIKE TWO YEARS OLD WHEN I LEFT, NINA. YOU WERE A FOETUS.
I WAS EIGHT! I GOT THE CUTTING FROM WHEN YOU LEFT!
"LOCAL GIRL JOINS AIR HEROES!"

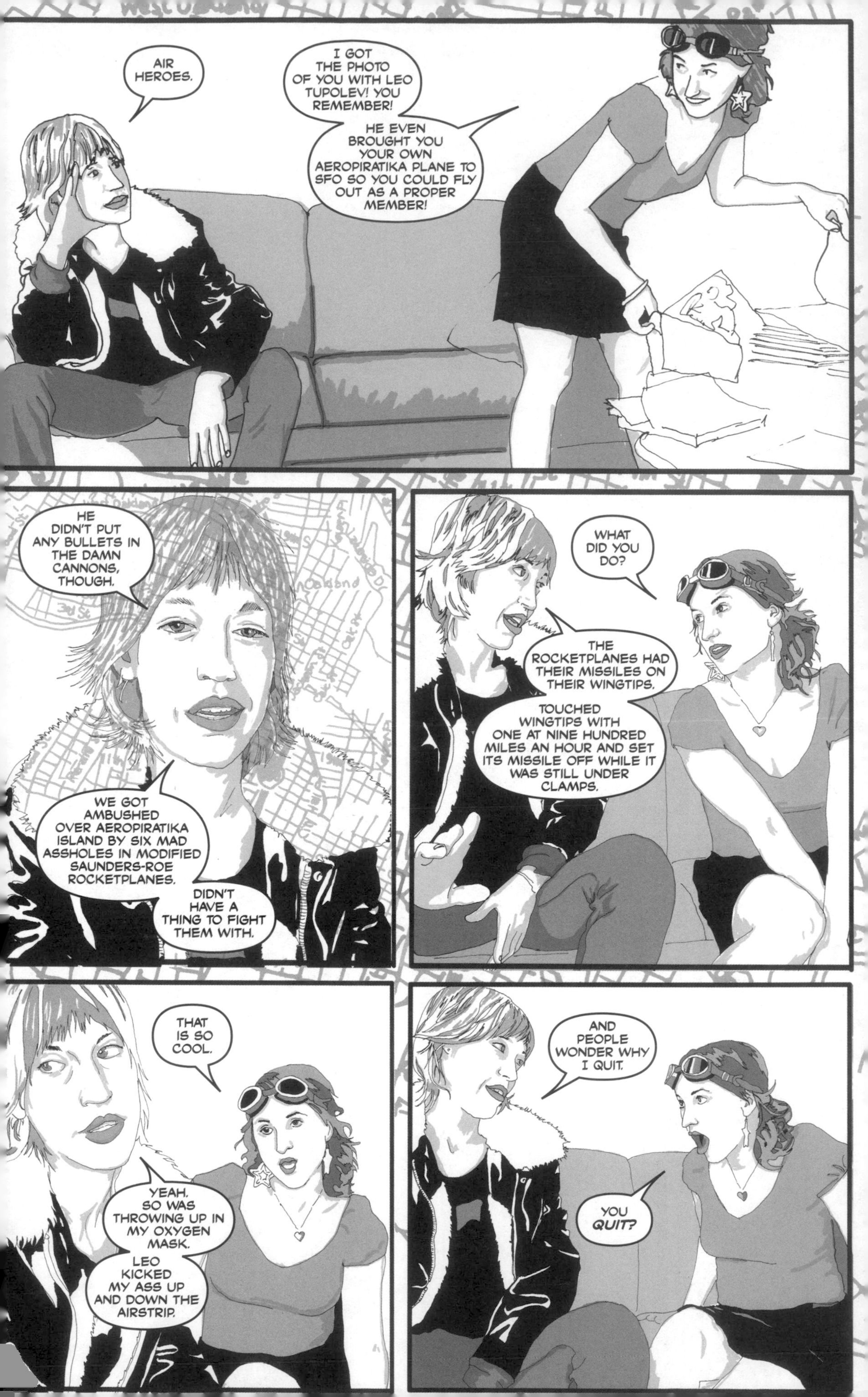
AIR HEROES.
I GOT THE PHOTO OF YOU WITH LEO TUPOLEV! YOU REMEMBER!
HE EVEN BROUGHT YOU YOUR OWN AEROPIRATIKA PLANE TO SFO SO YOU COULD FLY OUT AS A PROPER MEMBER!
HE DIDN'T PUT ANY BULLETS IN THE DAMN CANNONS, THOUGH.
WE GOT AMBUSHED OVER AEROPIRATIKA ISLAND BY SIX MAD ASSHOLES IN MODIFIED SAUNDERS-ROE ROCKETPLANES.
DIDN'T HAVE A THING TO FIGHT THEM WITH.
WHAT DID YOU DO?
THE ROCKETPLANES HAD THEIR MISSILES ON THEIR WINGTIPS.
TOUCHED WINGTIPS WITH ONE AT NINE HUNDRED MILES AN HOUR AND SET ITS MISSILE OFF WHILE IT WAS STILL UNDER CLAMPS.
THAT IS SO COOL.
YEAH. SO WAS THROWING UP IN MY OXYGEN MASK.
LEO KICKED MY ASS UP AND DOWN THE AIRSTRIP.
AND PEOPLE WONDER WHY I QUIT.
YOU *QUIT?*

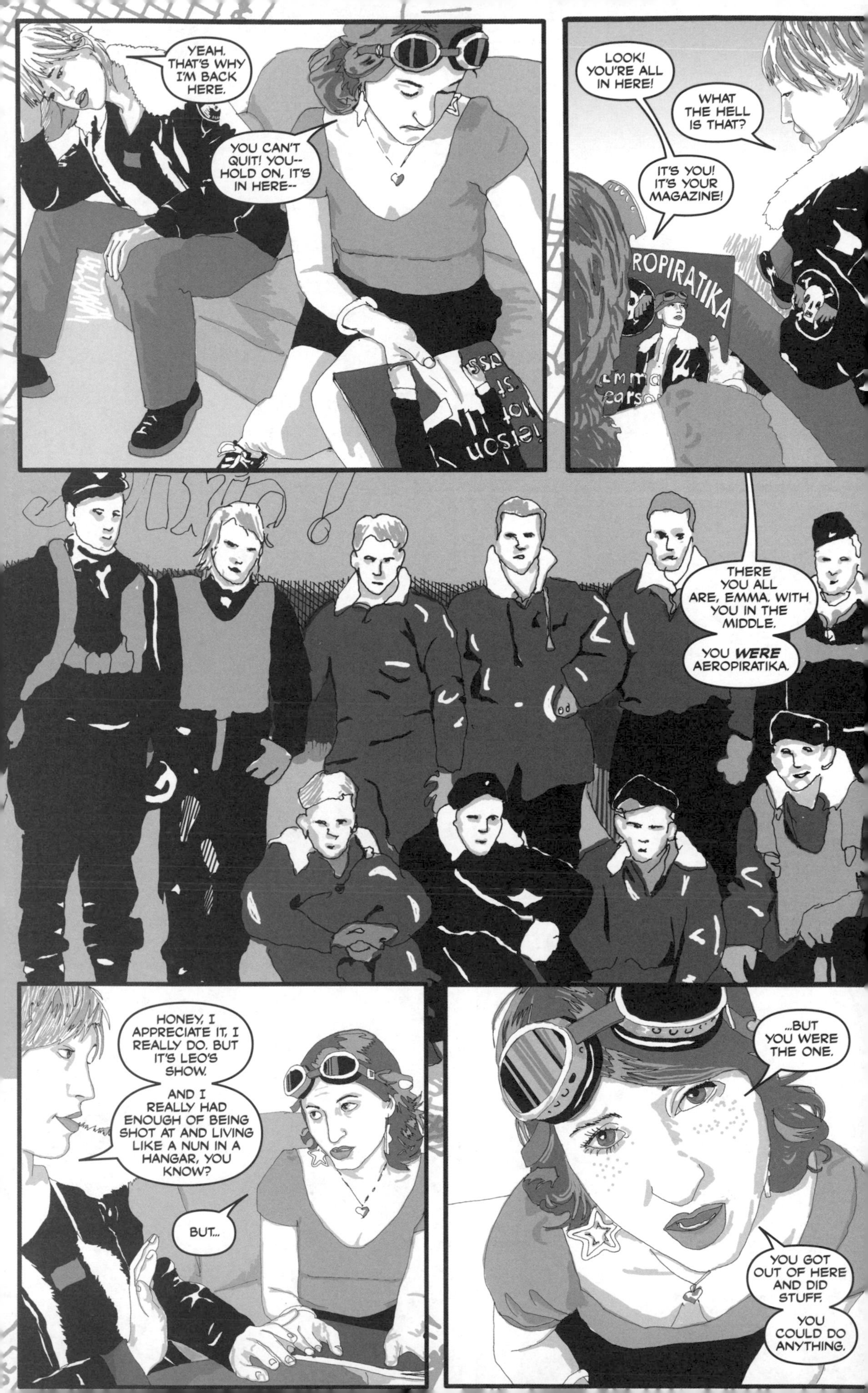
YEAH. THAT'S WHY I'M BACK HERE.
YOU CAN'T QUIT! YOU-- HOLD ON, IT'S IN HERE--
LOOK! YOU'RE ALL IN HERE!
WHAT THE HELL IS THAT?
IT'S YOU! IT'S YOUR MAGAZINE!
ROPIRATIKA
THERE YOU ALL ARE, EMMA. WITH YOU IN THE MIDDLE.
YOU *WERE* AEROPIRATIKA.
HONEY, I APPRECIATE IT, I REALLY DO. BUT IT'S LEO'S SHOW.
AND I REALLY HAD ENOUGH OF BEING SHOT AT AND LIVING LIKE A NUN IN A HANGAR, YOU KNOW?
BUT...
...BUT YOU WERE THE ONE.
YOU GOT OUT OF HERE AND DID STUFF.
YOU COULD DO ANYTHING.

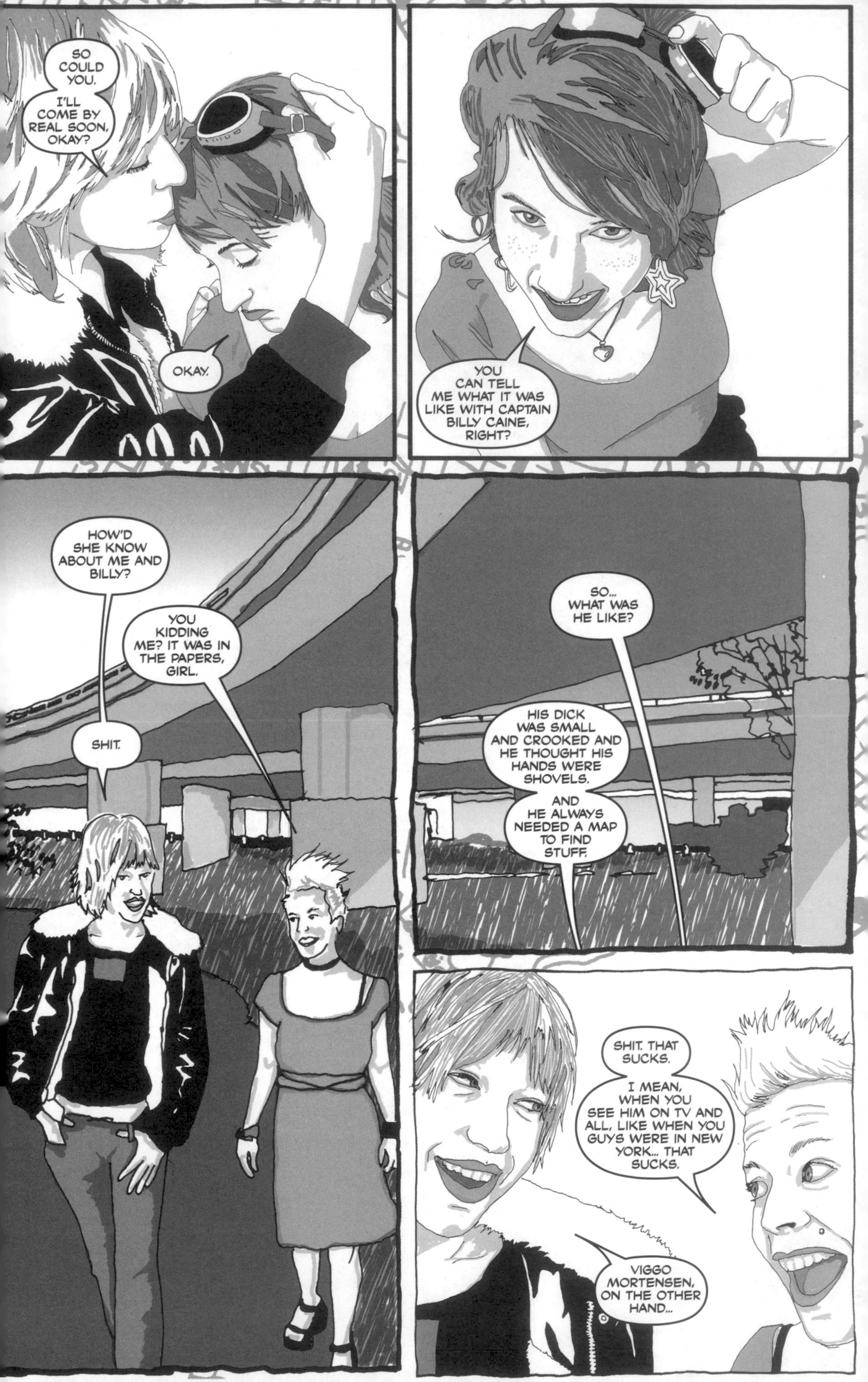

SO COULD YOU.
I'LL COME BY REAL SOON, OKAY?
OKAY.
YOU CAN TELL ME WHAT IT WAS LIKE WITH CAPTAIN BILLY CAINE, RIGHT?
HOW'D SHE KNOW ABOUT ME AND BILLY?
YOU KIDDING ME? IT WAS IN THE PAPERS, GIRL.
SHIT.
SO... WHAT WAS HE LIKE?
HIS DICK WAS SMALL AND CROOKED AND HE THOUGHT HIS HANDS WERE SHOVELS.
AND HE ALWAYS NEEDED A MAP TO FIND STUFF.
SHIT. THAT SUCKS.
I MEAN, WHEN YOU SEE HIM ON TV AND ALL, LIKE WHEN YOU GUYS WERE IN NEW YORK... THAT SUCKS.
VIGGO MORTENSEN, ON THE OTHER HAND...

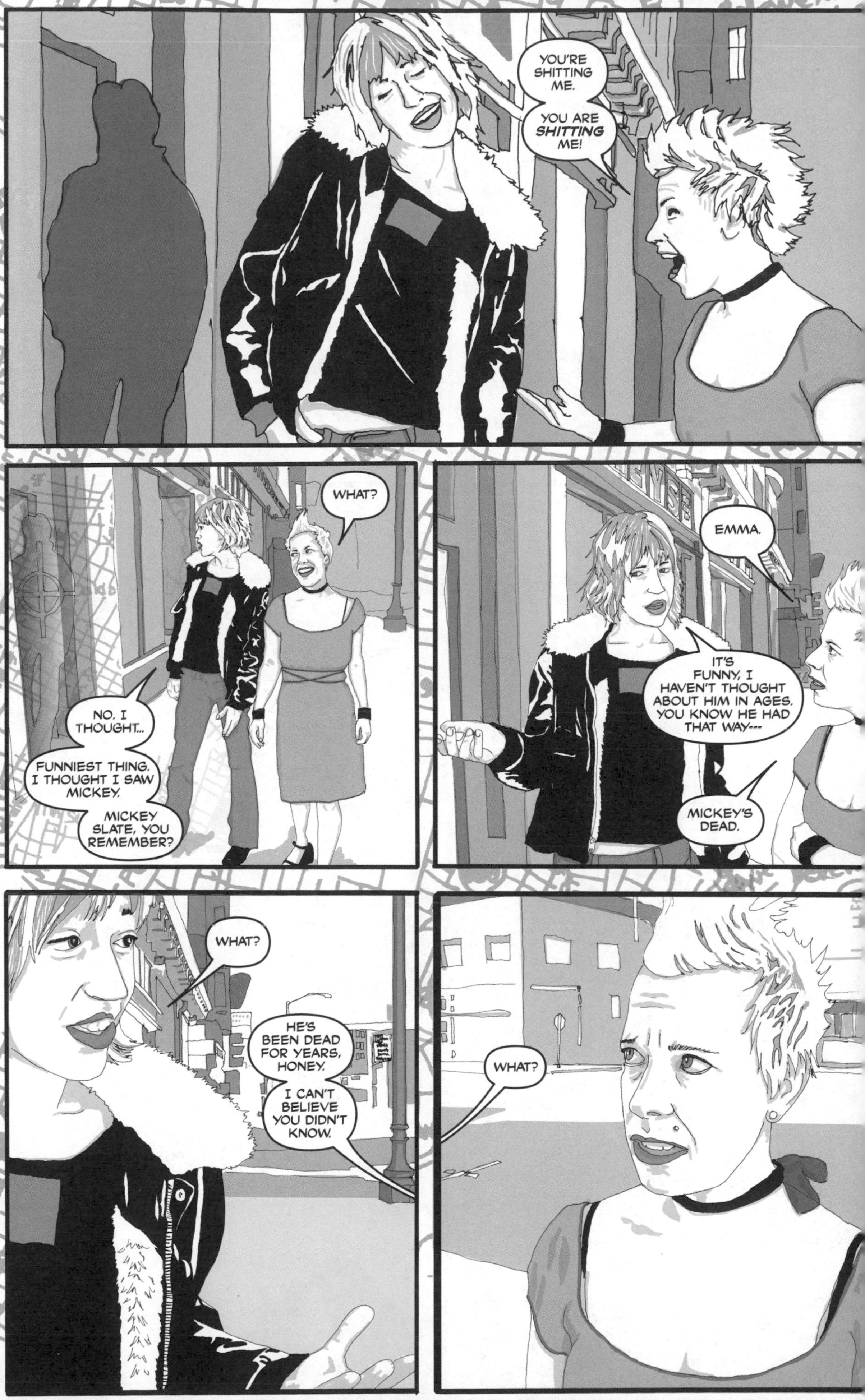
YOU'RE SHITTING ME.
YOU ARE *SHITTING* ME!
WHAT?
NO. I THOUGHT...
FUNNIEST THING. I THOUGHT I SAW MICKEY.
MICKEY SLATE, YOU REMEMBER?
EMMA.
IT'S FUNNY, I HAVEN'T THOUGHT ABOUT HIM IN AGES. YOU KNOW HE HAD THAT WAY---
MICKEY'S DEAD.
WHAT?
HE'S BEEN DEAD FOR YEARS, HONEY.
I CAN'T BELIEVE YOU DIDN'T KNOW.
WHAT?

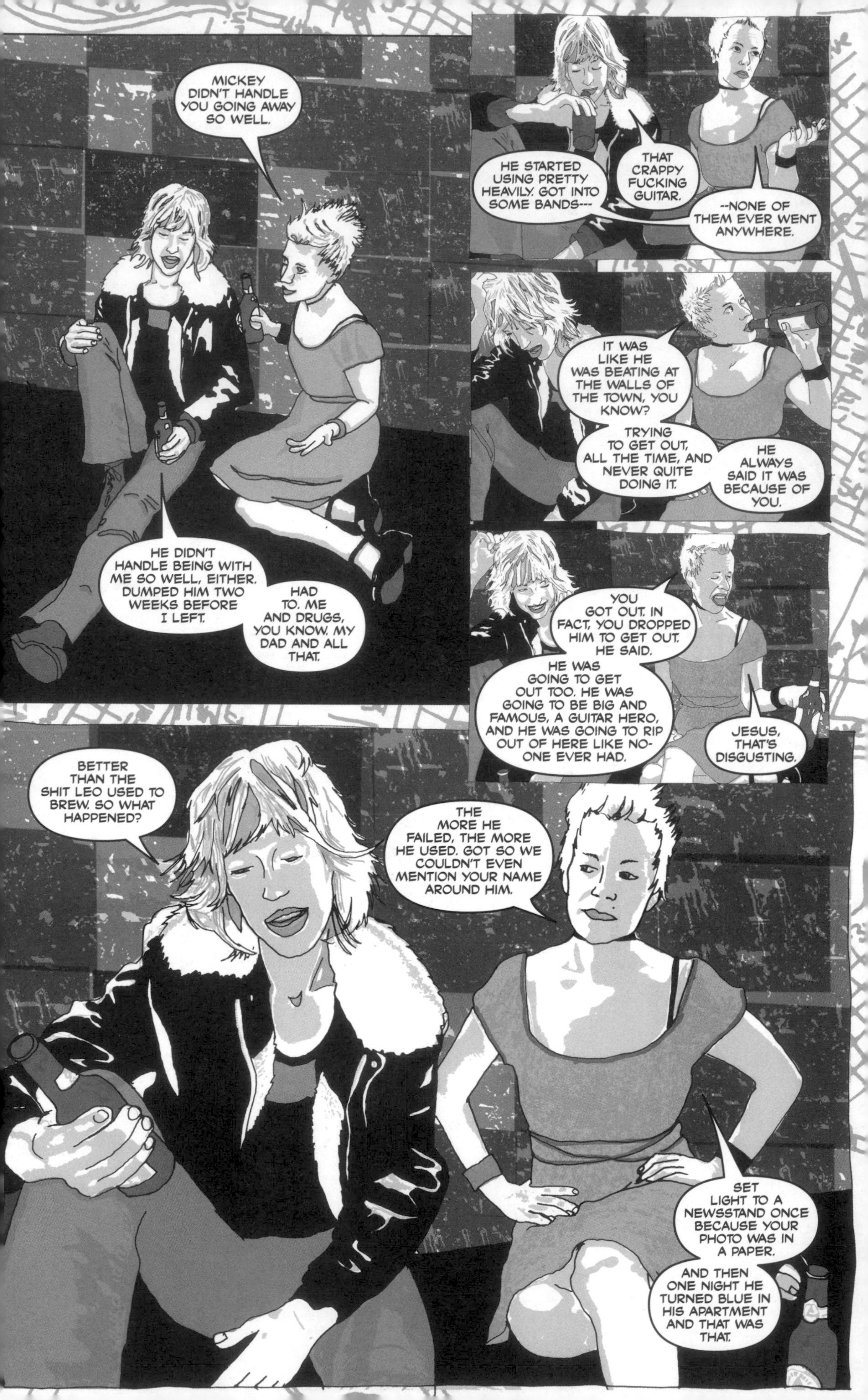
MICKEY DIDN'T HANDLE YOU GOING AWAY SO WELL.
HE DIDN'T HANDLE BEING WITH ME SO WELL, EITHER. DUMPED HIM TWO WEEKS BEFORE I LEFT.
HAD TO. ME AND DRUGS, YOU KNOW. MY DAD AND ALL THAT.
HE STARTED USING PRETTY HEAVILY. GOT INTO SOME BANDS---
THAT CRAPPY FUCKING GUITAR.
--NONE OF THEM EVER WENT ANYWHERE.
IT WAS LIKE HE WAS BEATING AT THE WALLS OF THE TOWN, YOU KNOW?
TRYING TO GET OUT, ALL THE TIME, AND NEVER QUITE DOING IT.
HE ALWAYS SAID IT WAS BECAUSE OF YOU.
YOU GOT OUT. IN FACT, YOU DROPPED HIM TO GET OUT. HE SAID.
HE WAS GOING TO GET OUT TOO. HE WAS GOING TO BE BIG AND FAMOUS, A GUITAR HERO, AND HE WAS GOING TO RIP OUT OF HERE LIKE NO-ONE EVER HAD.
JESUS, THAT'S DISGUSTING.
BETTER THAN THE SHIT LEO USED TO BREW. SO WHAT HAPPENED?
THE MORE HE FAILED, THE MORE HE USED. GOT SO WE COULDN'T EVEN MENTION YOUR NAME AROUND HIM.
SET LIGHT TO A NEWSSTAND ONCE BECAUSE YOUR PHOTO WAS IN A PAPER.
AND THEN ONE NIGHT HE TURNED BLUE IN HIS APARTMENT AND THAT WAS THAT.

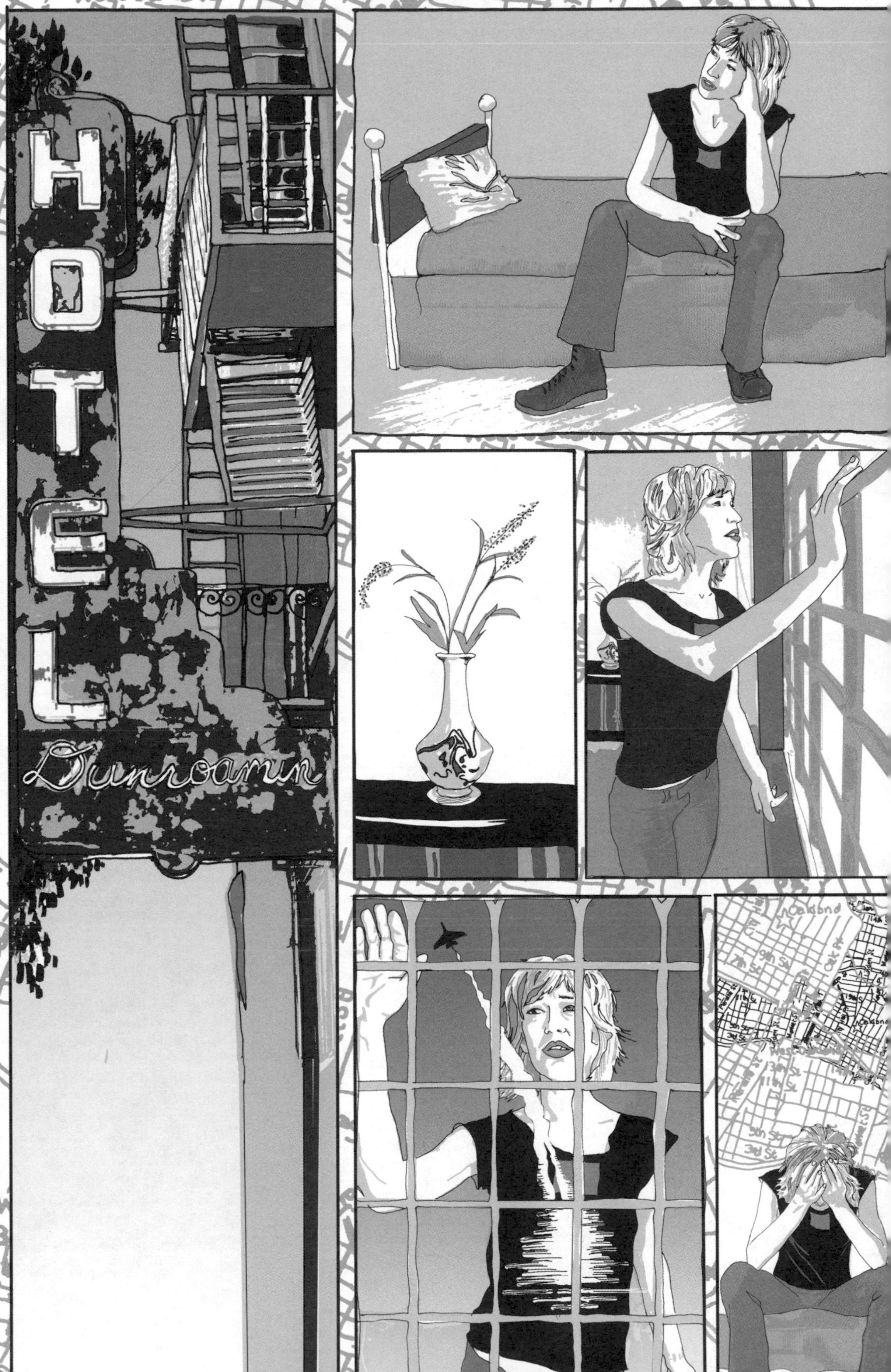
HOTEL
Dunroamin

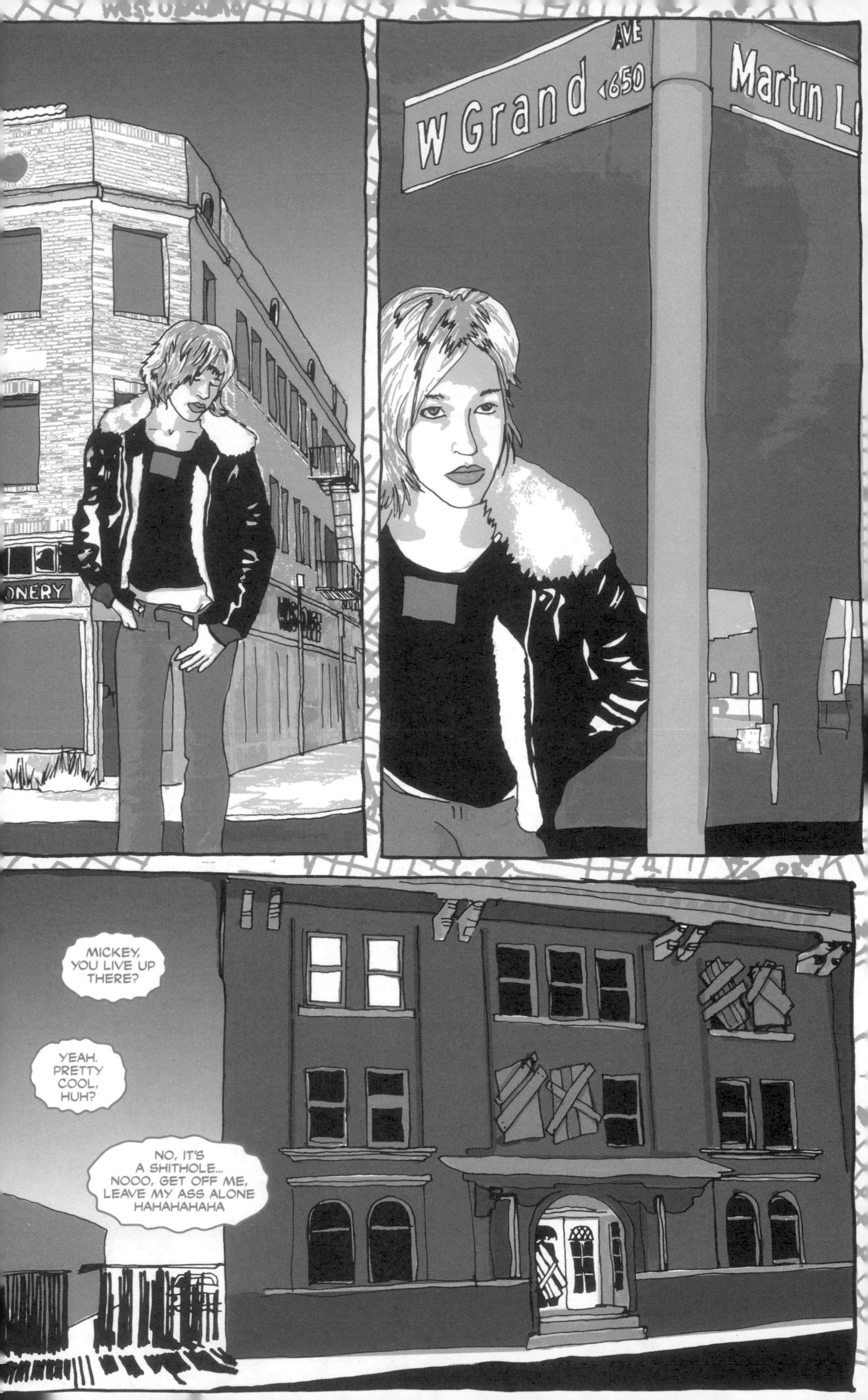
AVE
W Grand 1650
Martin L
ONERY
MICKEY, YOU LIVE UP THERE?
YEAH. PRETTY COOL, HUH?
NO, IT'S A SHITHOLE... NOOO, GET OFF ME, LEAVE MY ASS ALONE HAHAHAHAHA

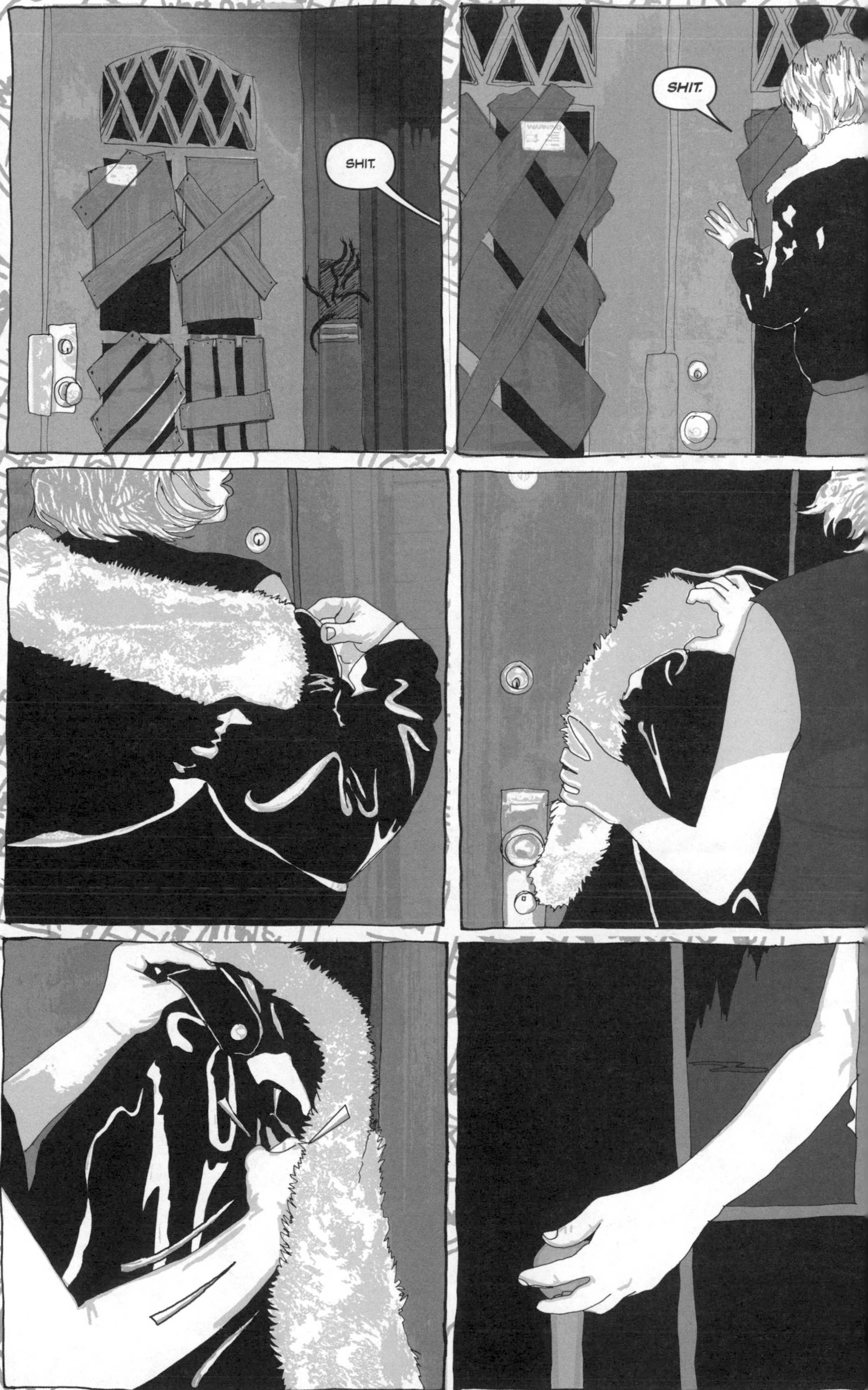
SHIT.
SHIT.

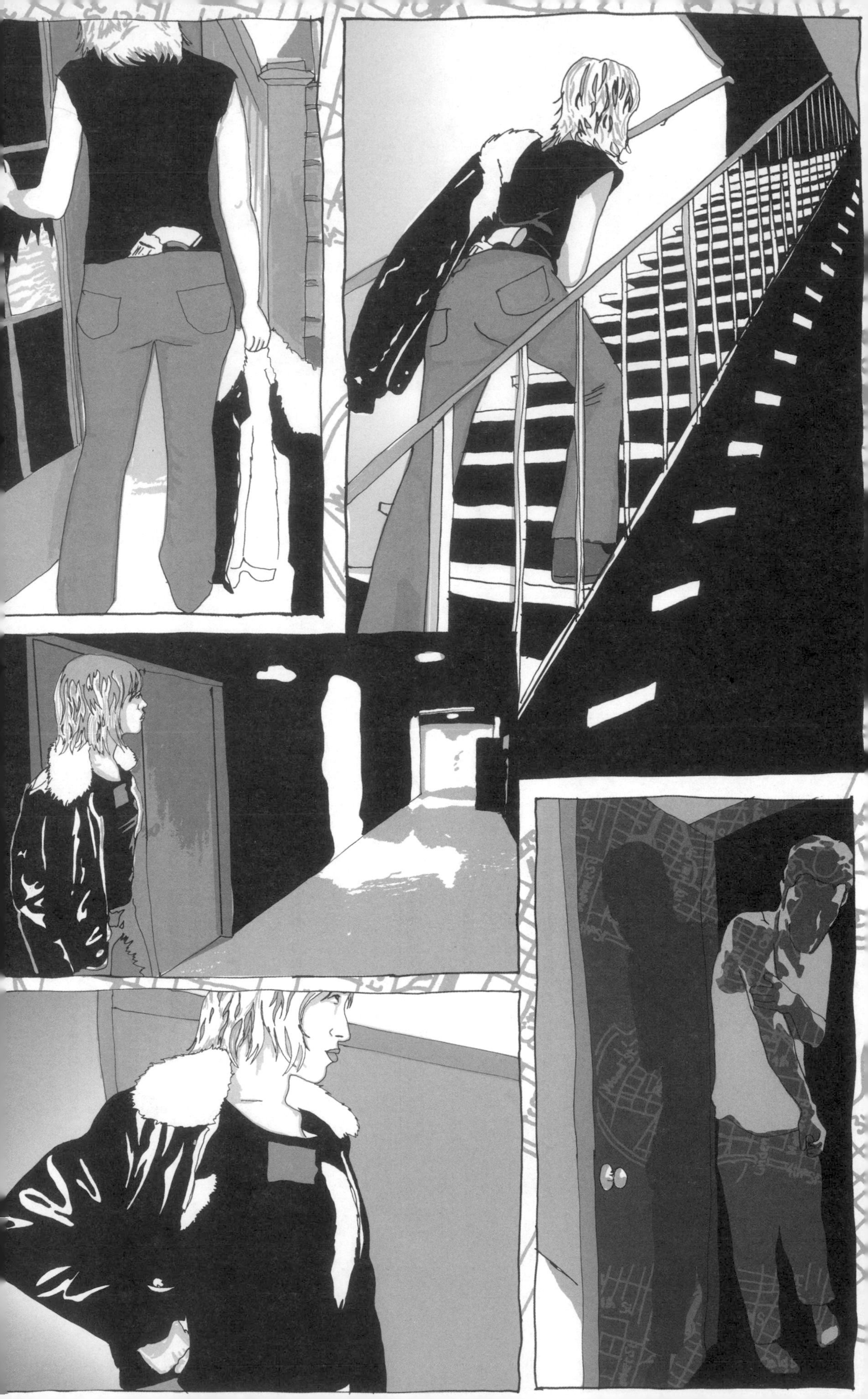

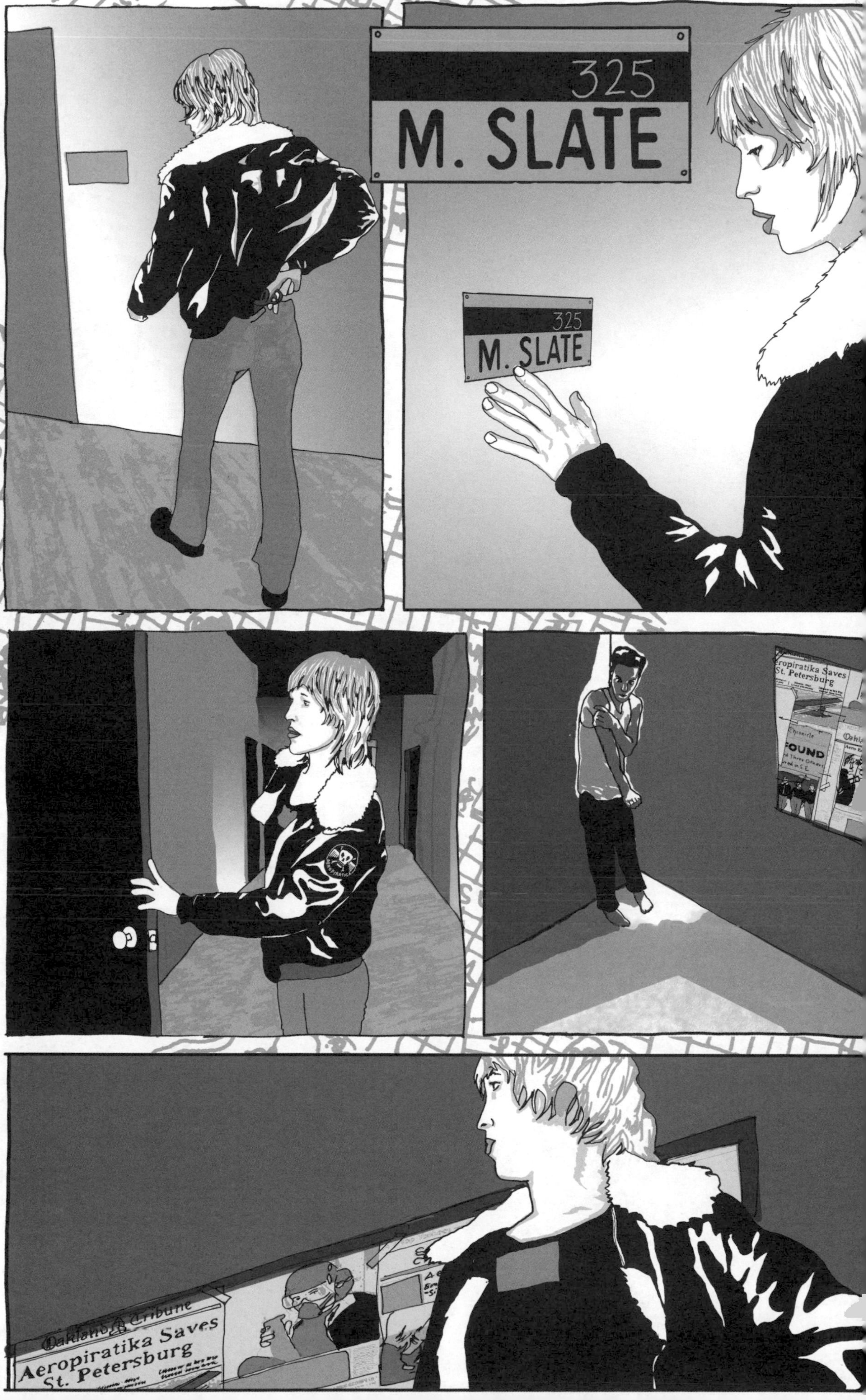

325
M. SLATE
325
M. SLATE
Aeropiratika Saves
St. Petersburg
Chronicle
FOUND
Oakland Tribune
Aeropiratika Saves
St. Petersburg

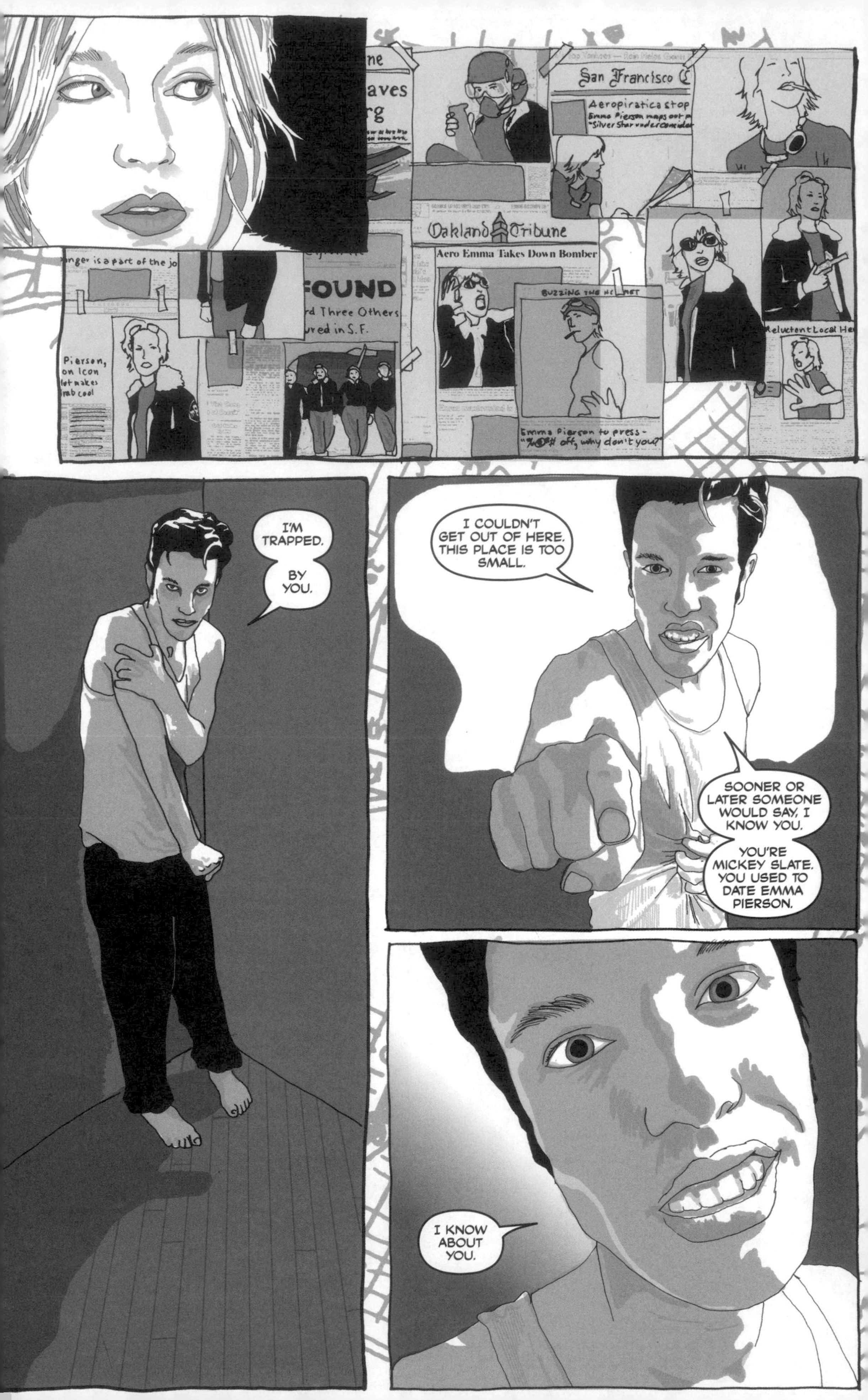
Oakland Tribune
Aero Emma Takes Down Bomber
FOUND
Emma Pierson to press - "%@# off, why don't you?"
I'M TRAPPED.
BY YOU.
I COULDN'T GET OUT OF HERE. THIS PLACE IS TOO SMALL.
SOONER OR LATER SOMEONE WOULD SAY, I KNOW YOU.
YOU'RE MICKEY SLATE. YOU USED TO DATE EMMA PIERSON.
I KNOW ABOUT YOU.

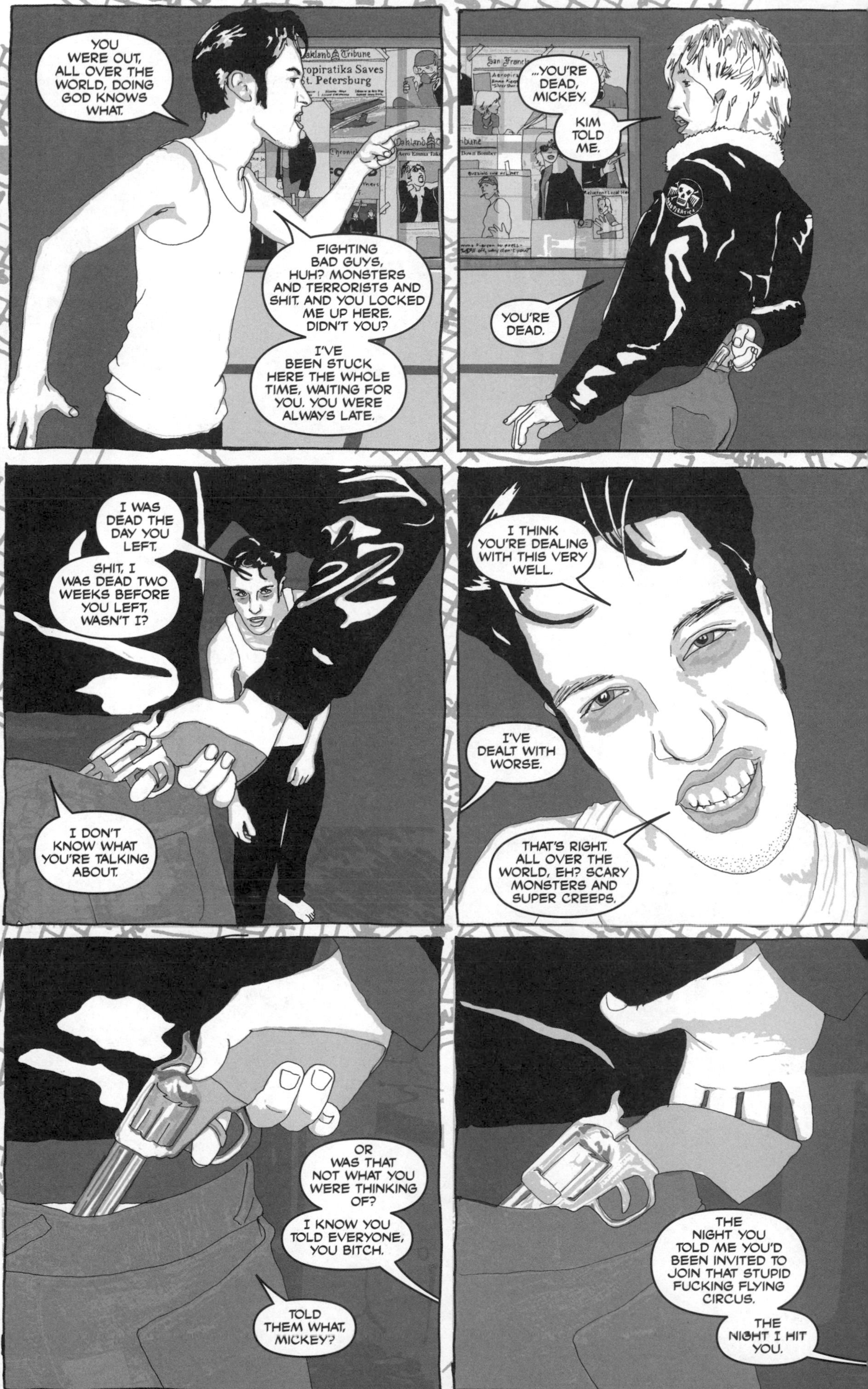
YOU WERE OUT, ALL OVER THE WORLD, DOING GOD KNOWS WHAT.
FIGHTING BAD GUYS, HUH? MONSTERS AND TERRORISTS AND SHIT. AND YOU LOCKED ME UP HERE. DIDN'T YOU?
I'VE BEEN STUCK HERE THE WHOLE TIME, WAITING FOR YOU. YOU WERE ALWAYS LATE.
...YOU'RE DEAD, MICKEY.
KIM TOLD ME.
YOU'RE DEAD.
I WAS DEAD THE DAY YOU LEFT.
SHIT, I WAS DEAD TWO WEEKS BEFORE YOU LEFT, WASN'T I?
I DON'T KNOW WHAT YOU'RE TALKING ABOUT.
I THINK YOU'RE DEALING WITH THIS VERY WELL.
I'VE DEALT WITH WORSE.
THAT'S RIGHT. ALL OVER THE WORLD, EH? SCARY MONSTERS AND SUPER CREEPS.
OR WAS THAT NOT WHAT YOU WERE THINKING OF?
I KNOW YOU TOLD EVERYONE, YOU BITCH.
TOLD THEM WHAT, MICKEY?
THE NIGHT YOU TOLD ME YOU'D BEEN INVITED TO JOIN THAT STUPID FUCKING FLYING CIRCUS.
THE NIGHT I HIT YOU.

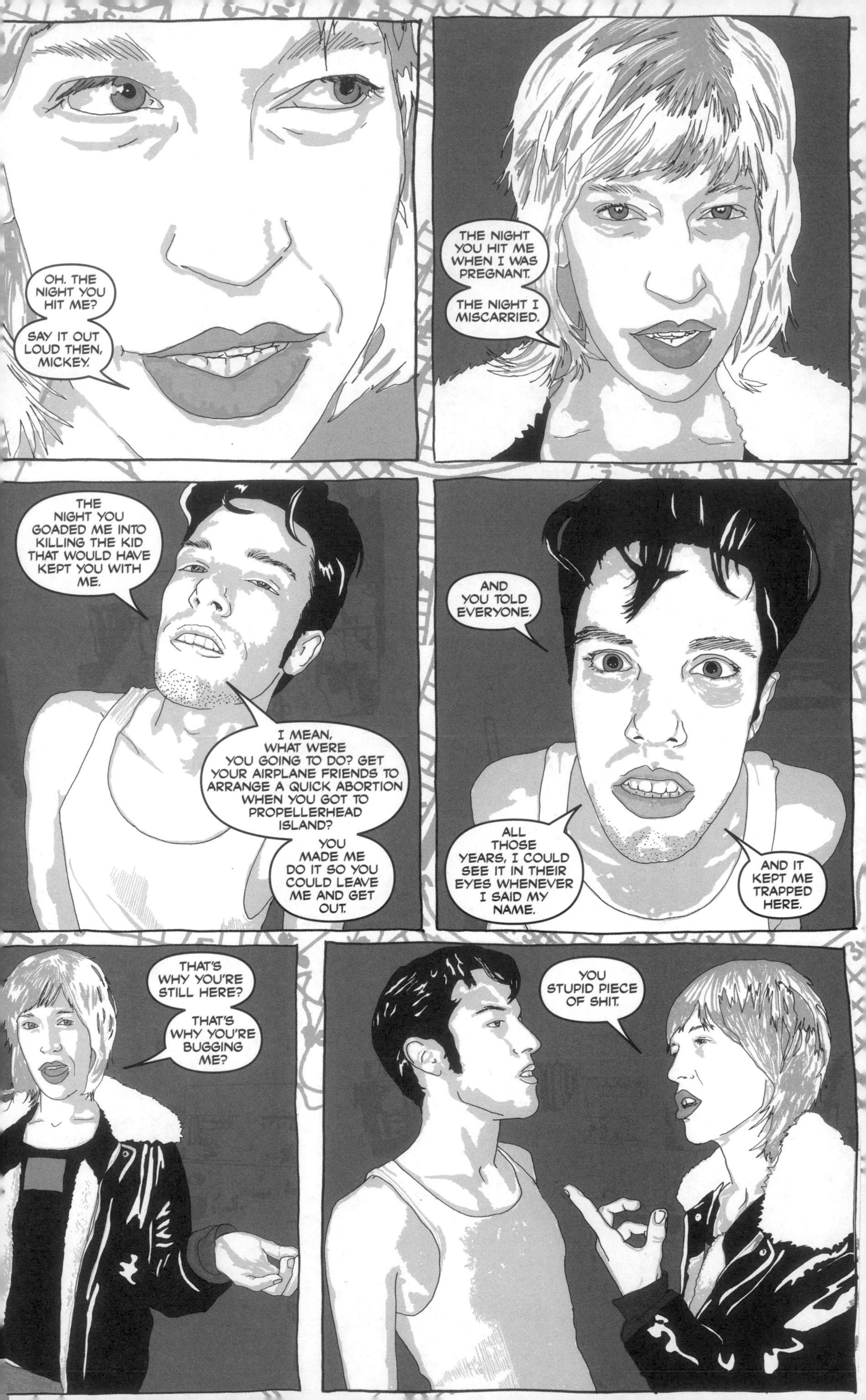
OH, THE NIGHT YOU HIT ME?
SAY IT OUT LOUD THEN, MICKEY.
THE NIGHT YOU HIT ME WHEN I WAS PREGNANT.
THE NIGHT I MISCARRIED.
THE NIGHT YOU GOADED ME INTO KILLING THE KID THAT WOULD HAVE KEPT YOU WITH ME.
I MEAN, WHAT WERE YOU GOING TO DO? GET YOUR AIRPLANE FRIENDS TO ARRANGE A QUICK ABORTION WHEN YOU GOT TO PROPELLERHEAD ISLAND?
YOU MADE ME DO IT SO YOU COULD LEAVE ME AND GET OUT.
AND YOU TOLD EVERYONE.
ALL THOSE YEARS, I COULD SEE IT IN THEIR EYES WHENEVER I SAID MY NAME.
AND IT KEPT ME TRAPPED HERE.
THAT'S WHY YOU'RE STILL HERE?
THAT'S WHY YOU'RE BUGGING ME?
YOU STUPID PIECE OF SHIT.

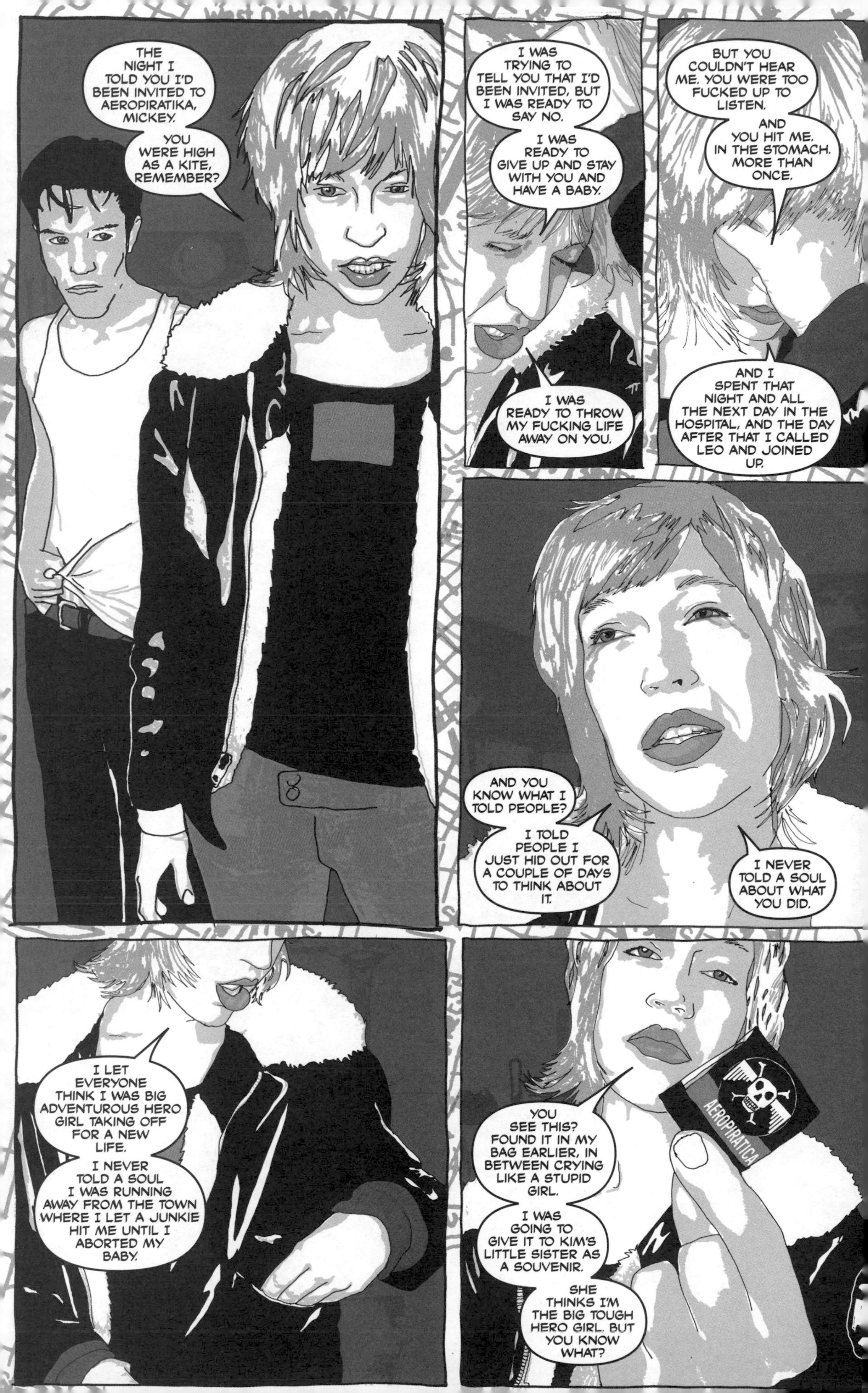
THE NIGHT I TOLD YOU I'D BEEN INVITED TO AEROPIRATIKA, MICKEY.
YOU WERE HIGH AS A KITE, REMEMBER?
I WAS TRYING TO TELL YOU THAT I'D BEEN INVITED, BUT I WAS READY TO SAY NO.
I WAS READY TO GIVE UP AND STAY WITH YOU AND HAVE A BABY.
I WAS READY TO THROW MY FUCKING LIFE AWAY ON YOU.
BUT YOU COULDN'T HEAR ME. YOU WERE TOO FUCKED UP TO LISTEN.
AND YOU HIT ME. IN THE STOMACH. MORE THAN ONCE.
AND I SPENT THAT NIGHT AND ALL THE NEXT DAY IN THE HOSPITAL, AND THE DAY AFTER THAT I CALLED LEO AND JOINED UP.
AND YOU KNOW WHAT I TOLD PEOPLE?
I TOLD PEOPLE I JUST HID OUT FOR A COUPLE OF DAYS TO THINK ABOUT IT.
I NEVER TOLD A SOUL ABOUT WHAT YOU DID.
I LET EVERYONE THINK I WAS BIG ADVENTUROUS HERO GIRL TAKING OFF FOR A NEW LIFE.
I NEVER TOLD A SOUL I WAS RUNNING AWAY FROM THE TOWN WHERE I LET A JUNKIE HIT ME UNTIL I ABORTED MY BABY.
YOU SEE THIS? FOUND IT IN MY BAG EARLIER, IN BETWEEN CRYING LIKE A STUPID GIRL.
AEROPIRATICA
I WAS GOING TO GIVE IT TO KIM'S LITTLE SISTER AS A SOUVENIR.
SHE THINKS I'M THE BIG TOUGH HERO GIRL. BUT YOU KNOW WHAT?

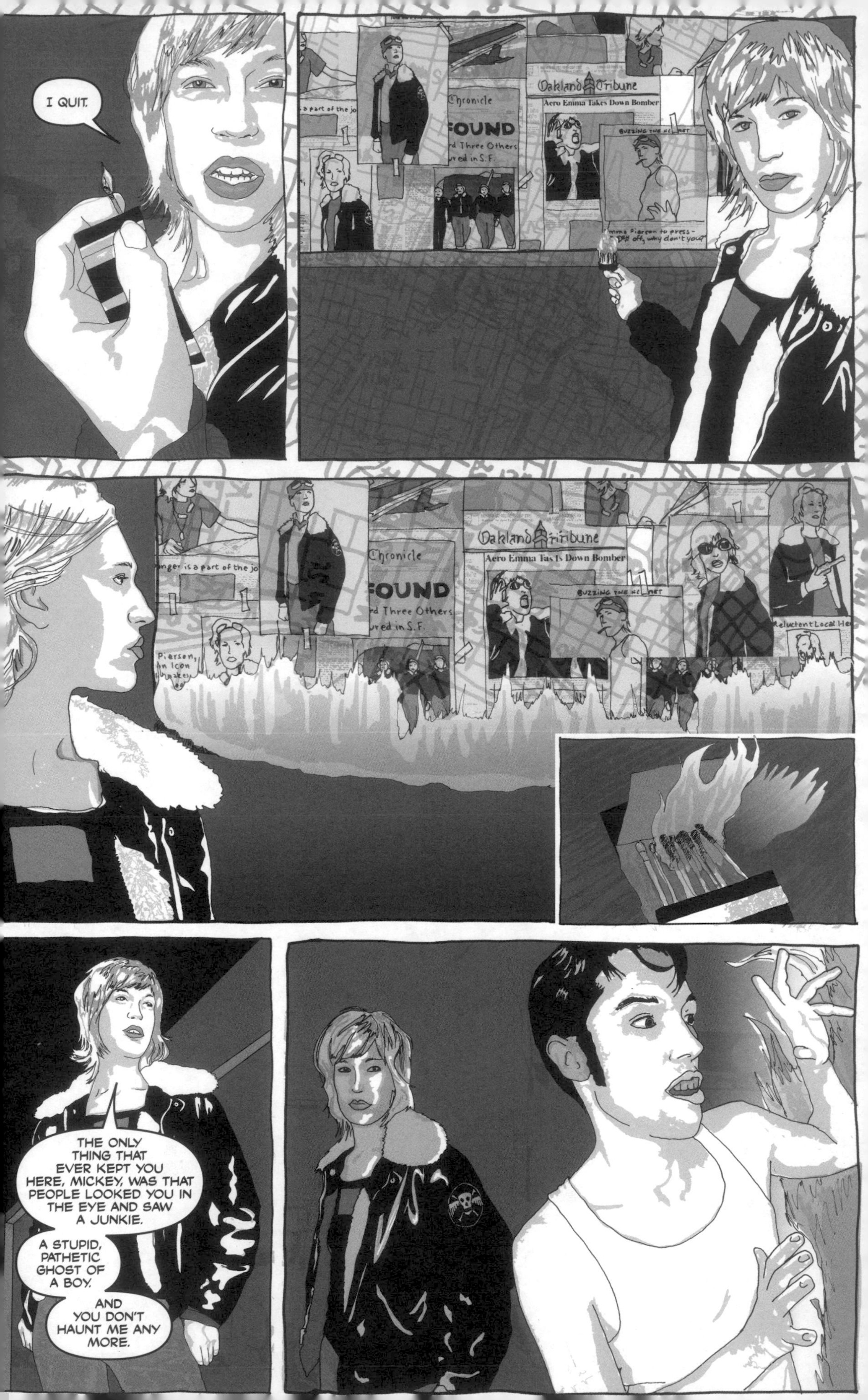
I QUIT.
Oakland Tribune
Aero Emma Takes Down Bomber
Chronicle
FOUND
THE ONLY THING THAT EVER KEPT YOU HERE, MICKEY, WAS THAT PEOPLE LOOKED YOU IN THE EYE AND SAW A JUNKIE.
A STUPID, PATHETIC GHOST OF A BOY.
AND YOU DON'T HAUNT ME ANY MORE.

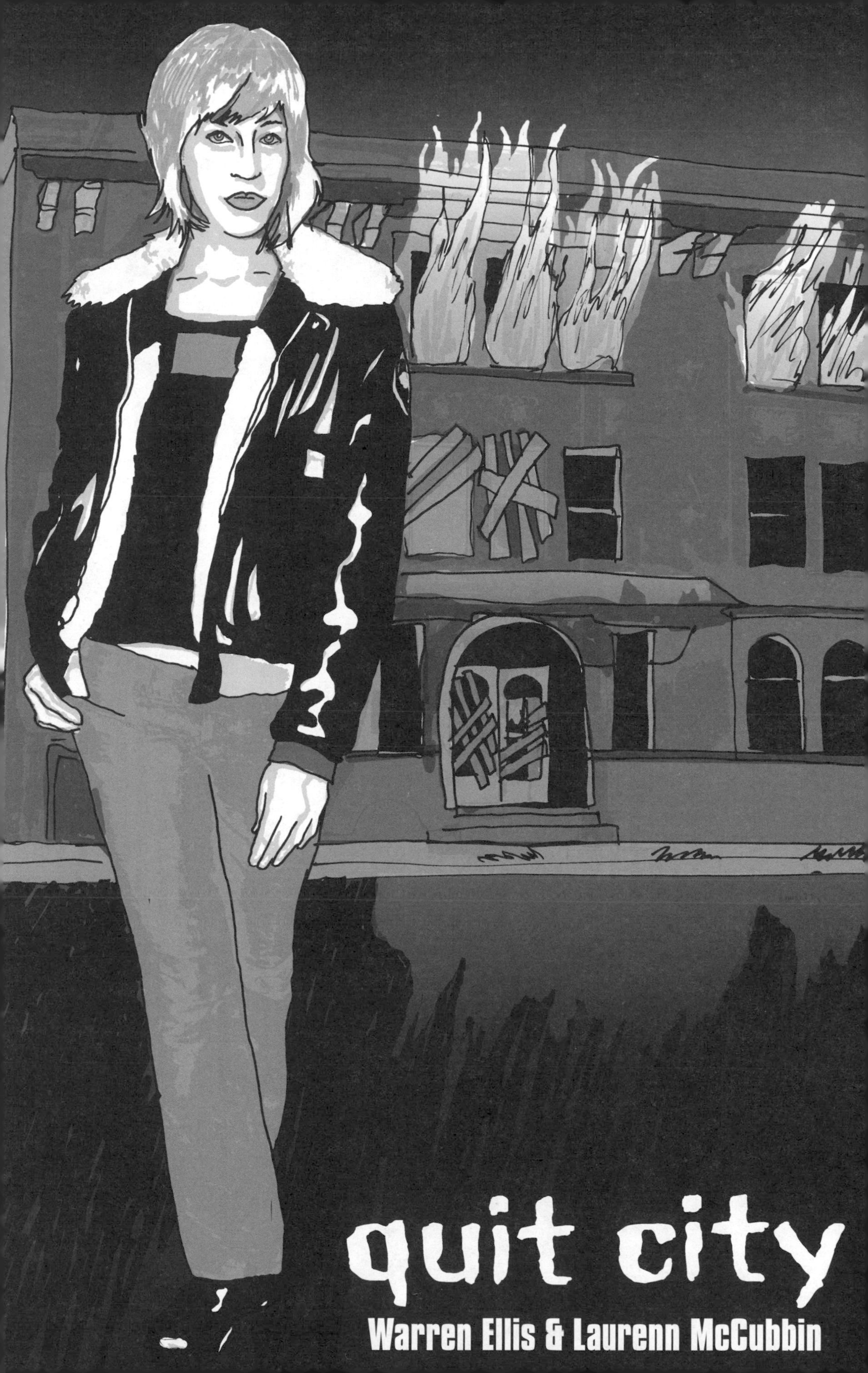
quit city
Warren Ellis & Laurenn McCubbin

quit city

YEARS AGO, I SAT DOWN AND THOUGHT ABOUT WHAT adventure comics might've looked like today if superhero comics hadn't have happened. If, in fact, the pulp tradition of Weird Thrillers had jumped straight into comics form without mutating into the superhero subgenre we know today. If you took away preconceptions about design and the dominant single form.

And then, a couple of years later, Alan Moore went ahead and did some of it with the America's Best Comics line. And Dan Jurgens did the rest with the Tangent line at DC.

The other day, I was thinking about response songs. Rappers taking shots at each other, covers that answer something in the original, art made in reaction to art. Which, you kind of hope, is not the same as being reactionary.

The small music labels 555 Recordings and Dark Beloved Cloud have singles clubs. People play down the importance of singles these days—they don't sell the way they used to, downloads bother the music business—but I love them. Sometimes one song contained on one object is all you need to move the axis of the world. Self-contained and saying all that needs to be said.

Singles and Tangent and ABC all kind of stuck together in my head, and I began conceiving of a response. The Apparat Singles Group. An imaginary line of comics singles. Four imaginary first issues of imaginary series from an imaginary line of comics, even.

This is what I think adventure comics would look like today if you blanked out the last sixty years of superhero comics. Yes, there would still be elements of great strangeness, because that's what the pulps traded on. There would be sf and high adventure and weird thrillers and occult journeys. But they would be of their time. The term "adventure" itself would have a dozen different definitions.

AIRBORNE

There was a time when aviators were heroes. They were an elite group, brave and skilled, technological explorers. Renaissance men like Antoine de St. Exupery, French poet of the air who wrote "The Little Prince." Dashing Lindbergh. And lost Amelia Earhart.

This was, naturally enough, reflected in pulp fiction. G-8 And His Battle Aces. Dusty Ayres And His Battle Birds. Not just combat pilots, but adventurers and heroes, fighting strangeness at altitude. Strange wars in the air. By the 1940s, the theme had found its way to comics in the likes of Blackhawk, an international team of pilot-adventurers, launching out of the

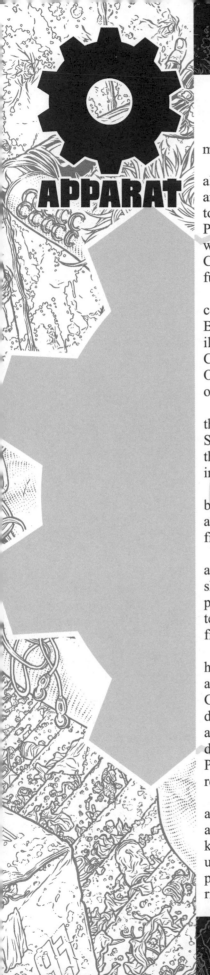

APPARAT

mysterious Blackhawk Island to fight Nazis and beasties.

The aviator hero couldn't survive the future, of course. Like all great leaps, they became old ground. Pilots are no longer rare and remarkable creatures. Hell, even I've flown a plane, thanks to my girlfriend's father, who took his hands off the controls of a Piper Cherokee at four thousand feet and said "fly the plane for a while, Warren." And there I am, flying a plane over the English Channel like Berlioz, without the benefit of little things like fucking flying lessons. The bastard.

The aviator hero went away. (Apart from me. As far as I'm concerned, it's St Exupery and then me. Shut up.) The Blackhawk comic has limped along the years—a beautifully illustrated but fairly incoherent graphic novel by Howard Chaykin, heroic but fruitless efforts by writers like John Ostrander—but has also pretty much gone away, an ageing film option from Hollywood notwithstanding.

Of all the main pulp themes, it's possibly the one that's aged the worst. We can still get behind the strange vigilantes like The Shadow or Doc Savage, the science fiction and the horror, and the hard-boiled crime fiction. But aviators... fiction about pilots in the present day tends to express as sitcom fodder.

So I'm sitting here, thinking that I want to address the theme, because I like the romance of it—but the romance has gone away. And that was the hook. The machinery of adventure fiction thrown into reverse. The aviator-adventurer who quit.

Because that, too, is part of the contemporary expression of adventure fiction. Throwing it into reverse. Flipping it over to show its human underpinnings. Setting the adventurer adrift, putting the form under a kind of interrogation—one of the basic tenets of the postmodern intention that made it into adventure fiction in the 1980s.

Cross Amelia Earhart with a Battle Ace or a Blackhawk, and have her walk away before that last flight. The aviator hero quits and tries to go back to her old life. An Air Pirate in West Oakland. Going all the way past the usual stabs at this kind of story and driving it all the distance into contemporary fiction, not even acknowledging the action scene that the postmodern action story drops in to serve the form. Just the smallest colouring of what Paul Di Filippo calls "the counterintuitive" to express the pulp roots, that little hit of the unusual that no other fiction deals.

Realism is comics isn't about photographic exactitude. It's about communicating the feeling of the authentic world. It's not about drawing a table so precisely that a drunken carpenter could knock up a copy from the page. It's about making you feel its used, textural, remembered presence. Real, flawed, inhabited people. For my money, there are only two people who do this right, right now, and those people are Laurenn McCubbin and

Eddie Campbell. And Laurenn's one of my best friends and draws the best women, so she was the only choice for this. I set *Quit City* in Oaktown because that's where she lives and works. When she's not illustrating and working as a photographer, she's Creative Director for the award-winning Oakland-based magazine *Kitchen Sink*. For me, she's as much a Renaissance figure as St Exupery. Nigh on six feet tall in her bare feet, with an irresistible crooked beauty, she's possessed of a work ethic that'd cripple an elephant and is an inspiration to everyone around her. She's also very probably hiding under her bed as she reads this. Jen Loy, the editor of *Kitchen Sink* and owner of the Mama Buzz cafe in Oakland, once took me aside and said to me very sternly, "Every moment you spend with her is a blessing. You know that, right?" Jen's about four foot tall, with eyes like targeting lasers and muscles like a young jaguar. You don't argue with Jen. Ever.

You write differently for Laurenn. Mostly because you know she's a better writer than you are. (I have the same problem writing for Colleen Doran.) But also because her pages work differently to other people. She works best with big images. She really brings it home to you that comics are a bastard fusion of at least eight other things (the French call bande dessinée the Ninth Art, and it's hard to deny them the point just because they're French). Single-panel cartoons, photographic composition, pure illustration, prose and poetry, even, as the writer Si Spencer once suggested, advertising art and copy and t-shirt slogans. That's how Laurenn works. She'll tend to frame a single line of text against a single image, using the photographer, illustrator, writer and graphic designer parts of her brain simultaneously. Every panel punches hard.

You're an idiot if you don't adapt to your artist. You'll never get the best out of them if you just run them over. I'm not talking about collaboration so much as I'm talking about sitting down and studying their work and deciding how to tell the story so that it plays to their strengths and makes them look good.

Hopefully, all the Apparat books have a different feel to each other. But *Quit City,* I think, would look unusual anywhere.

I think that everyone, at some point, entertains the notion of going home again. As bad as it might have been. Wounds heal over. Scars fade with years. Even the most remarkable of people—and the protagonist of *Quit City,* to me, is a remarkable woman—sometimes need to throw everything into reverse and go back to where they once belonged. Everyone had a place where they once were safe. Or, at least, once *felt* safe.

For some people, Air Wonder Stories aren't enough.

—Warren Ellis

SIMON SPECTOR™

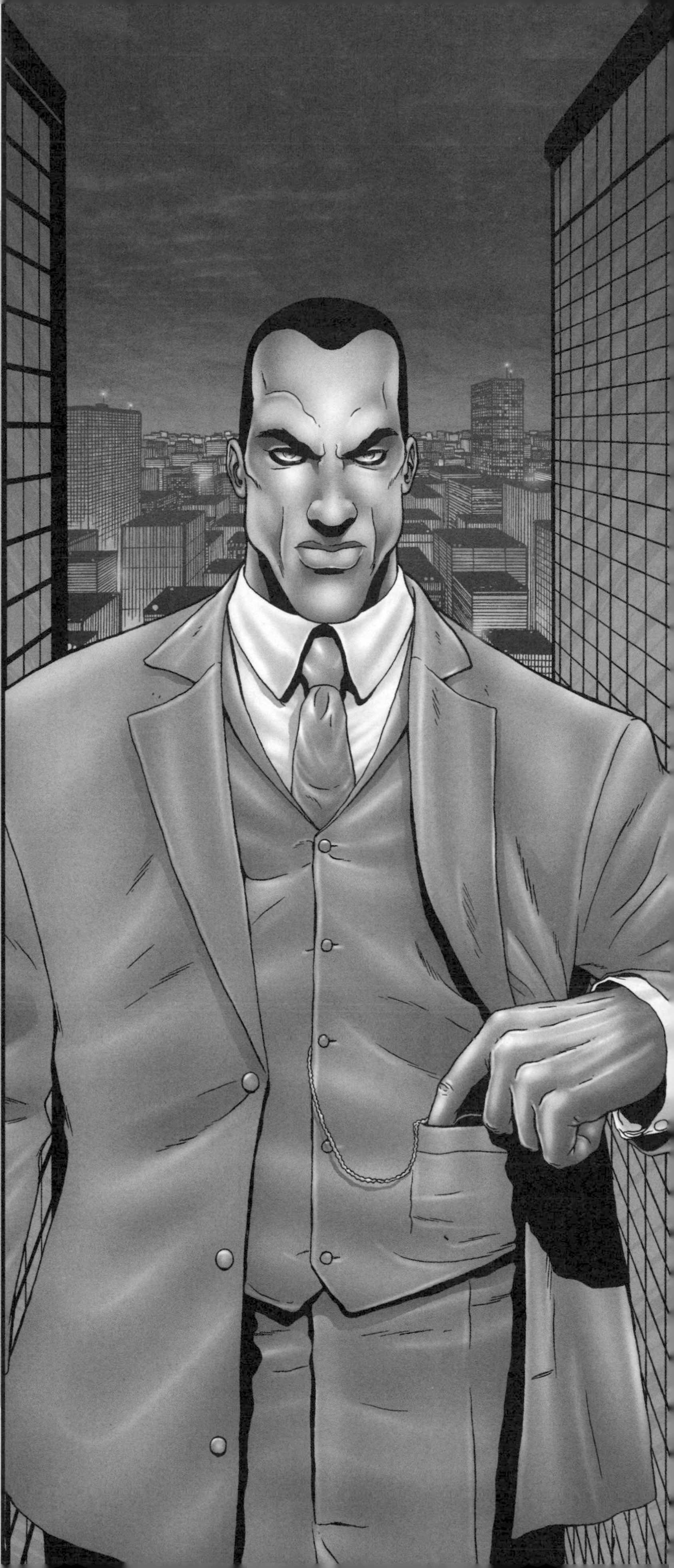

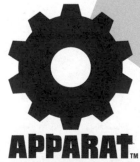

APPARAT™

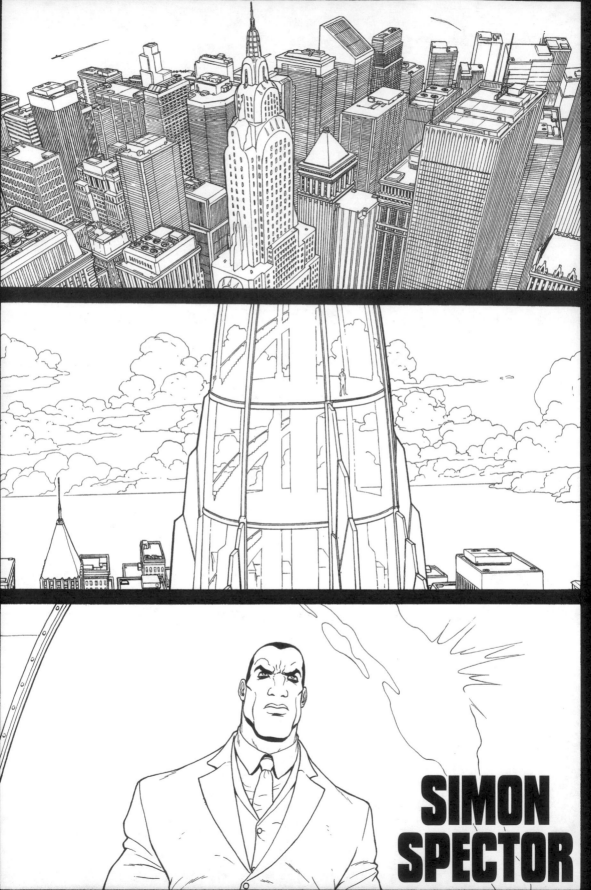

SIMON
SPECTOR

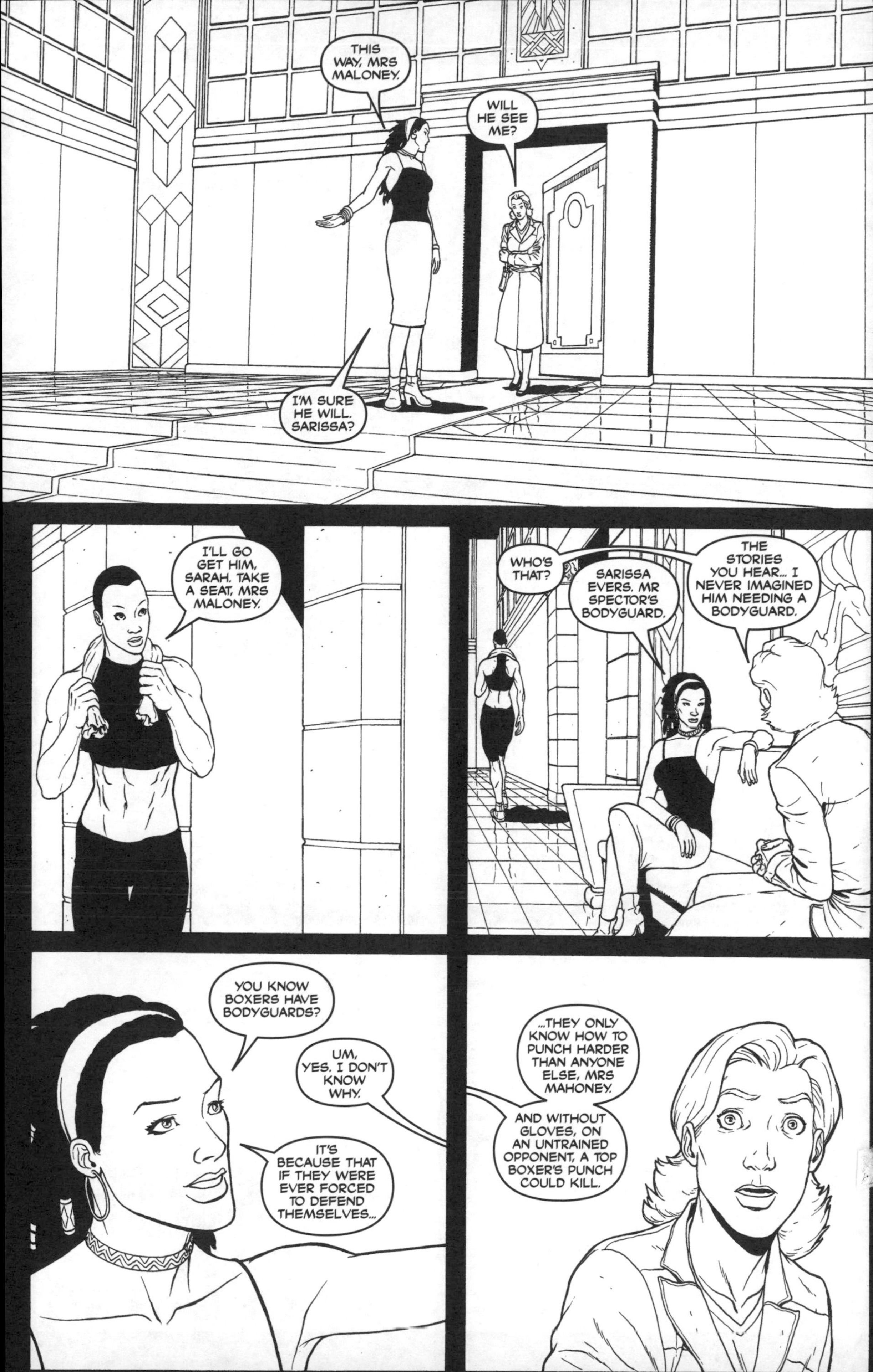
THIS WAY, MRS MALONEY.
WILL HE SEE ME?
I'M SURE HE WILL. SARISSA?
I'LL GO GET HIM, SARAH. TAKE A SEAT, MRS MALONEY.
WHO'S THAT?
SARISSA EVERS. MR SPECTOR'S BODYGUARD.
THE STORIES YOU HEAR... I NEVER IMAGINED HIM NEEDING A BODYGUARD.
YOU KNOW BOXERS HAVE BODYGUARDS?
UM, YES. I DON'T KNOW WHY.
IT'S BECAUSE THAT IF THEY WERE EVER FORCED TO DEFEND THEMSELVES...
...THEY ONLY KNOW HOW TO PUNCH HARDER THAN ANYONE ELSE, MRS MAHONEY.
AND WITHOUT GLOVES, ON AN UNTRAINED OPPONENT, A TOP BOXER'S PUNCH COULD KILL.

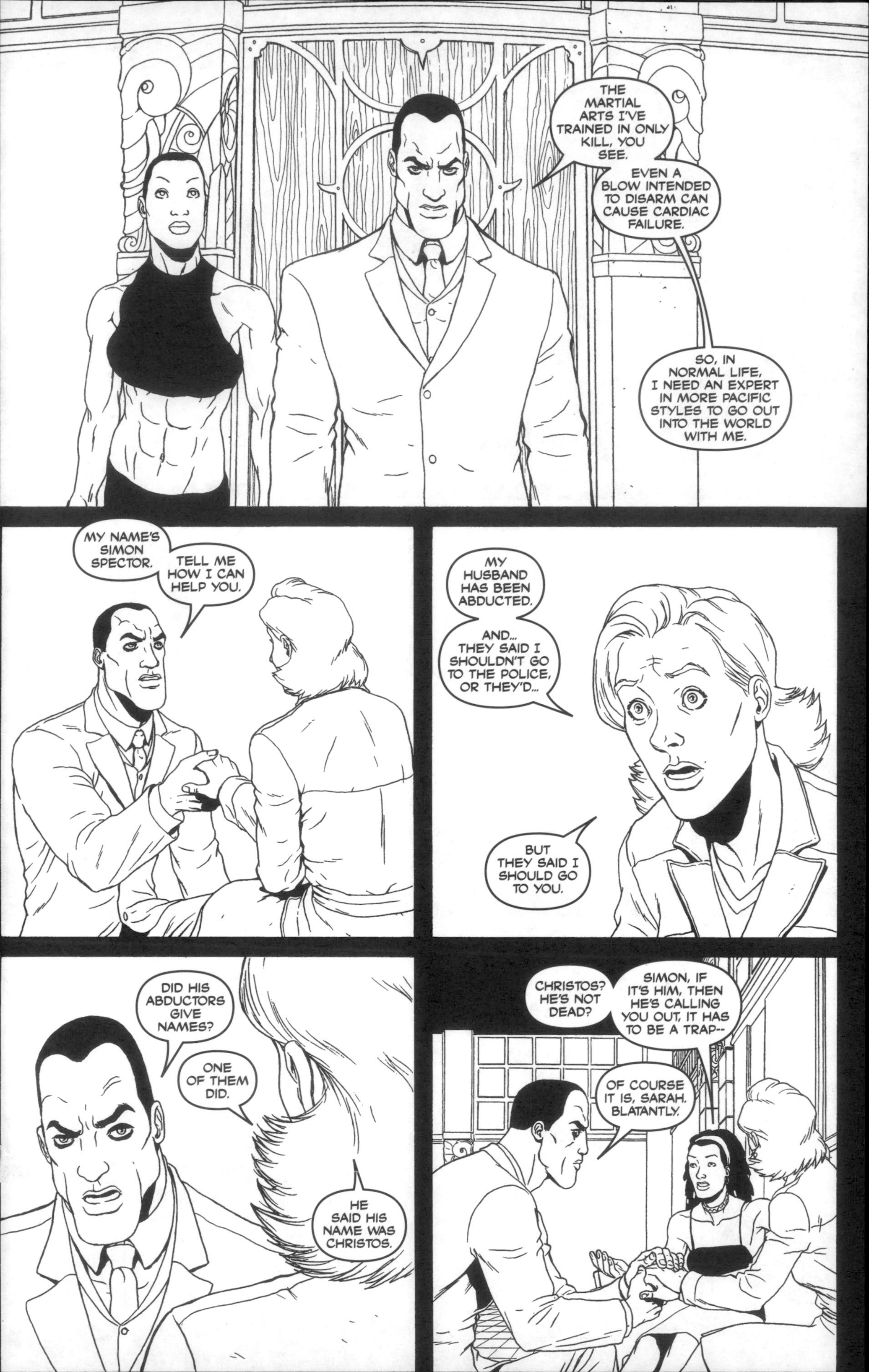
THE MARTIAL ARTS I'VE TRAINED IN ONLY KILL, YOU SEE.
EVEN A BLOW INTENDED TO DISARM CAN CAUSE CARDIAC FAILURE.
SO, IN NORMAL LIFE, I NEED AN EXPERT IN MORE PACIFIC STYLES TO GO OUT INTO THE WORLD WITH ME.
MY NAME'S SIMON SPECTOR.
TELL ME HOW I CAN HELP YOU.
MY HUSBAND HAS BEEN ABDUCTED.
AND... THEY SAID I SHOULDN'T GO TO THE POLICE, OR THEY'D...
BUT THEY SAID I SHOULD GO TO YOU.
DID HIS ABDUCTORS GIVE NAMES?
ONE OF THEM DID.
HE SAID HIS NAME WAS CHRISTOS.
CHRISTOS? HE'S NOT DEAD?
SIMON, IF IT'S HIM, THEN HE'S CALLING YOU OUT, IT HAS TO BE A TRAP--
OF COURSE IT IS, SARAH. BLATANTLY.

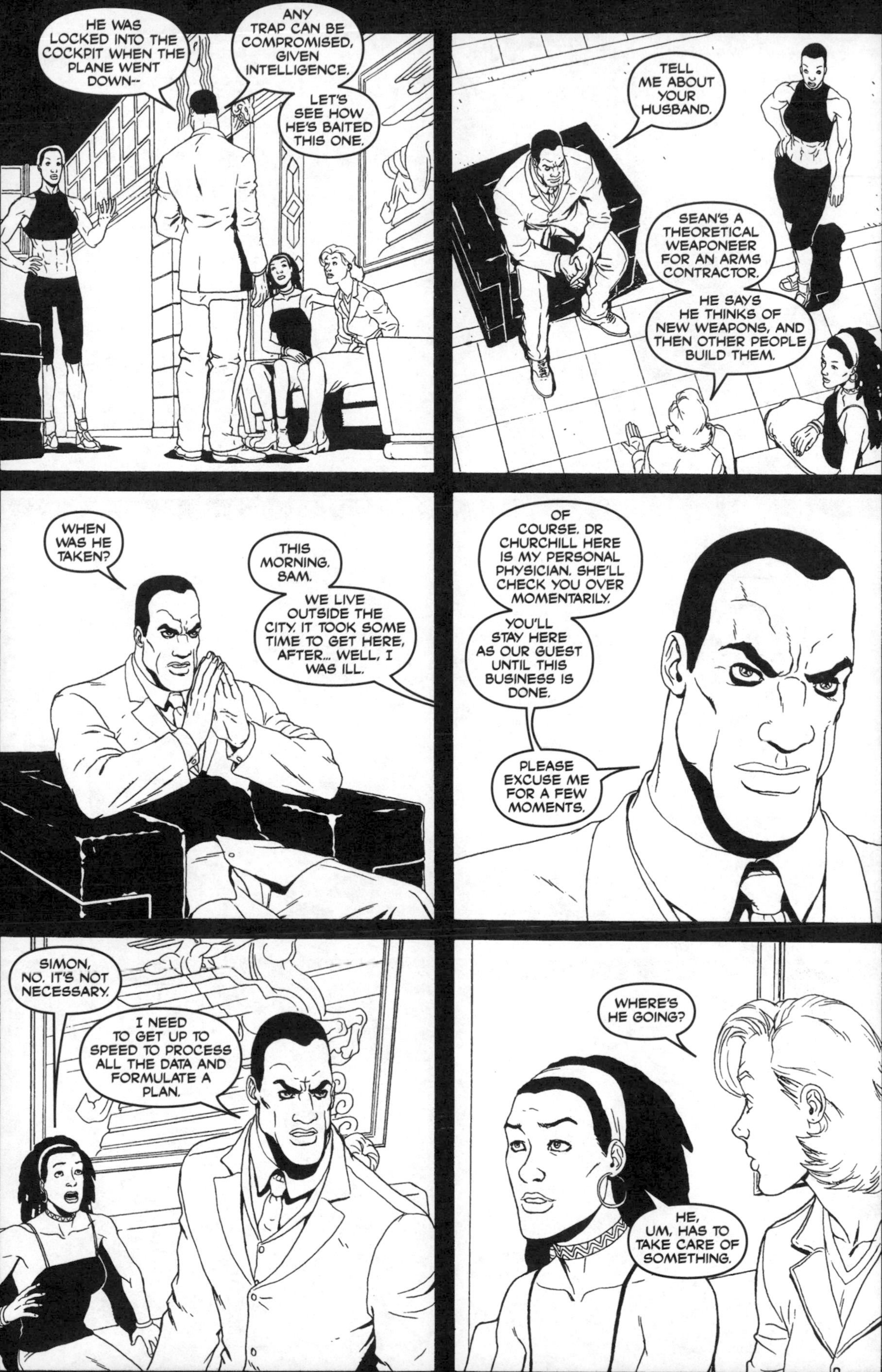
HE WAS LOCKED INTO THE COCKPIT WHEN THE PLANE WENT DOWN--
ANY TRAP CAN BE COMPROMISED, GIVEN INTELLIGENCE.
LET'S SEE HOW HE'S BAITED THIS ONE.
TELL ME ABOUT YOUR HUSBAND.
SEAN'S A THEORETICAL WEAPONEER FOR AN ARMS CONTRACTOR.
HE SAYS HE THINKS OF NEW WEAPONS, AND THEN OTHER PEOPLE BUILD THEM.
WHEN WAS HE TAKEN?
THIS MORNING, SAM.
WE LIVE OUTSIDE THE CITY. IT TOOK SOME TIME TO GET HERE, AFTER... WELL, I WAS ILL.
OF COURSE. DR CHURCHILL HERE IS MY PERSONAL PHYSICIAN. SHE'LL CHECK YOU OVER MOMENTARILY.
YOU'LL STAY HERE AS OUR GUEST UNTIL THIS BUSINESS IS DONE.
PLEASE EXCUSE ME FOR A FEW MOMENTS.
SIMON, NO. IT'S NOT NECESSARY.
I NEED TO GET UP TO SPEED TO PROCESS ALL THE DATA AND FORMULATE A PLAN.
WHERE'S HE GOING?
HE, UM, HAS TO TAKE CARE OF SOMETHING.

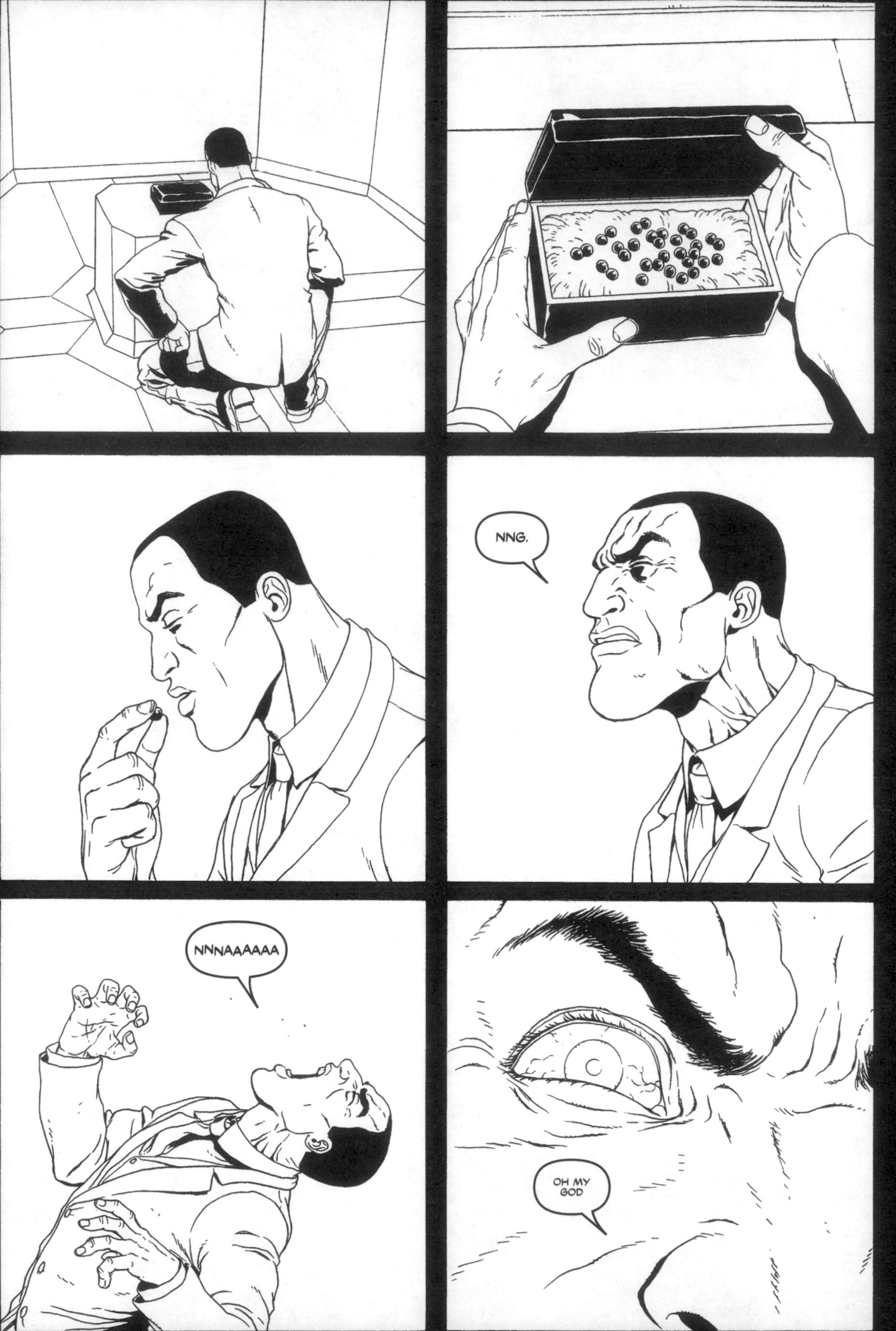
NNG.
NNNAAAAAA
OH MY GOD

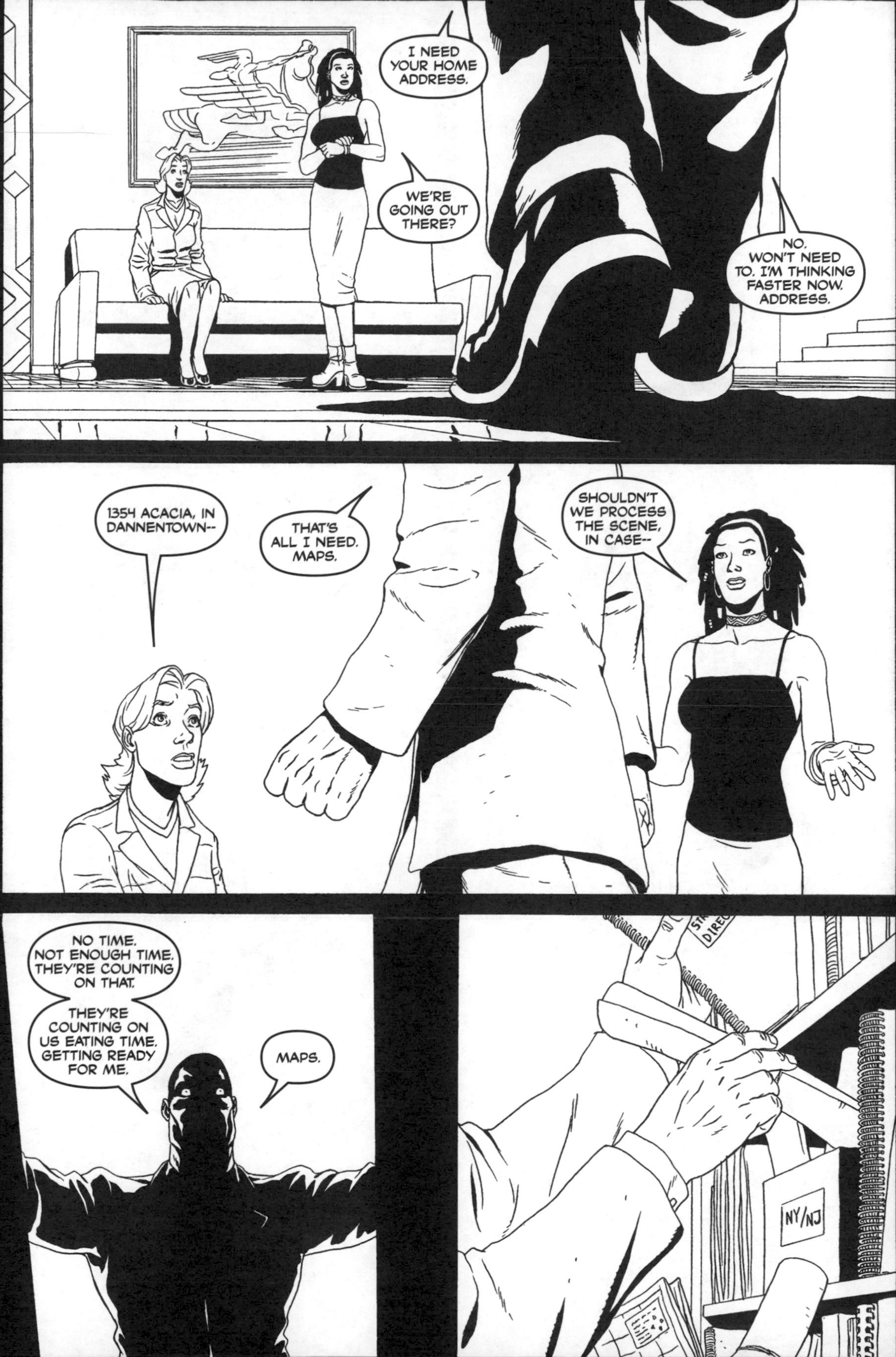
I NEED YOUR HOME ADDRESS.
WE'RE GOING OUT THERE?
NO. WON'T NEED TO. I'M THINKING FASTER NOW. ADDRESS.
1354 ACACIA, IN DANNENTOWN--
THAT'S ALL I NEED. MAPS.
SHOULDN'T WE PROCESS THE SCENE, IN CASE--
NO TIME. NOT ENOUGH TIME. THEY'RE COUNTING ON THAT.
THEY'RE COUNTING ON US EATING TIME. GETTING READY FOR ME.
MAPS.
NY/NJ

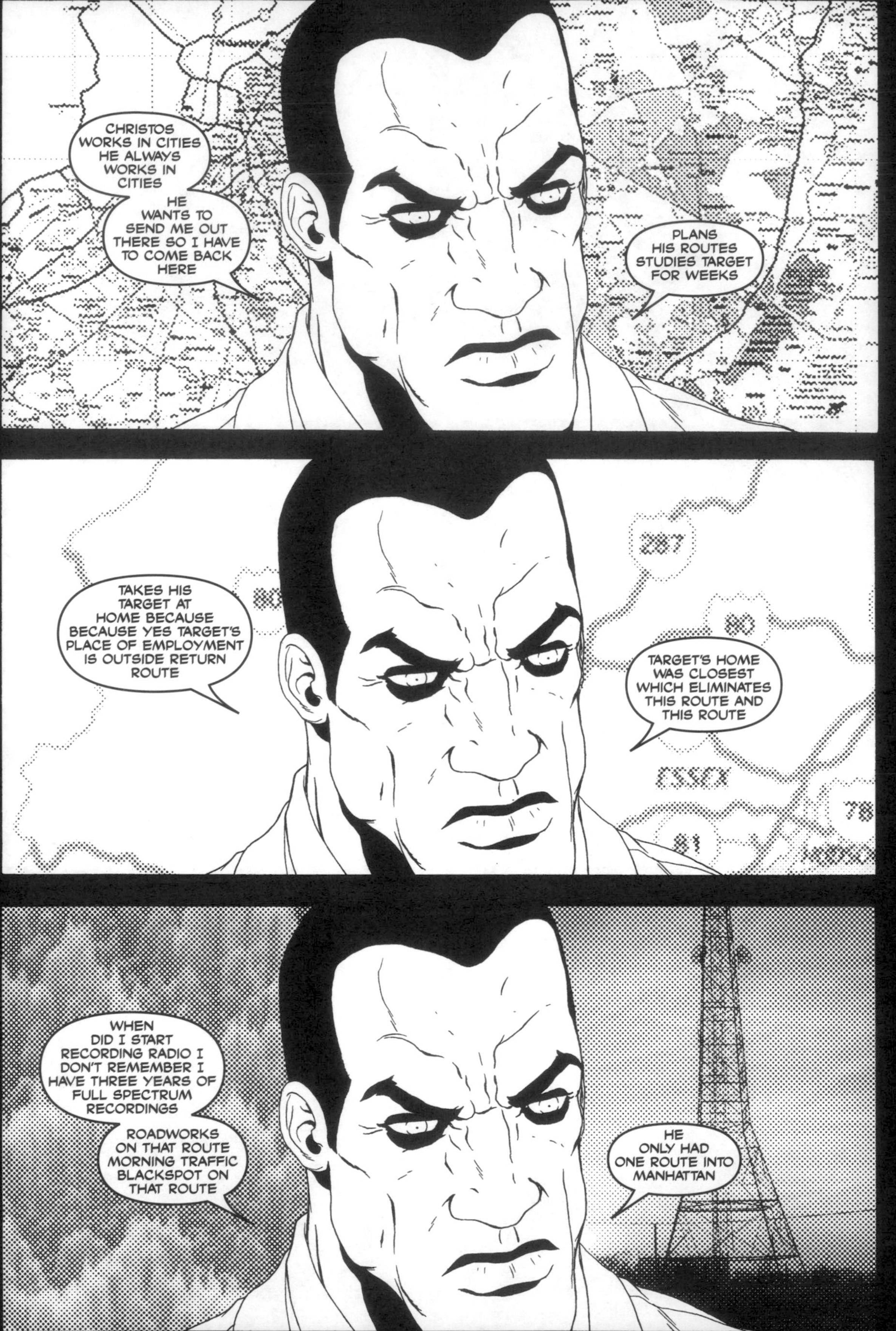
CHRISTOS WORKS IN CITIES HE ALWAYS WORKS IN CITIES
HE WANTS TO SEND ME OUT THERE SO I HAVE TO COME BACK HERE
PLANS HIS ROUTES STUDIES TARGET FOR WEEKS
287
80
TAKES HIS TARGET AT HOME BECAUSE BECAUSE YES TARGET'S PLACE OF EMPLOYMENT IS OUTSIDE RETURN ROUTE
TARGET'S HOME WAS CLOSEST WHICH ELIMINATES THIS ROUTE AND THIS ROUTE
WHEN DID I START RECORDING RADIO I DON'T REMEMBER I HAVE THREE YEARS OF FULL SPECTRUM RECORDINGS
ROADWORKS ON THAT ROUTE MORNING TRAFFIC BLACKSPOT ON THAT ROUTE
HE ONLY HAD ONE ROUTE INTO MANHATTAN

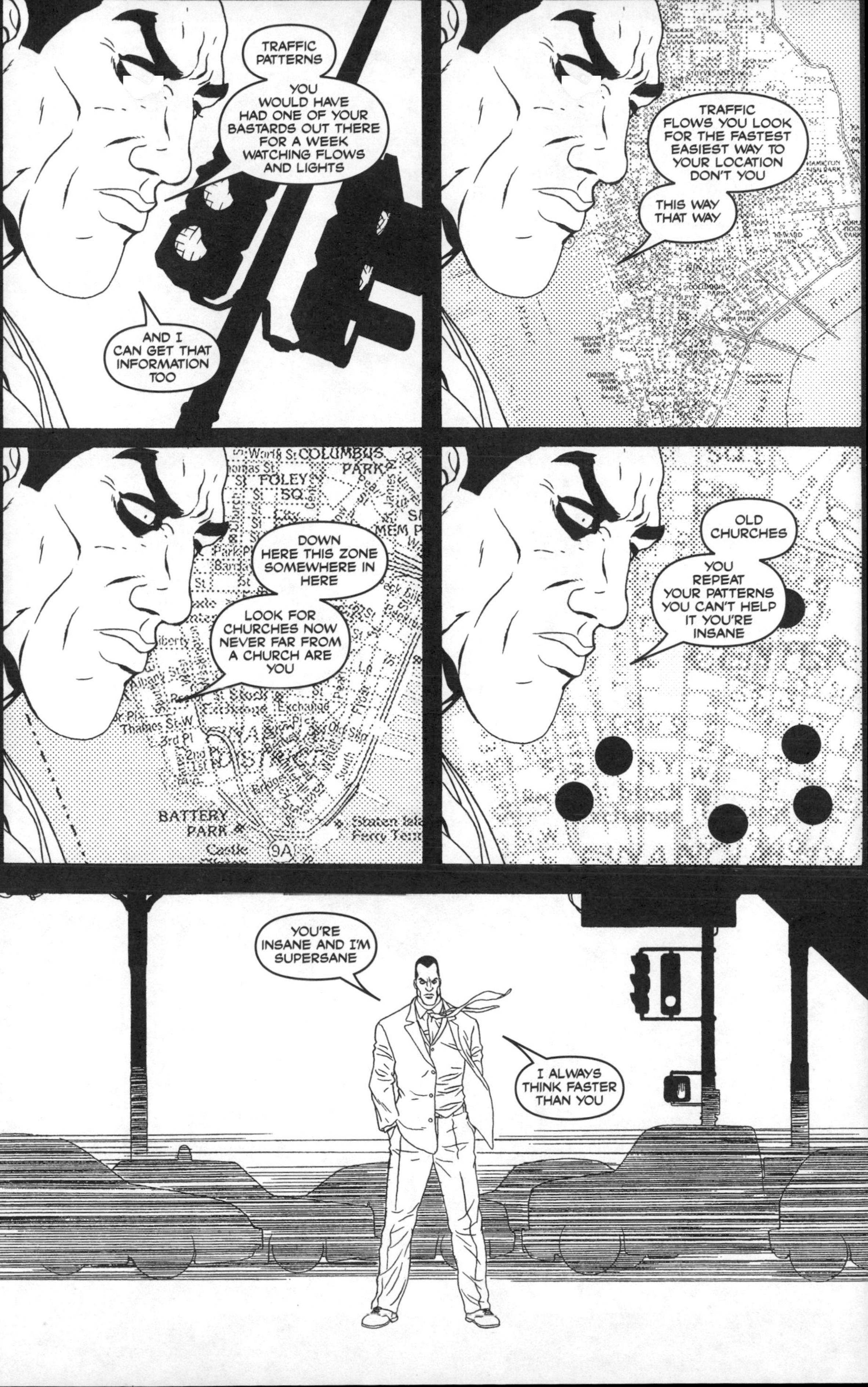
TRAFFIC PATTERNS
YOU WOULD HAVE HAD ONE OF YOUR BASTARDS OUT THERE FOR A WEEK WATCHING FLOWS AND LIGHTS
AND I CAN GET THAT INFORMATION TOO
TRAFFIC FLOWS YOU LOOK FOR THE FASTEST EASIEST WAY TO YOUR LOCATION DON'T YOU
THIS WAY THAT WAY
COLUMBUS PARK
FOLEY SQ
DOWN HERE THIS ZONE SOMEWHERE IN HERE
LOOK FOR CHURCHES NOW NEVER FAR FROM A CHURCH ARE YOU
BATTERY PARK
OLD CHURCHES
YOU REPEAT YOUR PATTERNS YOU CAN'T HELP IT YOU'RE INSANE
YOU'RE INSANE AND I'M SUPERSANE
I ALWAYS THINK FASTER THAN YOU

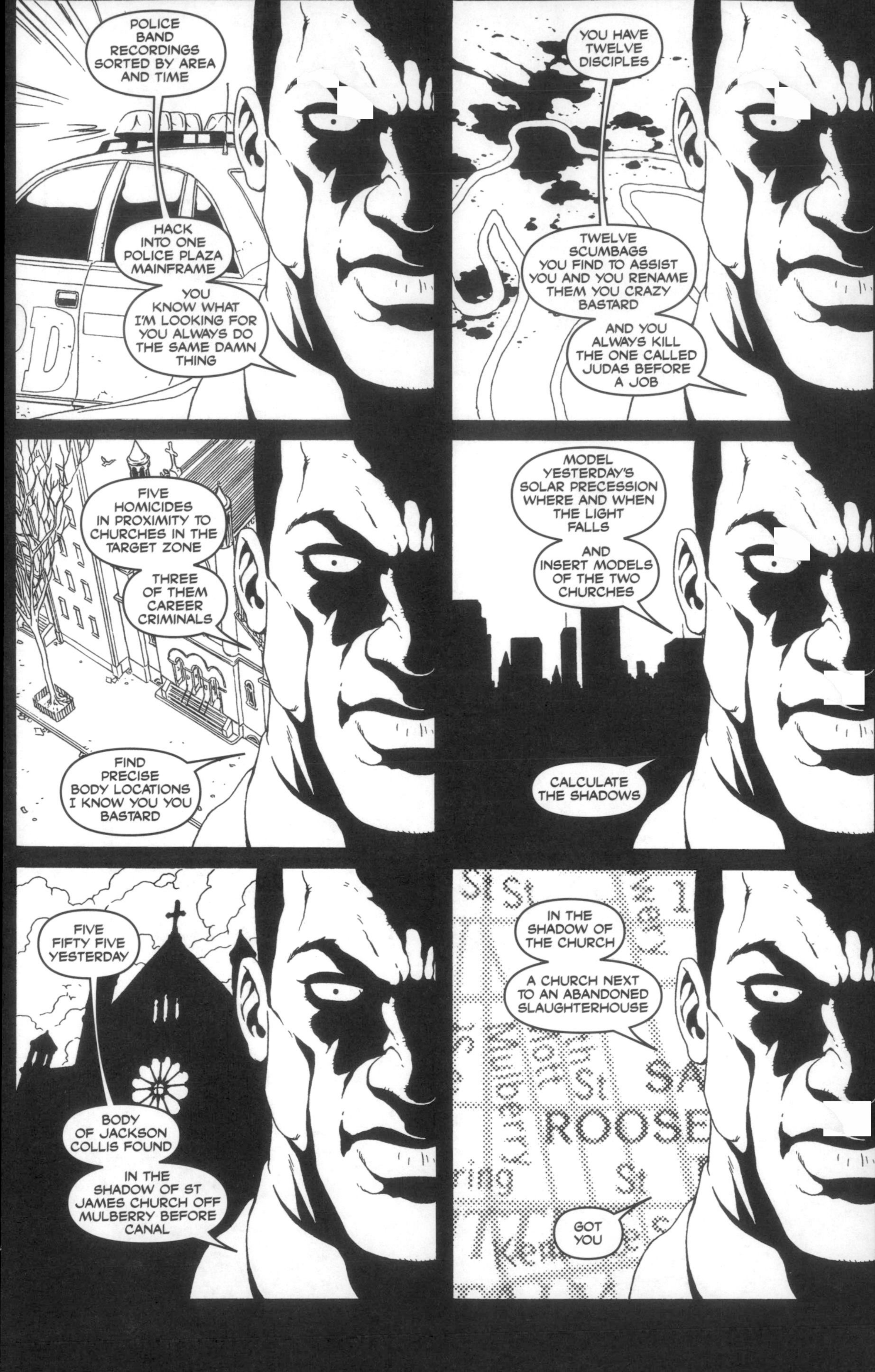
POLICE BAND RECORDINGS SORTED BY AREA AND TIME
HACK INTO ONE POLICE PLAZA MAINFRAME
YOU KNOW WHAT I'M LOOKING FOR YOU ALWAYS DO THE SAME DAMN THING
YOU HAVE TWELVE DISCIPLES
TWELVE SCUMBAGS YOU FIND TO ASSIST YOU AND YOU RENAME THEM YOU CRAZY BASTARD
AND YOU ALWAYS KILL THE ONE CALLED JUDAS BEFORE A JOB
FIVE HOMICIDES IN PROXIMITY TO CHURCHES IN THE TARGET ZONE
THREE OF THEM CAREER CRIMINALS
FIND PRECISE BODY LOCATIONS I KNOW YOU YOU BASTARD
MODEL YESTERDAY'S SOLAR PRECESSION WHERE AND WHEN THE LIGHT FALLS
AND INSERT MODELS OF THE TWO CHURCHES
CALCULATE THE SHADOWS
FIVE FIFTY FIVE YESTERDAY
BODY OF JACKSON COLLIS FOUND
IN THE SHADOW OF ST JAMES CHURCH OFF MULBERRY BEFORE CANAL
IN THE SHADOW OF THE CHURCH
A CHURCH NEXT TO AN ABANDONED SLAUGHTERHOUSE
ROOSE
GOT YOU

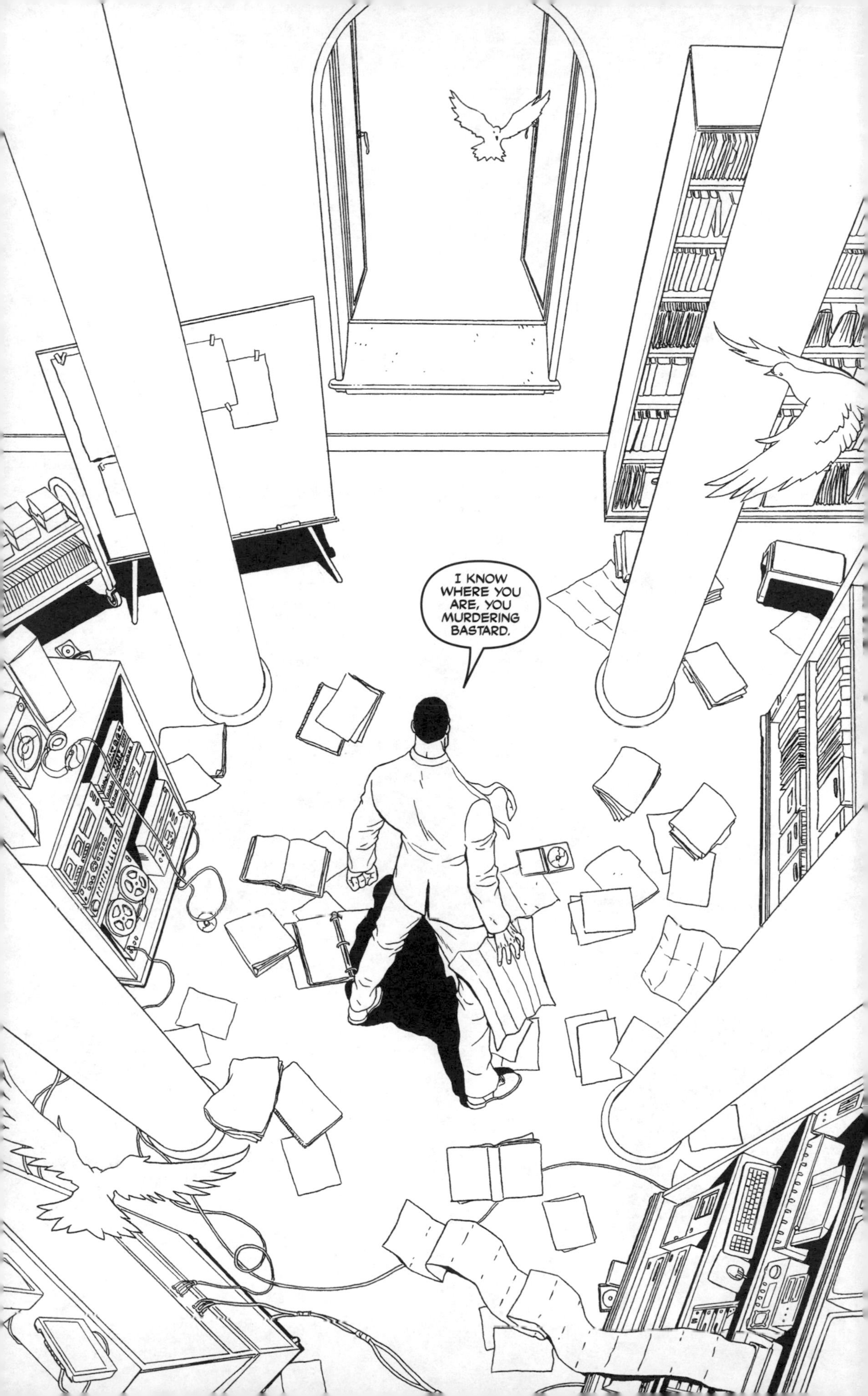
I KNOW WHERE YOU ARE, YOU MURDERING BASTARD.

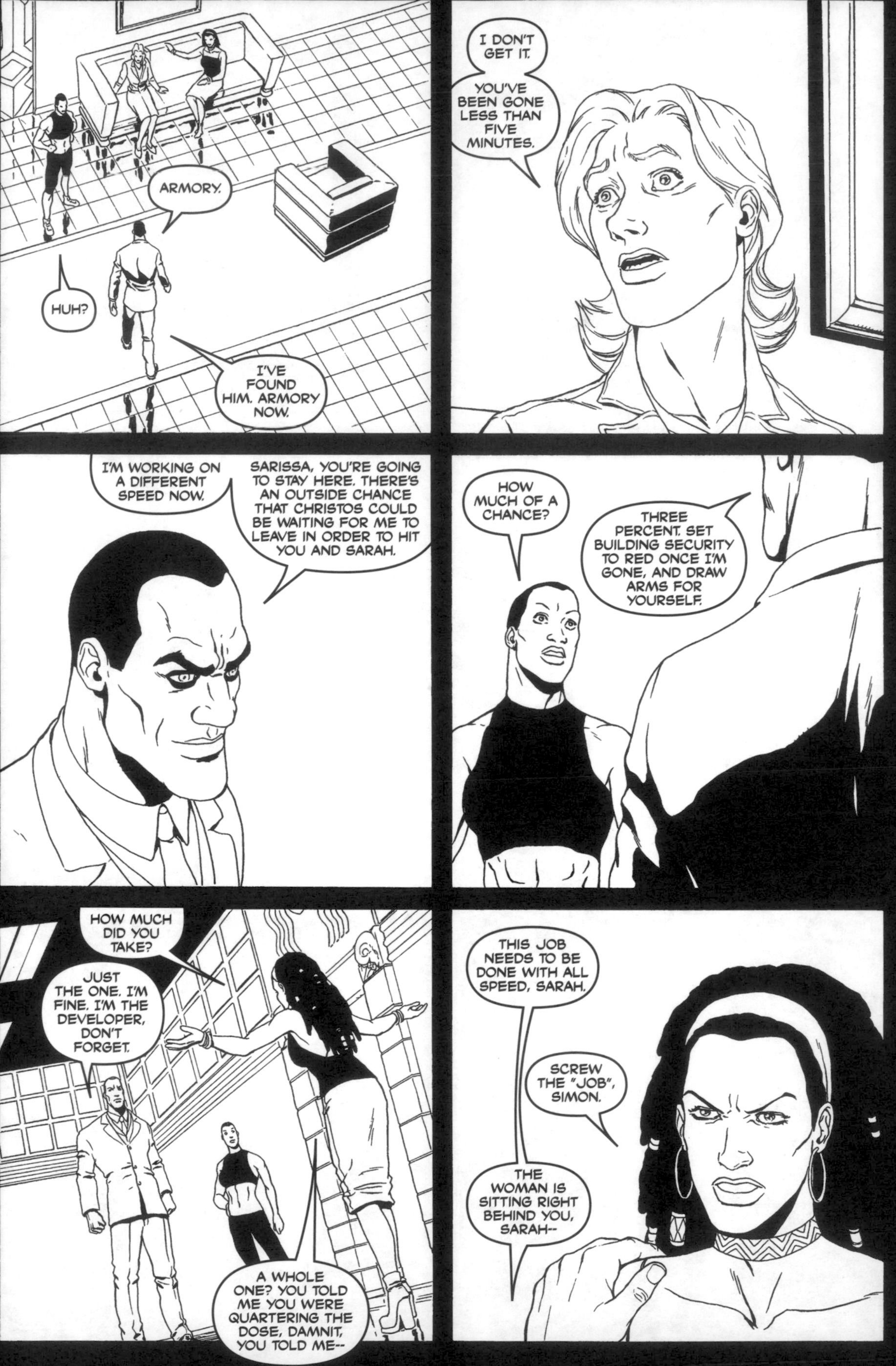
ARMORY.
HUH?
I'VE FOUND HIM. ARMORY NOW.
I DON'T GET IT.
YOU'VE BEEN GONE LESS THAN FIVE MINUTES.
I'M WORKING ON A DIFFERENT SPEED NOW.
SARISSA, YOU'RE GOING TO STAY HERE. THERE'S AN OUTSIDE CHANCE THAT CHRISTOS COULD BE WAITING FOR ME TO LEAVE IN ORDER TO HIT YOU AND SARAH.
HOW MUCH OF A CHANCE?
THREE PERCENT. SET BUILDING SECURITY TO RED ONCE I'M GONE, AND DRAW ARMS FOR YOURSELF.
HOW MUCH DID YOU TAKE?
JUST THE ONE. I'M FINE. I'M THE DEVELOPER, DON'T FORGET.
A WHOLE ONE? YOU TOLD ME YOU WERE QUARTERING THE DOSE, DAMNIT, YOU TOLD ME--
THIS JOB NEEDS TO BE DONE WITH ALL SPEED, SARAH.
SCREW THE "JOB", SIMON.
THE WOMAN IS SITTING RIGHT BEHIND YOU, SARAH--

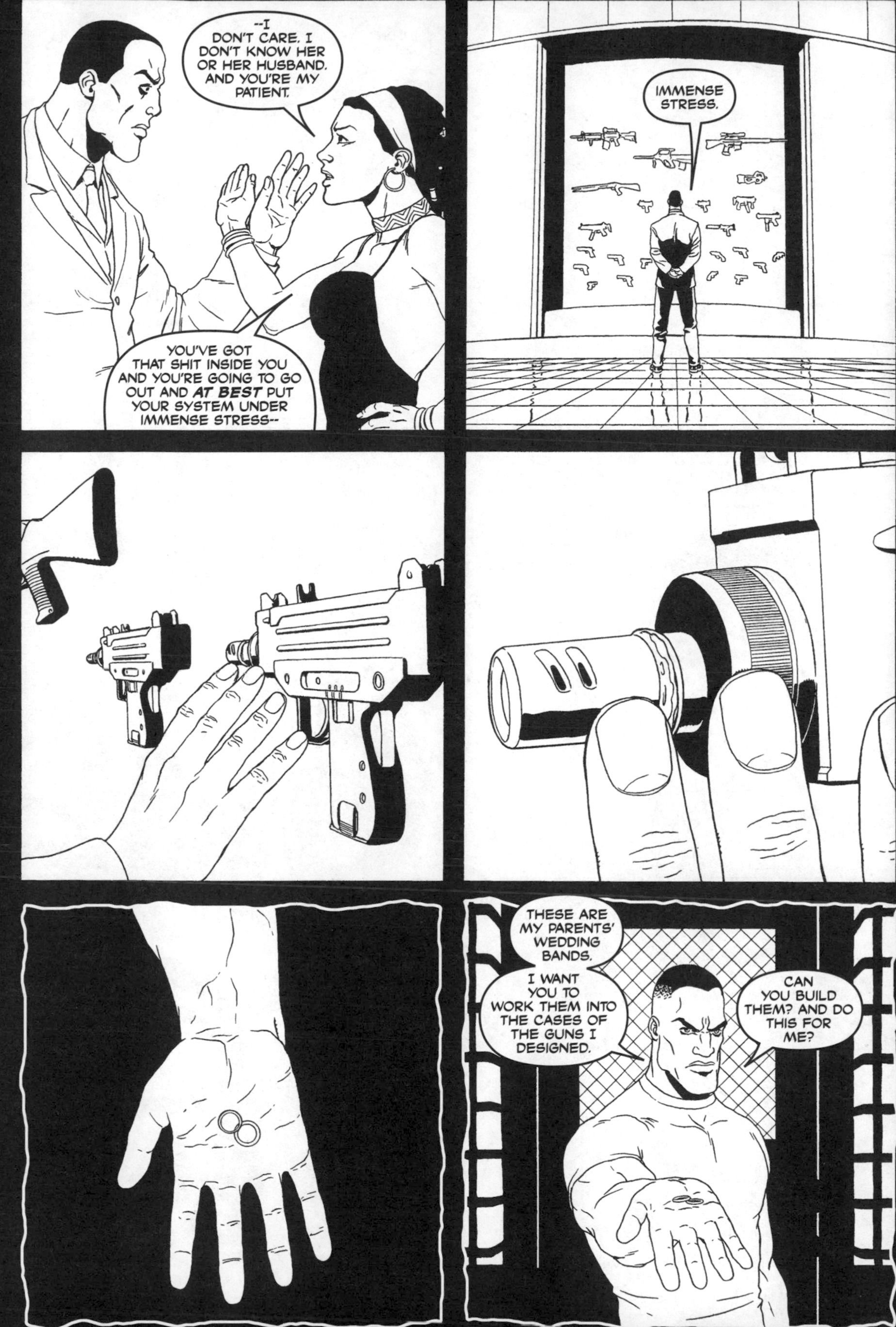
--I DON'T CARE. I DON'T KNOW HER OR HER HUSBAND. AND YOU'RE MY PATIENT.
YOU'VE GOT THAT SHIT INSIDE YOU AND YOU'RE GOING TO GO OUT AND AT BEST PUT YOUR SYSTEM UNDER IMMENSE STRESS--
IMMENSE STRESS.
THESE ARE MY PARENTS' WEDDING BANDS.
I WANT YOU TO WORK THEM INTO THE CASES OF THE GUNS I DESIGNED.
CAN YOU BUILD THEM? AND DO THIS FOR ME?

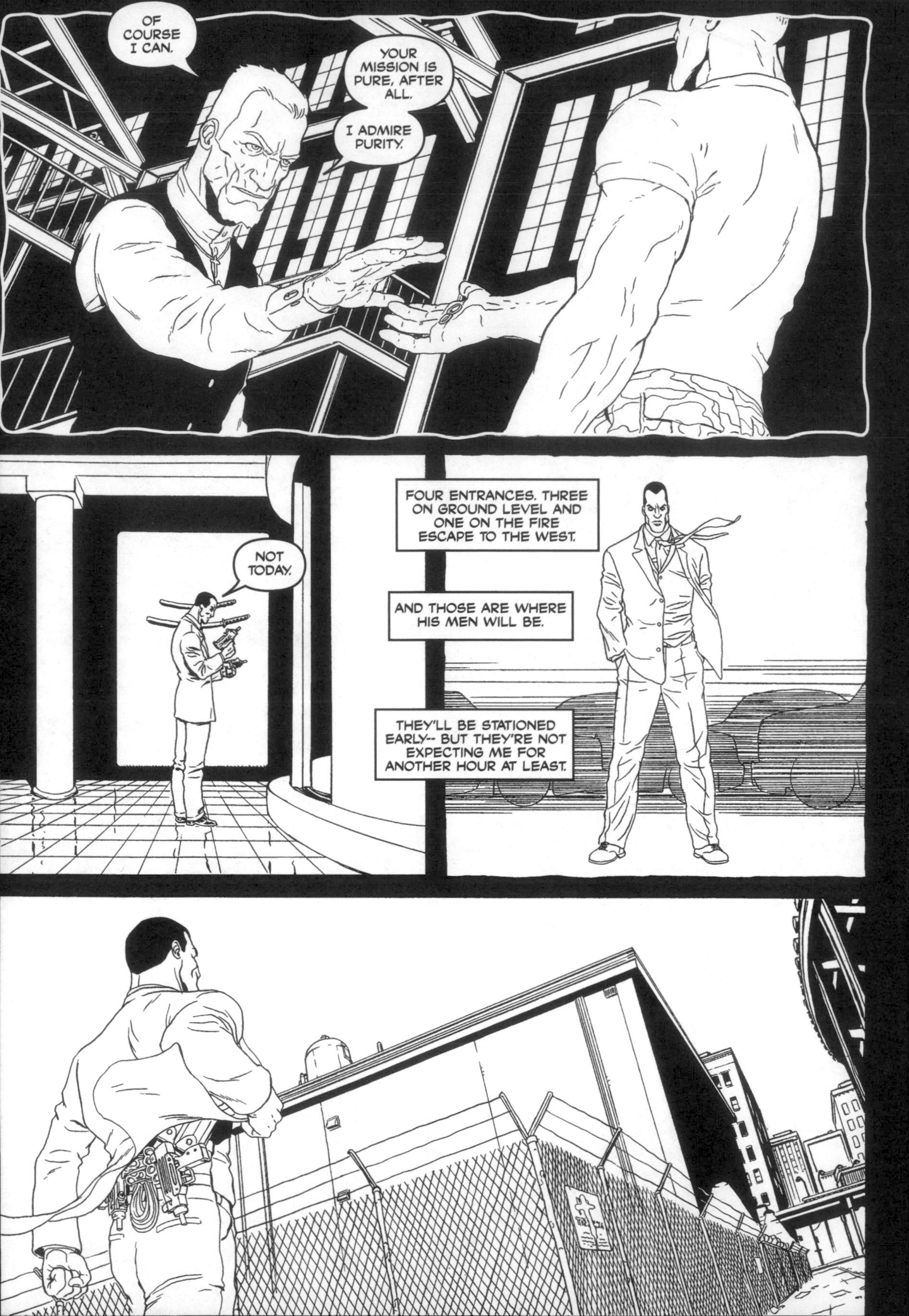

OF COURSE I CAN.
YOUR MISSION IS PURE, AFTER ALL.
I ADMIRE PURITY.
NOT TODAY.
FOUR ENTRANCES. THREE ON GROUND LEVEL AND ONE ON THE FIRE ESCAPE TO THE WEST.
AND THOSE ARE WHERE HIS MEN WILL BE.
THEY'LL BE STATIONED EARLY-- BUT THEY'RE NOT EXPECTING ME FOR ANOTHER HOUR AT LEAST.

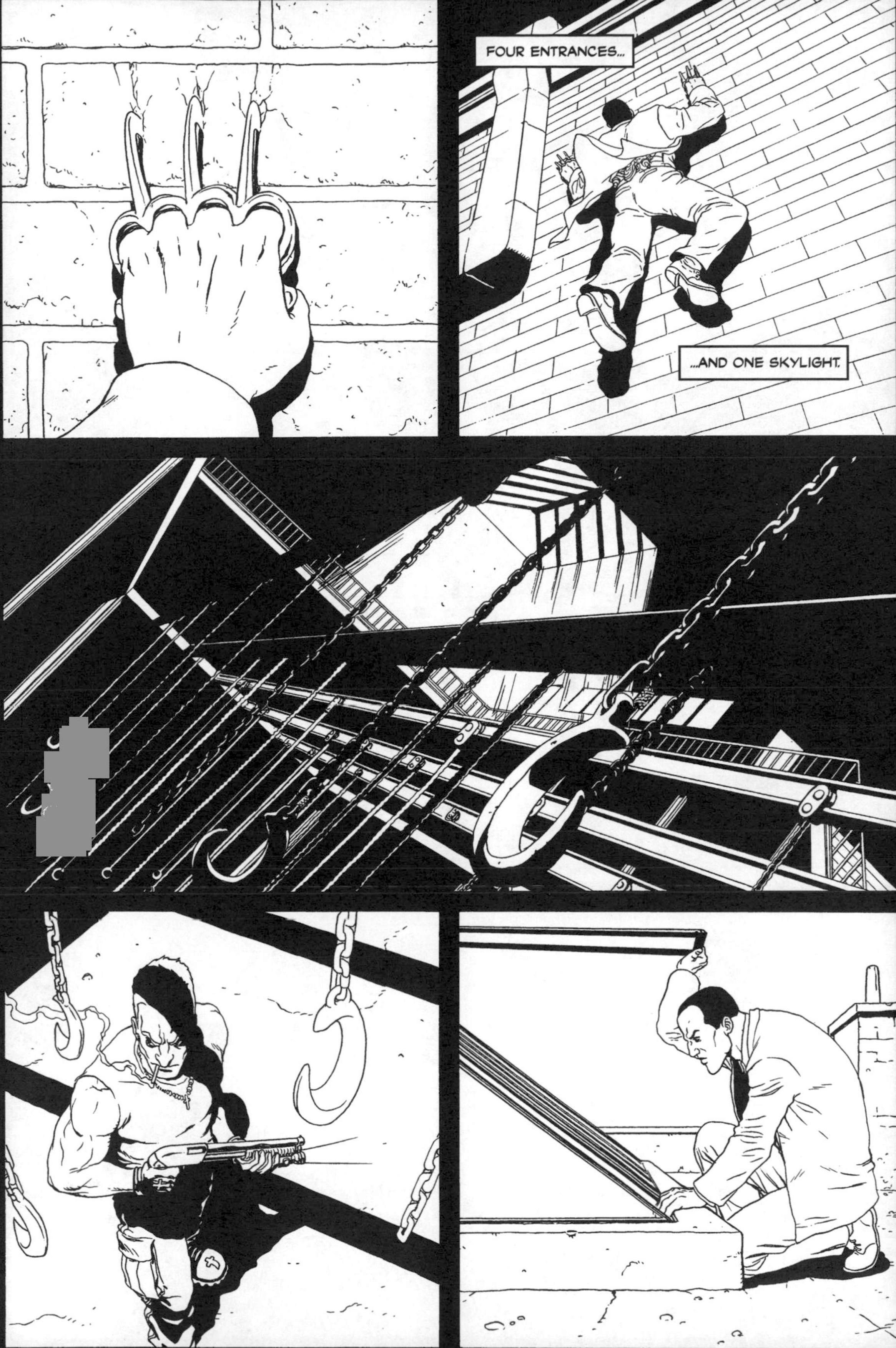
FOUR ENTRANCES...
...AND ONE SKYLIGHT.

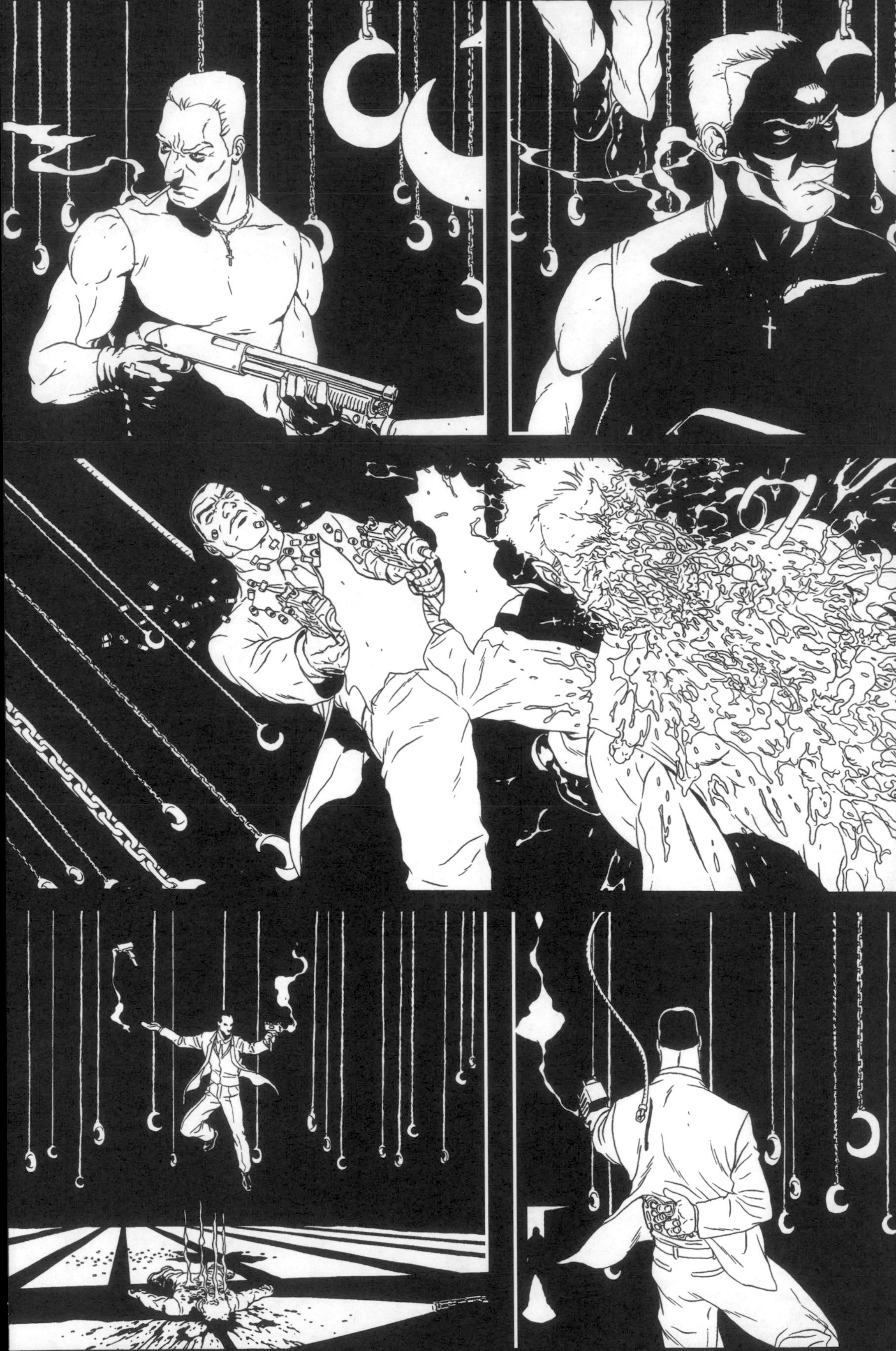

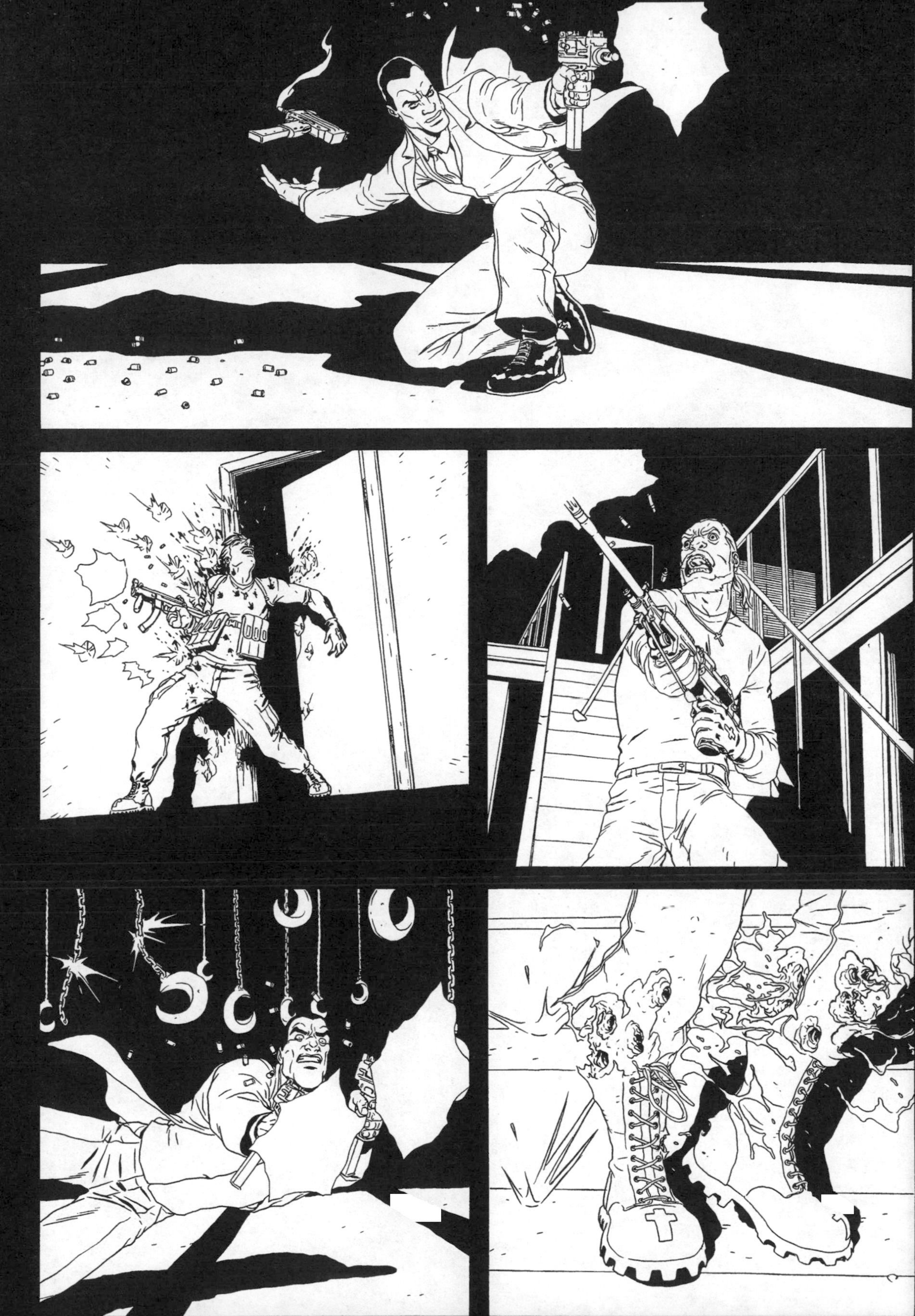

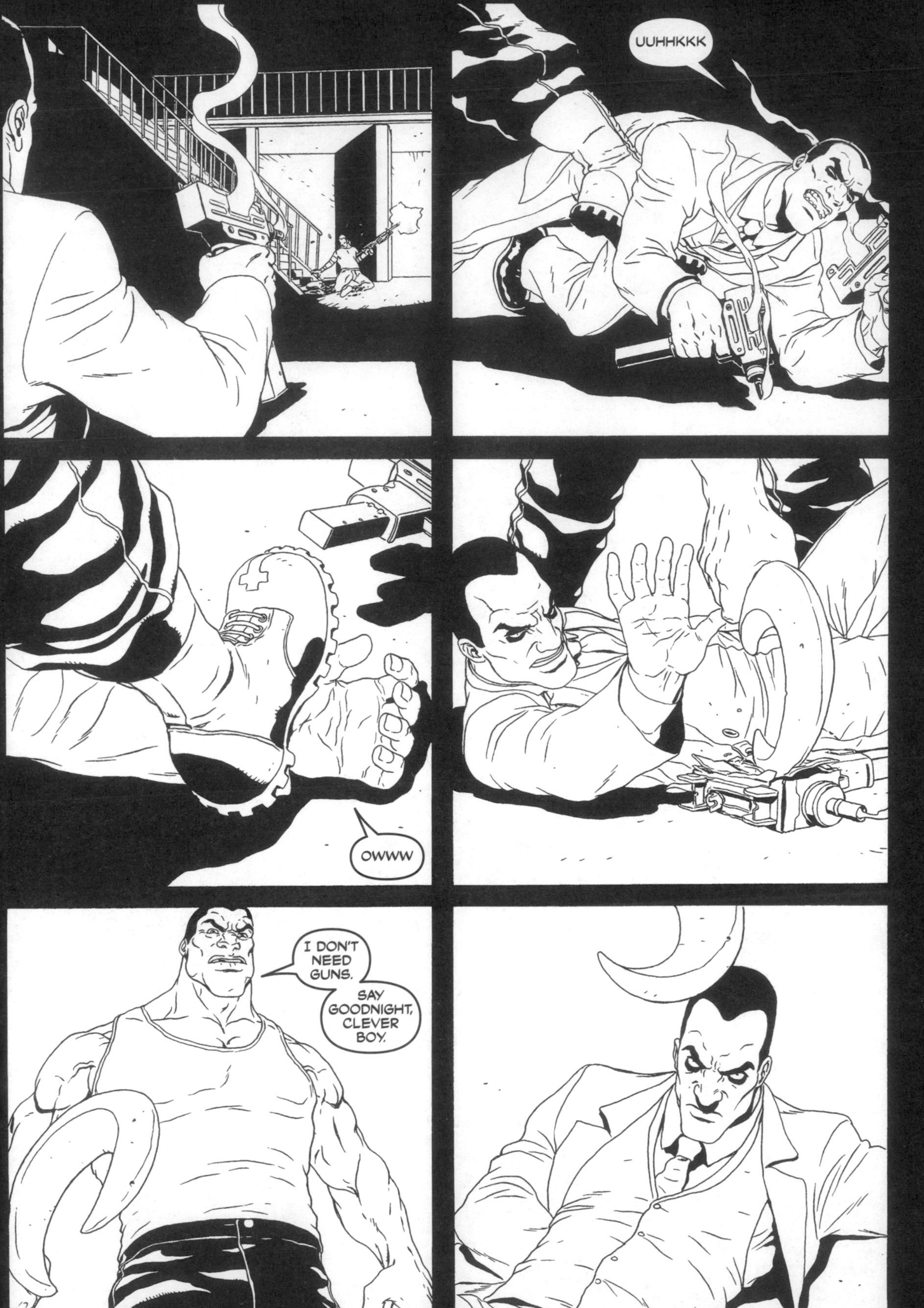
UUHHKKK
OWWW
I DON'T NEED GUNS.
SAY GOODNIGHT, CLEVER BOY.

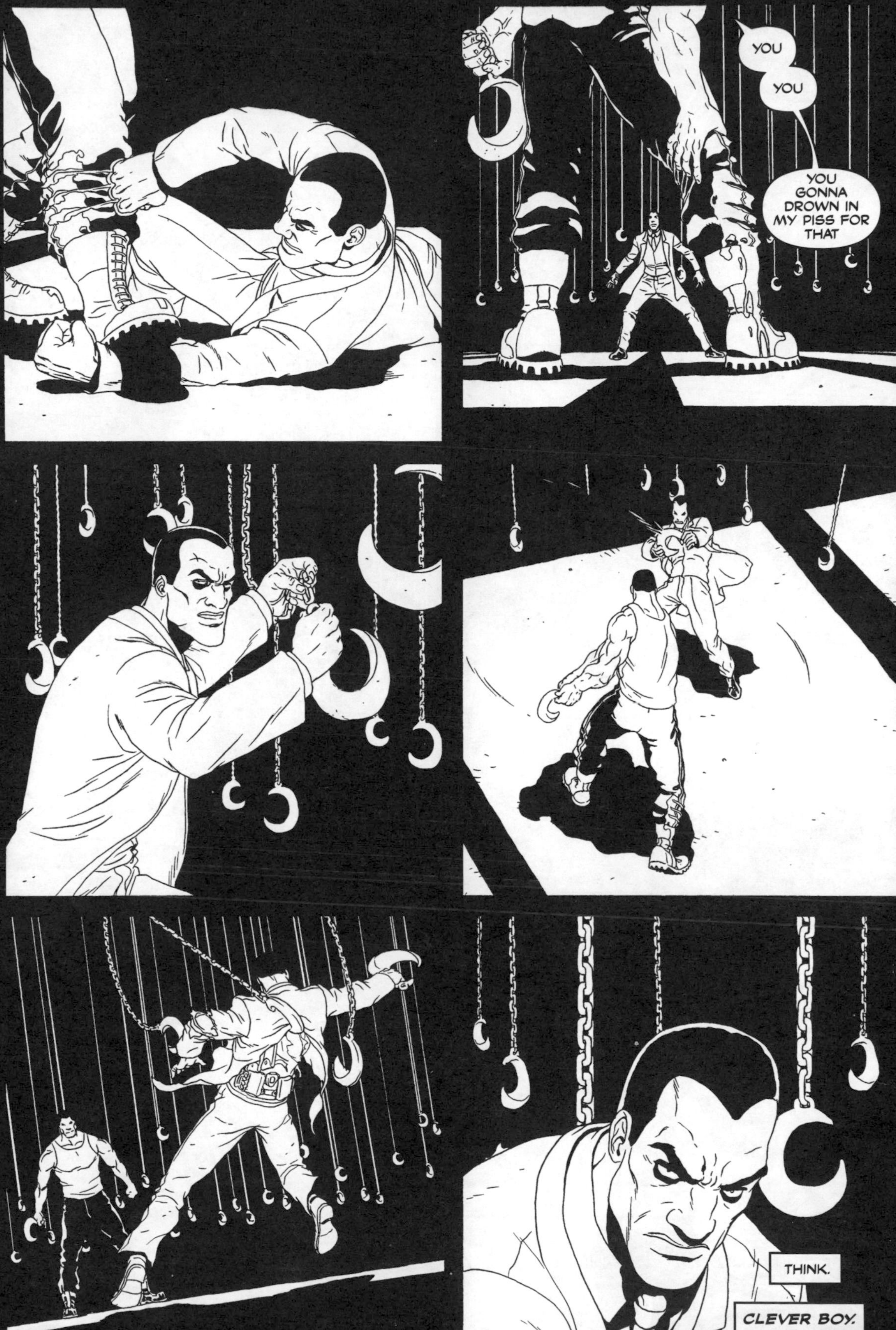
YOU
YOU
YOU GONNA DROWN IN MY PISS FOR THAT
THINK.
CLEVER BOY.